Exploring Windows 10

May 2020 Edition

Kevin Wilson

Elluminet Press
www.elluminetpress.com

Exploring Windows 10: May 2020 Edition

Publisher: Elluminet Press
Director: Kevin Wilson
Lead Editor: Steven Ashmore
Technical Reviewer: Mike Taylor, Robert Ashcroft
Copy Editors: Joanne Taylor, James Marsh
Proof Reader: Mike Taylor
Indexer: James Marsh
Cover Designer: Kevin Wilson

eBook versions and licenses are also available for most titles. Any source code or other supplementary materials referenced by the author in this text is available to readers at

www.elluminetpress.com/resources

For detailed information about how to locate your book's resources, go to

www.elluminetpress.com/resources

Table of Contents

About the Author

With over 15 years' experience in the computer industry, Kevin Wilson has made a career out of technology and showing others how to use it. After earning a master's degree in computer science, software engineering, and multimedia systems, Kevin has held various positions in the IT industry including graphic & web design, building & managing corporate networks, training, and IT support.

He currently serves as Elluminet Press Ltd's senior writer and director, he periodically teaches computer science at college in South Africa and serves as an IT trainer in England. His books have become a valuable resource among the students in England, South Africa and our partners in the United States.

Kevin's motto is clear: "If you can't explain something simply, then you haven't understood it well enough." To that end, he has created the Exploring Technology Series, in which he breaks down complex technological subjects into smaller, easy-to-follow steps that students and ordinary computer users can put into practice.

Acknowledgements

Thanks to all the staff at Luminescent Media & Elluminet Press for their passion, dedication and hard work in the preparation and production of this book.

To all my friends and family for their continued support and encouragement in all my writing projects.

To all my colleagues, students and testers who took the time to test procedures and offer feedback on the book

Finally thanks to you the reader for choosing this book. I hope it helps you to use your computer with greater understanding.

Have fun!

Windows 10

Windows 10 is the latest operating system from Microsoft Corporation and is one that represents a major shift in the devices we use. In other words Windows is designed to adapt to the device it's installed on, so you'll get a point and click environment on desktop PCs, workstations, laptops, and all-in-one PCs called desktop mode, and a touch screen environment on tablets, hybrid laptop/tablet, and other small screen devices called tablet mode.

So what's an Operating System? An Operating System is a computer program that manages the computer's hardware resources such as memory, processor and disk drives.

The Operating System also provides a platform for you to run apps such as word processors, web browsers, games, open files, and so on. These are represented as graphical icons on the screen. Apps open up in a window allowing you to interact with them using either a mouse, keyboard or touch-screen. Commands and options are organised into menus for you to select. This is called a graphic user interface.

Windows Editions

There are two editions of Windows 10 available to consumers: Home and Pro.

Windows 10 Home is designed for use on PCs, laptops and tablets. This edition is intended for the every day home user. If you bought a laptop or tablet device from a computer store, then this is the version you're most likely to have.

Windows 10 Pro is the same as the home edition, except it has additional features that are oriented towards business environments and power users.

Microsoft subsequently released other editions of Windows 10 aimed at different markets.

Windows 10 Enterprise is aimed at medium to large scale organisations that have hundreds or even thousands of computers in their offices and networks. This edition is very similar to Windows 10 Pro except it has a couple of extra features.

Windows 10 Education is very much like Windows 10 Pro and Windows 10 Enterprise but is distributed to educational establishments such as schools, colleges, and universities.

Windows 10 S is a feature-limited edition of Windows 10 designed primarily for low-end devices and the education market. Windows 10 S only allows the installation of software from the Windows Store. You can only use Microsoft Edge as the web browser and Bing as the search engine.

Windows 10 Pro for Workstations is designed for high-end hardware for intensive computing tasks and supports Intel Xeon or AMD Opteron processors, up to 4 CPUs, 6TB RAM, the ReFS file system.

The May 2020 Update

Windows 10 - May 2020 Update, Version 2004, also known as 20H1, introduces some new features and improvements over the previous update.

What's New?

There is a new cloud download option for reinstalling windows, making it a bit easier to download and install windows if you run into problems.

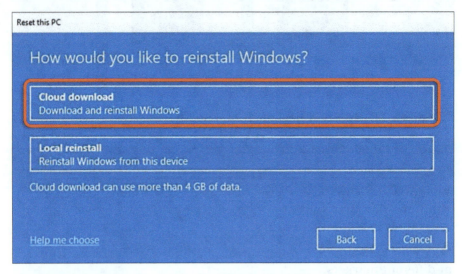

Cortana now has a chat feature, and you can move the window.

You can rename your virtual desktops, instead of desktop 1, desktop 2, desktop 3, etc.

Windows Ink Workspace has had a few tweaks and now takes up less screen space.

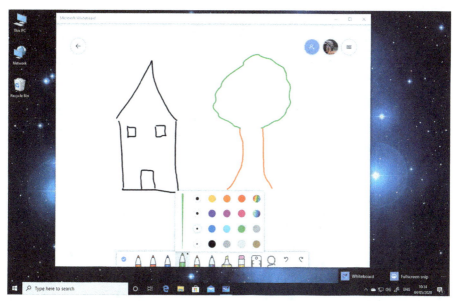

Windows ink workspace has been streamlined so now when you click the icon on the taskbar you either select the 'whiteboard' app or the 'fullscreen snip' app.

Chapter 1: Windows 10

Windows Search experience is a little faster, and the File Explorer search experience makes it easier to find your files.

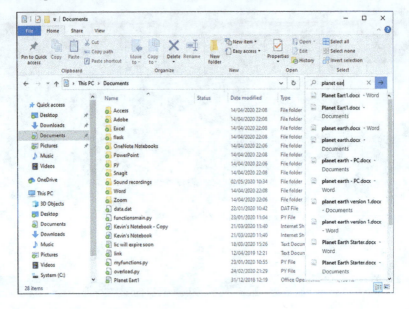

A better touch experience in desktop mode for convertible PCs such as the surface tablet, surface pro, or lenovo yoga etc. *Not to be confused with full tablet mode.*

Icons on the task bar are more spaced and optimised for touch screen interfaces.

Bluetooth pairing has been improved making it easier to connect bluetooth devices to your machine.

Windows now allows users to add IP cameras to their PC, enabling photo capture and streaming of video in camera applications.

Some other minor tweaks give you more control over Optional Updates in Windows Update, you now need a PIN to enter Safe mode, and you can make some devices passwordless allowing you to use a PIN code, finger print scan or facial recognition cameras.

There is also a restart apps option which allows you to manage whether apps that aren't closed during shutdown are reopened automatically on the next start up.

Windows Subsystem for Linux (WSL) has also had a few improvements

```
user@insider: ~                                                        —   □   ×
Welcome to Ubuntu 20.04 LTS (GNU/Linux 4.4.0-19628-Microsoft x86_64)

 * Documentation:  https://help.ubuntu.com
 * Management:     https://landscape.canonical.com
 * Support:        https://ubuntu.com/advantage

  System information as of Mon Jun  1 14:03:11 BST 2020

  System load:   0.52      Users logged in:        4
  Usage of /home: unknown   IPv4 address for eth2:  172.21.160.28
  Memory usage:  30%       IPv4 address for eth3:  172.28.48.28
  Swap usage:    0%        IPv4 address for wifi0: 192.168.1.35
  Processes:     7

This message is shown once once a day. To disable it please create the
/home/user/.hushlogin file.
user@insider:~$
```

Setting up Windows 10

New PC laptops, tablets and computers will come with Windows 10 already installed, usually the home edition. If you are running an older system such as Windows 7 or Windows 8 you should upgrade your system to Windows 10.

Microsoft's free upgrade may be over, but since they want as many people on Windows 10 as possible, those with activated versions of Windows 7 and Windows 8 can still upgrade for free. If you are running either of those two operating systems, you should upgrade as soon as possible.

In this chapter we'll take a look at how to upgrade - you can do this using the media creation tool, available from Microsoft's website.

Also we'll go through system settings, monitoring child accounts and family safety, blue tooth devices, and various other features in Windows 10.

We'll also take a look at running Windows 10 for the first time as well as setting it up, installing printers, connecting to WiFi and Windows 10's many other features.

Let's begin with a look at upgrading to the latest Windows 10 update...

Upgrading to Windows 10

If you have a fully licensed version of Windows 7 or 8 installed on your machine, you can still upgrade for free using the Media Creation Tool - see section on upgrading from Windows 7 & 8.

If you're upgrading, make sure your PC meets the following specification. A computer with the minimum spec recommended by Microsoft will run painfully slow, so I've included a recommended minimum spec below that I've tested.

- 2GHz or faster CPU
- At least 4GB of RAM
- At least 32GB Hard Disk Space
- At least 1152x864 screen resolution
- Graphics card with WDDM support and DirectX 9 or above.

If you Already have Windows 10

If you are already running Windows 10 and simply want to get the May 2020 Update, then you should automatically receive a notification on Windows Update.

Go to Start Menu, click Settings icon. Select 'Update & Security' then 'Windows Update'. Click 'check for updates'.

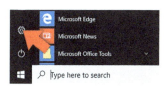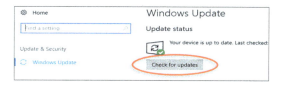

Windows 10 will check for any available updates. The May update is version 2004. When it's available, you'll see a 'feature update' notification in windows update. Click 'download and install now'.

To complete the update, you'll need to restart your machine when it's finished. Go to Start > Power > 'Update & Restart'. If you only see 'restart' on the menu, then the update hasn't finished downloading yet.

Buying Windows 10

If you can't upgrade free for whatever reason, you can buy Windows 10 from any computer store or online retailer. The installation media for Windows 10 will either come as a download, a DVD disk or a flash/usb drive.

The best place is to buy a copy from Microsoft's Online Store, using your Microsoft Account. Head over to the following website.

```
www.microsoftstore.com/windows
```

Scroll down and click 'Windows 10 Home', or 'Windows 10 Pro', for most users the home edition is fine.

Select 'how do you want to get Windows 10'. You can select either Download disk image or a USB stick. Having Windows 10 installer on a USB stick is useful for installing and is easier to use than a disk image.

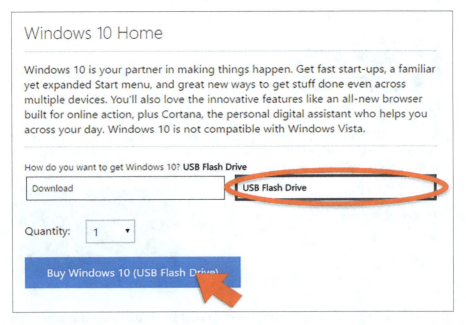

Click 'buy and download'.

You'll see a summary of your order and how much it is going to cost. Click 'checkout', when you're happy.

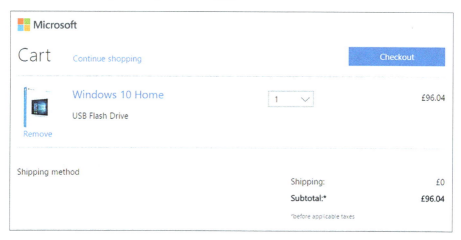

Click 'sign in and checkout'. Sign in with your Microsoft Account email address and password.

Run through the steps to enter payment details and confirm order. You'll be able to download Windows 10 and Microsoft will send you a copy on a USB stick.

This will associate your Windows 10 license with your Microsoft Account and the device you're installing it on. This means that when you log into Windows 10 with your Microsoft Account email address and password, Windows will automatically activate on your device, even if you have to re-install Windows.

To install Windows 10, insert the USB stick, open up your file explorer, navigate to the USB stick and run the 'setup.exe' file; see next section. You can also upgrade using the Media Creation Tool; see page 40.

If your device, laptop or PC came with Windows 10, you don't need to buy a copy, unless for example, you have Windows 10 Home and want to upgrade to Windows 10 Pro.

Upgrading from Windows 7 & 8

At the time of writing, if you have an activated version of Windows 7 or Windows 8, you can still upgrade to Windows 10 for free. To do this, go to the following website and download the media creation tool.

www.microsoft.com/software-download/windows10

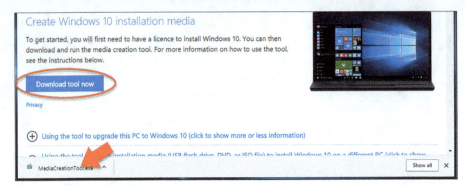

Double click on mediacreationtool.exe, or click 'run' when prompted by your browser. If you don't see it, the file will be in your downloads folder on your file explorer.

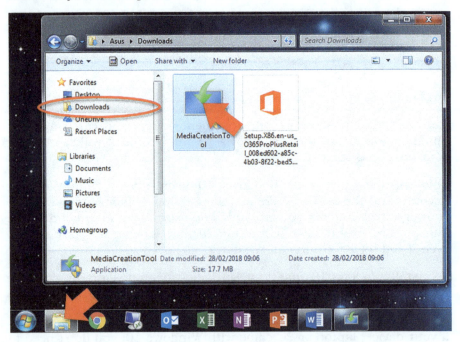

On the opening blue screen, make sure 'upgrade this PC now' is selected and click 'next'.

Follow the instructions on screen. Leave the setting selected; 'download and install updates'. This will insure you get the latest release of Windows 10. Click 'next'.

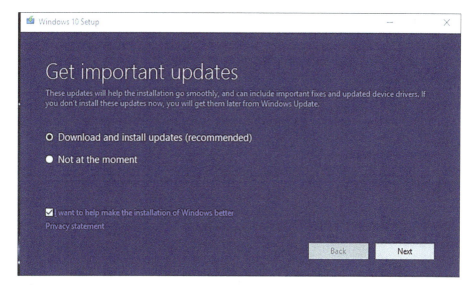

Click 'Accept' to accept the licence terms.

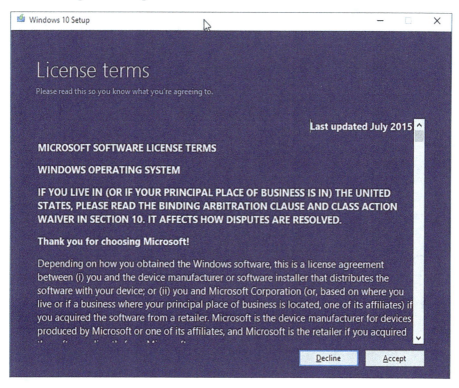

On the next screen, choose what data you want to keep. You have three options.

Keep personal files, apps and Windows settings

This upgrades everything to Windows 10 and transfers all your installed apps, settings and personal files.

Keep personal files only

Use this option if you want to remove installed apps, old windows settings and applications but keep all your personal files. If you choose this option you will need to re-install your applications. This is usually the best option to select.

Keep Nothing

This will wipe all your files, applications and settings. Only do this if you have backed up all your personal files. Useful if you want a fresh install of Windows 10.

If in doubt click 'keep personal files, apps and windows settings' to keep everything. This will keep all your files, any compatible applications and windows settings such as Edge/Explorer browser histories, contacts, desktop themes/backgrounds and so on.

Click Next.

Windows will shut down and restart. Once restarted windows update will kick in and configure the updates. This will take a while.

Setup will restart and Windows will proceed with the install. This will also take a while.

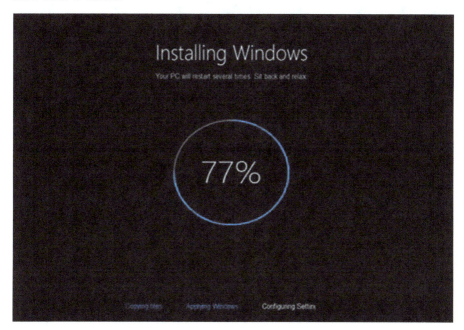

Once Windows 10 is installed, you'll see the 'welcome to windows 10' screen.

Chapter 2: Setting up Windows 10

Welcome to Windows 10. You will notice Windows 10 has imported your username from Windows 7/8. Click next.

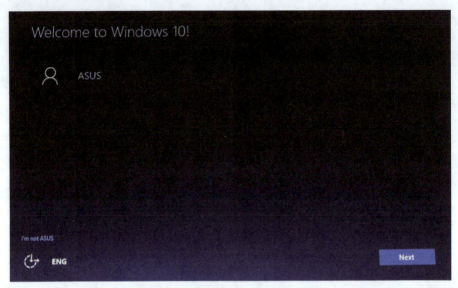

Select 'use express settings' to let Windows 10 use the default settings.

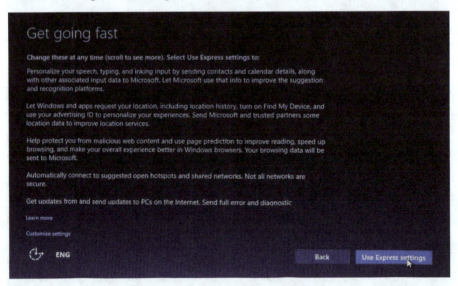

Click next on the following screen. Windows will start to configure itself and restart. Once it restarts you will land on the new Windows 10 desktop. You may need to go through 'running windows the first time' section, if you selected 'keep nothing' and decided to do a fresh install.

Upgrading from Windows 8 the same procedure.

Once you see the desktop you should switch to your Microsoft Account if Windows doesn't do it for you.

To check, go to the start menu and select settings on the bottom left.

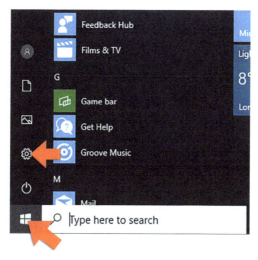

From the settings dialog box that appears, select accounts. Select 'your info' from the panel on the left.

If you see 'Local Account' then click 'Sign in with a Microsoft Account' - follow the instructions on screen.

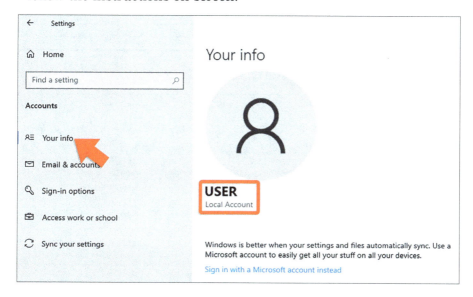

If you see 'Microsoft Account', you don't need to do anything here and can skip this step.

Update Assistant

The Update Assistant downloads and installs the latest version of Windows 10.

Open your web browser and navigate to the following website.

> www.microsoft.com/software-download/windows10

You'll need to purchase a license from the Microsoft Store, if you don't already have one. On the webpage click 'update now'.

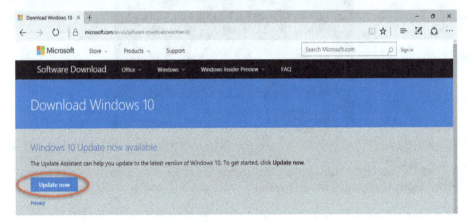

Click 'run' when prompted by your browser

Once the update assistant starts, click 'update now'.

Update Assistant will do a check on your device to make sure it is able to run the update.

Click 'next' on the bottom right when the check is complete.

The Update Assistant will now download and install the update.

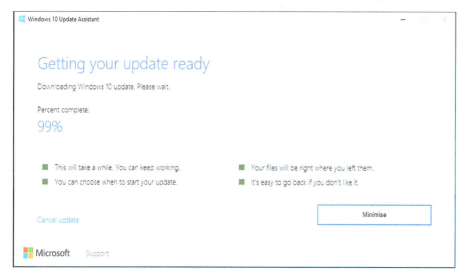

You can leave the Update Assistant open or you can minimise it and carry on working.

To minimise the assistant and run it in the background, click 'minimise'.

Once the update has been configured, click 'restart now'. You'll also notice a countdown on the left hand side of the screen. This means your device will restart automatically when the countdown hits zero.

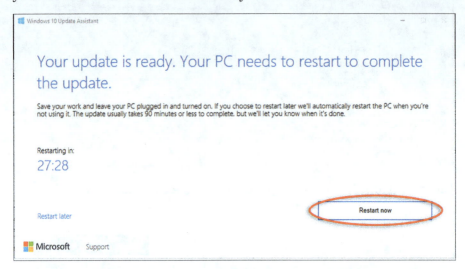

Your device will restart and installation will begin. This can take a while to complete.

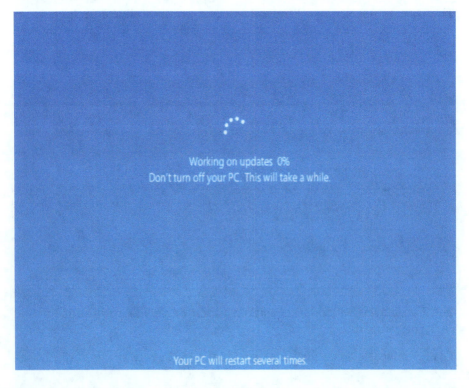

Once the installation is complete, you'll need to run through some settings.

You can turn them all on, but keep diagnostic information to 'basic', then click 'accept'. Select your username, if there is more than one, then click 'next'.

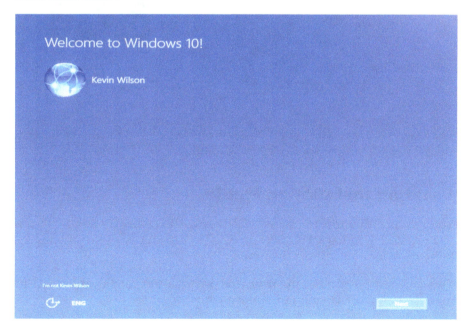

Click 'next' on the following screen. You can then log in when prompted.

Media Creation Tool

Microsoft has released a tool that you can download and run on your computer. This will allow you to create an install DVD or USB stick. These can be useful if your machine fails or has problems and will allow you to reinstall Windows 10 on your PC.

Open your web browser and navigate to the following website. You'll need to purchase a license from the Microsoft Store, if you don't already have one.

```
www.microsoft.com/software-download/windows10
```

Scroll down the page and at the bottom click 'download tool now'.

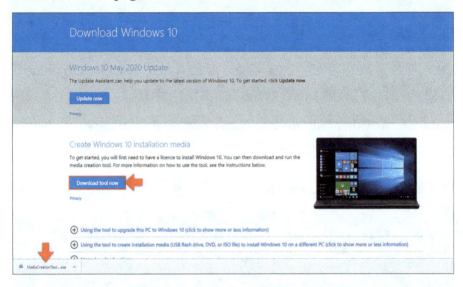

The download will appear on the bottom left of your browser screen. Click on it to run the tool.

Creating Installation Media

You can use this tool to create a DVD or a USB stick that you can use to re-install Windows 10 on your PC. This media is useful if your PC fails to start or your hard disk fails.

You can start your PC up from the installation media and run the installation process again to restore your computer.

To create the installation media, we are going to use a USB stick. Make sure your USB stick is at least 8GB.

First, plug your USB stick into your PC.

From the media creation tool, select 'create installation media (USB flash drive, DVD, or ISO file) for another PC'

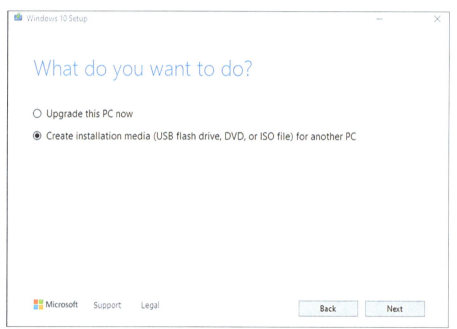

Click 'next'.

The media creation tool will start to download windows 10 and create the installation media. This might take a while...

Chapter 2: Setting up Windows 10

Select your language, edition of Windows 10 (home or pro) and your computer's architecture (either 32bit for older machines and 64bit for machines purchased in the last 10 years).

Most of the time, the media creation tool will automatically select these settings based on your current version of windows and hardware.

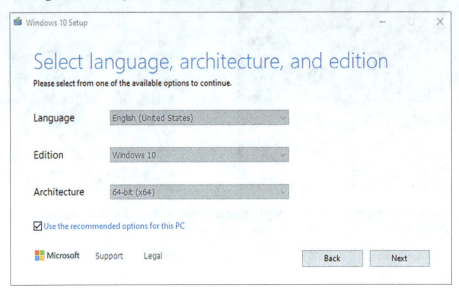

Click 'next'.

Select your installation media. In this case, we are using a USB stick, so select 'USB flash drive'.

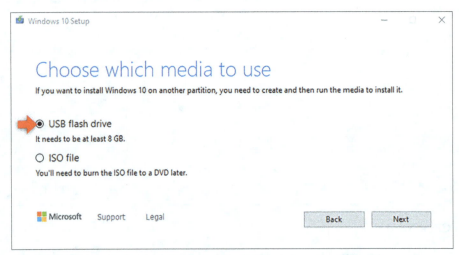

Click next.

The media creation tool will scan for your USB stick and will display what it finds in the next window.

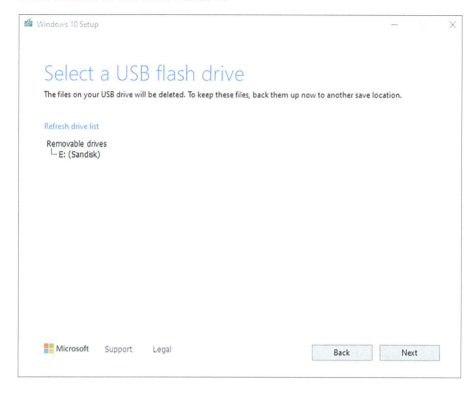

Click 'next' to start the process.

This process can take a while depending on the speed of your PC. Once it has finished, store your USB stick in a safe place, as you probably won't need it unless you have problems or want to install a fresh copy of Windows 10.

If you run into problems with your PC, you can always start it up using the USB stick you just created. See "Re-install Windows from USB Installation Media" on page 437.

Take a look at the 'media creation tool' demos in the maintenance section of the accompanying video resources. Go to the following website:

```
videos.tips/win-10-sys
```

Chapter 2: Setting up Windows 10

Media Creation Tool to Upgrade your PC

Open your web browser and navigate to the following website. Note *you'll need to purchase a license from the Microsoft Store, if you don't already have one.*

www.microsoft.com/software-download/windows10

Scroll down the page and at the bottom click 'download tool now'.

The download will appear on the bottom left of your browser screen. Click on it to run the tool.

From the main screen select 'upgrade this PC now'.

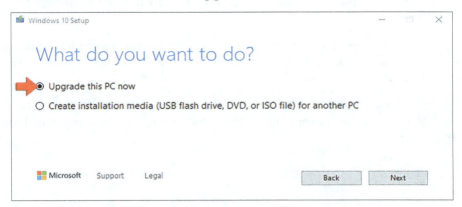

Click 'next'. Windows 10 installation files will be downloaded. This may take a while depending on your internet connection speed.

Once downloaded, accept the license terms. Windows creation tool will now download any updates it needs to install.

On the 'ready to install' screen, click 'change what to keep'.

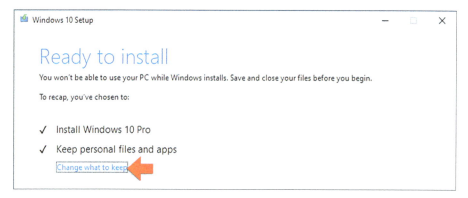

Select an option from the 'choose what to keep' screen.

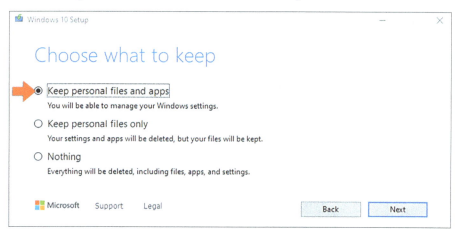

Select 'keep personal files and apps'. This will keep all your personal files, apps and current windows settings. For normal upgrades select this option.

Select 'keep personal files only' if you want to remove installed apps but keep all your personal files, removing all old windows settings and applications. If you choose this option you will need to re-install your applications.

Select 'keep nothing' to clean install windows 10. This will wipe all your files, applications and settings. Only do this if you have backed up all your personal files.

Click 'next'.

On the 'ready to install' screen, click 'install'.

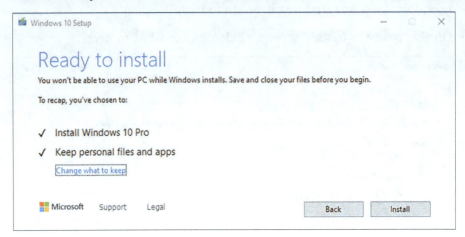

Windows will start the install. Your machine will restart a few times before it sorts itself out. Once installed, windows will run you through the initial setup - running windows the first time.

Take a look at the media creation tool demos in the maintenance section of the accompanying video resources.

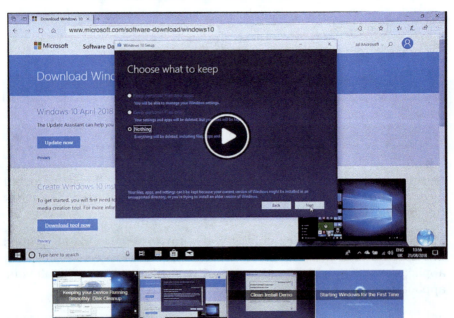

Open your web browser and navigate to:

```
videos.tips/win-10-sys
```

Running Windows the First Time

If you've just bought a new computer with Windows 10, or just installed a fresh copy, you'll need to run through the initial set up procedure.

Regional Settings

Select your country or region from the list and click 'yes'.

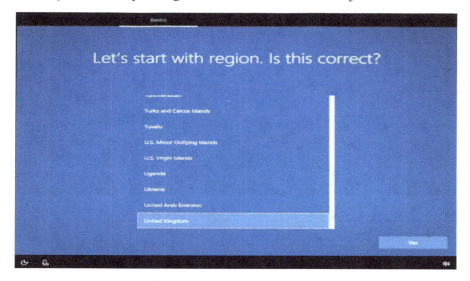

Select keyboard layout for your country, then click 'yes'. Skip secondary keyboard if you don't have one.

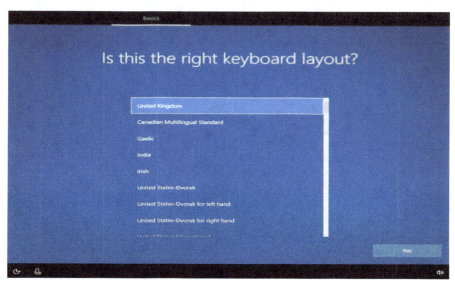

Terms Of Use

On the terms and agreements page click on 'Accept'.

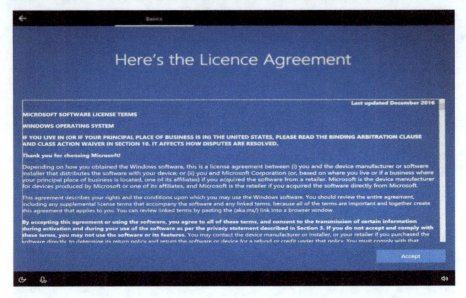

Connect to your WiFi

Select your WiFi network from the list of detected networks. This is usually printed on your router/modem or you can find out from your service provider. Click 'connect' from the box that appears.

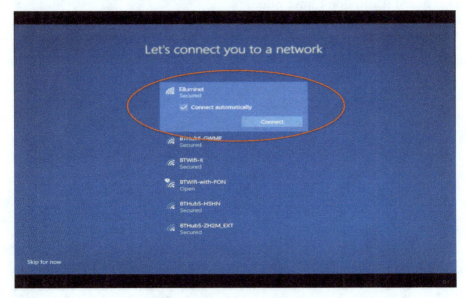

Enter WiFi Password

Enter the password for your WiFi network. This will be printed on the back of your router/modem, or you can find out from your service provider.

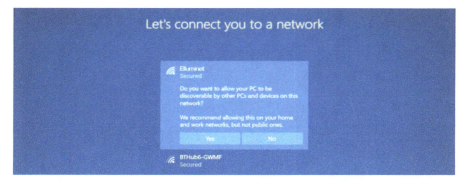

Click 'yes' to the prompt if you are on your home WiFi network. Click 'no' if you're using a public wifi hotspot such as a library, coffee shop or airport - you don't want other people to see you on a public network.

Sign in for the First Time

Sign in with your Microsoft Account email address and password, then click 'next'. This allows you to make use of OneDrive, email, purchase apps from the App Store, buy music and films.

If you don't have one, click 'create one', and fill in the form.

Set a PIN Code

Click 'Set a PIN code', then tap in your code, if you want the extra security. This means you can enter a 4 digit pin code instead of a password.

Link your Phone

This allows you access text messages, photos, contacts from your phone, and works best with android devices. Type in your phone number and hit 'send'. Click 'next' to continue.

Set up OneDrive

OneDrive is your online storage where you can store your files and access them from any of your devices. Click 'yes' to enable OneDrive.

Meet Cortana

Here you can enable your digital assistant and use voice commands.

Click 'yes' to enable Cortana, or click 'no' if you can't be bothered talking to your computer.

Do More with your Voice

If you're using Cortana, select 'use speech recognition', this helps Cortana understand you better. Select 'accept'.

Location

This allows windows to determine your physical location. This enables you to use location based apps such as weather, local interest, news as well as maps, and getting directions. To turn it on select 'yes'. If you don't plan on using any of these apps, then turn it off. Select 'accept'.

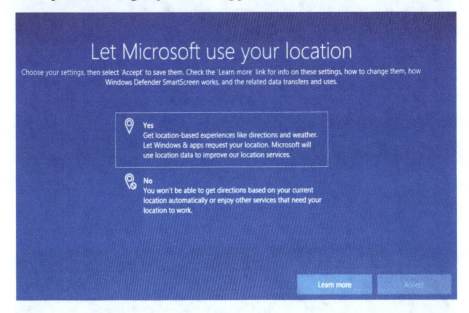

Find my Device

This is useful if you're setting up a tablet and allows windows to periodically report its location. This can help if you lose your device or it is stolen. You'll be able to see its location in your Microsoft Account settings. Select 'yes', then 'accept'.

Send Diagnostic Data

Diagnostic data is what Microsoft uses to troubleshoot problems and make improvements to its services. I'd suggest you select 'basic', so the only data that is sent to Microsoft is your device settings and its current state of operation, select 'accept'.

Improve Inking & Typing

This is data collected when you use Windows Ink and allows Microsoft to use the data to improve its product. Leaving this feature on is usually ok. Select 'yes' then 'accept'.

Get Tailored Experiences with Diagnostic Data

Allow Windows to tailor your computing experience to your personal tastes. This will give you tips and recommendations based on how you use Windows. To enable this, select 'yes', then 'accept'.

Let Apps use Advertising ID

This means any ads that appear will be tailored to your personal computing habits. Select 'yes', then 'accept'.

Chapter 2: Setting up Windows 10

Once Windows has all your preferences and details, it will configure your computer. Time for a coffee... this will take a while.

Once the configuration is complete, you'll land on the Windows 10 desktop.

Take a look at the "running windows for the first time" demos in the maintenance section of the accompanying video resources. Go to:

`videos.tips/win-10-sys`

Adjusting System Settings

To open the settings app, click the start button on the bottom left, then select the settings app icon on the left hand side of the start menu.

Here you'll see a window with different categories. Settings for different features and options are grouped into these categories.

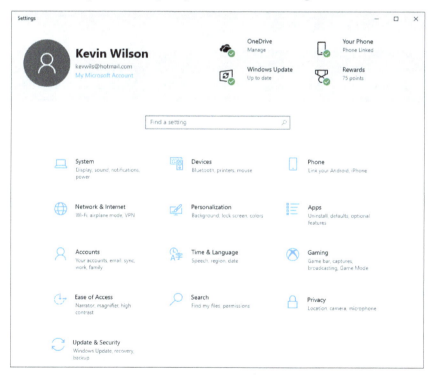

For example, all settings to do with devices such as printers, mice and keyboards can be found in the devices category. All system settings are found in the system category. Windows updates, backup and security settings are found in the update & security category.

Chapter 2: Setting up Windows 10

Lets take a look at the different categories of settings...

System: Display, sound, notifications & actions, focus, assist, power & sleep, battery, storage, tablet mode, multitasking/timeline, projecting to this PC, shared experiences, clipboard, remote desktop, about/ system info.

Devices: Bluetooth devices, printers & scanners, mouse, typing/ keyboard settings, pen & ink, autoplay, USB.

Phone: Link your iPhone or Android phone here.

Network & Internet: Network status, ethernet, wifi, dialup, VPN, airplane mode, mobile hotspot, proxy

Personalisation: Desktop background, colour schemes - light/dark mode, lock screen, themes - desktop icons, fonts, start menu, taskbar, recently used lists.

Apps: Apps & features, default apps, offline maps, apps for websites, video playback, startup apps.

Accounts: Your Microsoft Account info, email accounts, sign in options, connect to work or school network, add family members or additional user accounts, sync settings across devices, enable/disable kiosk mode.

Time & Language: Set date, time timezone, region & language, text to speech settings.

Gaming: Game bar, game DVR, broadcasting, game mode settings.

Ease of Access: On-screen narrator, magnifier, high contrast, closed captions, keyboard accessibility, mouse pointers and other visual & audio options.

Search: search permissions and history, safe search, searching windows - classic or enhanced, exclude folders from search.

Privacy: Windows permissions, app permissions. Diagnostics & feedback permissions. App permissions - location, cam, microphone, voice activation, notifications, calendar, phone calls, email, tasks, messaging, radio, other devices, background apps, documents, downloads folder, pictures, videos, file system, screen capture border

Update & Security: Windows update, windows security, backup, update downloads from other PCs, troubleshooting, windows recovery, activation, find my device, developer settings, programmatic screen capture.

The quickest way to change a setting is to search for it using the search field on the settings app.

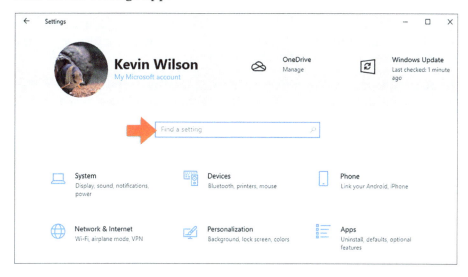

For example, if I wanted to change the printer settings, I could just type 'printer' into the search field where it says 'find a setting'.

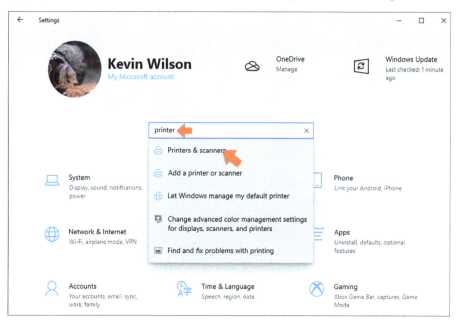

Click on 'Printers & Scanners' in the list of suggestions in the drop down box.

You can do this for any setting you need to change.

Screen Resolution

The screen resolution is the number of horizontal pixels by the number of vertical pixels on a screen. For example a full HD screen is 1920x1080. Windows 10 does its best to automatically select the correct screen resolution for any screens it detects.

If you need to change the screen resolution for any reason, type `display settings` into the search field on the bottom left of the taskbar. Select 'display settings' from the search results.

Select the screen whose resolution you want to change if you are using multiple screens. If you only have one screen you'll only have one choice.

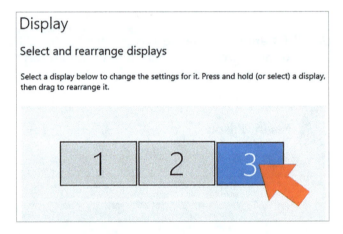

Scroll down to 'resolution', click the drop down box and select a resolution from the list.

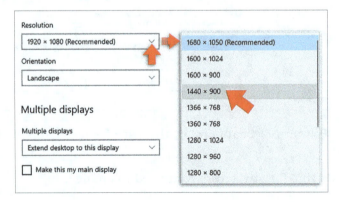

Power Options

If you need to change the power save settings, type `power & sleep` into the search field on the bottom left of the taskbar. Select 'power & sleep settings' from the search results.

Here, you can set the amount of time before your computer turns off the screen and the amount of time before your computer goes into sleep mode. These times mean the length of time your computer is left unattended. Click the drop down box and select a time.

To change your power schemes, click 'additional power settings' on the right hand side of the screen.

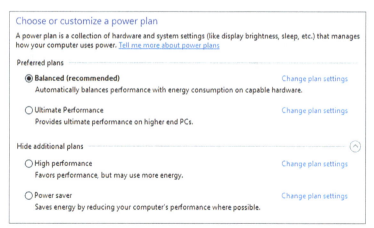

The balanced plan is great for laptops and tablets as it gives you a balance between performance and power efficiency.

Ultimate performance, and high performance plans are great for workstations and desktop PCs.

Date and Time

If you need to change the power save settings, type `date & time` into the search field on the bottom left of the taskbar. Select 'date & time settings' from the search results.

Here, you can select your time zone. Windows will automatically set the time when it connects to the internet.

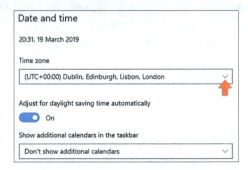

Regional Settings

If you need to change the power save settings, type `regional settings` into the search field on the bottom left of the taskbar. Select 'regional settings' from the search results.

Here, you can select your country or region and regional format.

Regional format means the format of dates, times, and the calendar you use.

Verifying Accounts

If you have signed into a new computer with your Microsoft Account, you'll need to verify your identity on that new computer. This is done as a security procedure.

To do this, go to the Settings App and click 'accounts'.

If you see 'you need to verify your identity on this PC', then you need to run through the verification process. Click 'verify'.

Enter the recovery email address you added when you signed up for your Microsoft Account. Click 'next'.

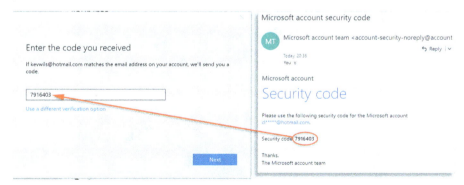

Check the recovery email account and enter the code from the 'Microsoft Account Team' email message. Click 'Next' to finish.

Connecting to WiFi Networks

To locate nearby WiFi networks, tap the WiFi icon on the bottom right of the screen or open the action centre and tap 'network'.

 **or**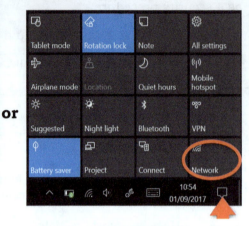

Tap the name of the network you want to join, then tap 'connect'

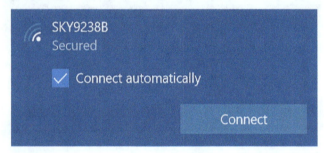

Enter the WiFi password or network key.

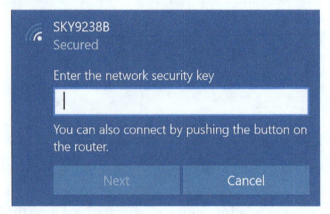

Once you have done that tap 'next' or 'ok'.

For your home WiFi, the network key or password is usually printed on the back of your router. Select network name and enter security key (password) when prompted.

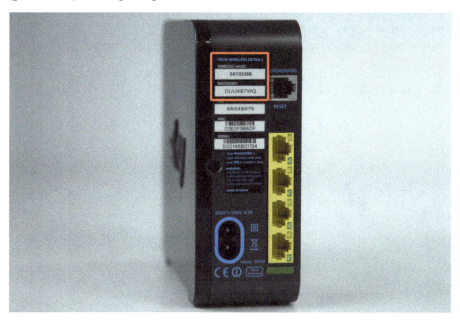

Sometimes the network name is called an SSID.

Use the same procedure if you are on a public hotspot such as in a cafe, library, hotel, airport and so on. You'll need to find the network key if they have one. Some are open networks and you can just connect.

When using public hotspots, keep in mind that most of them don't encrypt the data you send over the internet and aren't secure. So don't start checking your online banking account or shop online while using an unsecured connection, as anyone who is on the public wifi hotspot potentially can gain access to anything you do.

If you're really concerned about security or use your devices on public hotspots for work, then you should consider a VPN or Virtual Private Network. A VPN essentially encrypts all the data you send and receive over a network. There are a few good ones to choose from, some have a free option with a limited amount of data and others you pay a subscription.

Take a look at www.tunnelbear.com, windscribe.com & speedify.com

To set up a VPN, open Action Centre > VPN > Add VPN Connection

Enter the connection details from one of the VPN providers above.

Linking your Phone

You can link to any smartphone such as an iPhone, Android or Windows Phone. On an Android phone, you can view and respond to text messages, see photos, sync contacts, and so on. This feature works best if you have an Android phone running Android 7 or later.

The first thing you'll need to do is open the 'your phone' app on your PC. You'll find the app on your start menu.

Here, you can select your phone.

Android Phones

In the 'your phone' app on your PC, select 'android' and click 'continue'.

To link your phone, enter your phone number.

Click 'send'.

On your phone, check your text/sms messages, there should be one from Microsoft. Tap on the link.

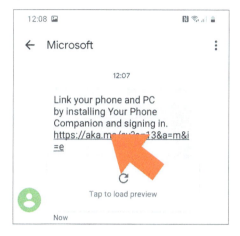

The link will take you to the Play Store where you can download the app. Tap 'install' on the product page.

Once installed tap 'open'.

For future reference, you'll find the 'Your Phone Companion' on your home screen, but because this app runs in the background, once signed in, you won't normally need to open it again.

Once the app starts on your phone, tap 'is there a QR code on your PC'. Tap 'allow' to any permission prompts.

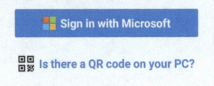

Scan the QR code on your PC's screen.

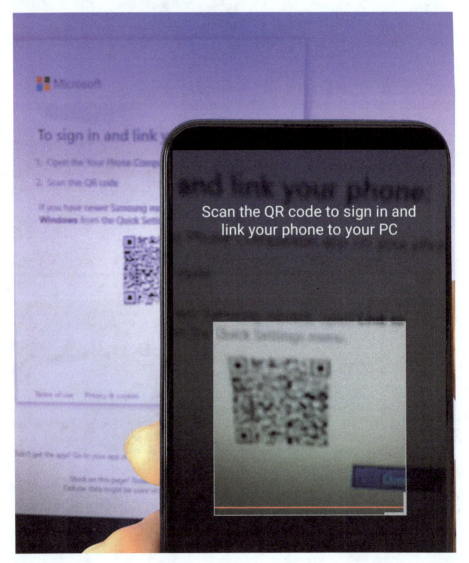

Tap 'continue', then tap 'allow' on any permission prompts.

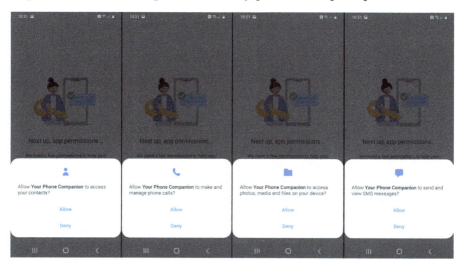

Tap 'continue'.

Now, on your PC, click 'done'.

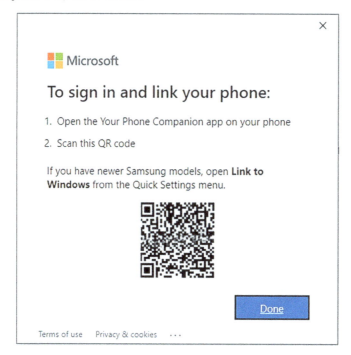

Allow your phone to connect to your PC.

iPhones

On your phone, go to the app store, open the search and type:

    Microsoft Edge

Tap 'get' to download the app to your phone.

Open Edge on your iPhone and sign in with your Microsoft Account email address and password

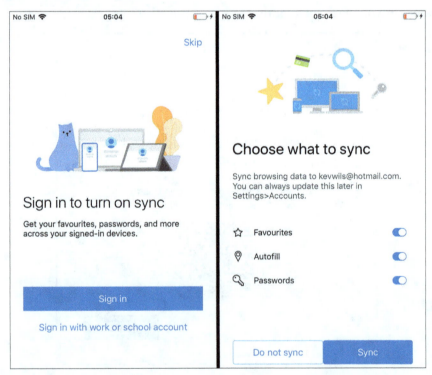

Choose what to sync. Tap 'share data', then tap 'allow' on any permission prompts.

Create a Microsoft Account

To set up a new Microsoft Account, open your web browser and navigate to the following address:

```
signup.live.com
```

Enter an email address you'd like to use for your Microsoft Account, click 'next'. Next, enter a password for the account. *Remember passwords must have at least 8 characters and contain at least one uppercase letter, lowercase letter, number, and a symbol (eg: *, $, #, etc).* Click 'next'.

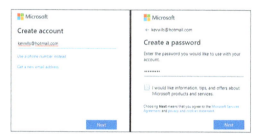

Enter your first and last names in the fields, click 'next'. Then enter the country you're living in and your date of birth.

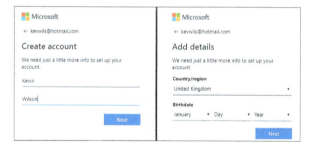

Enter the captcha code in the field at the bottom

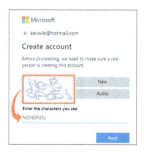

Click 'next'. Your account will be created. Close the browser window and you're good to go.

Setting up Additional Users

You can set up multiple users for different people on your computer. This will allow them to sign into your computer with their own username and have access to their own OneDrive, calendar, and email.

There are three different types of user: administrators, standard users and child users.

Administrators have complete access to your computer. They can install software and change settings. Administrator accounts should only be used to change settings and install software, not for everyday use.

Standard users can use apps and make limited changes to the system settings and are best for everyday use. This is the type of account you should be using for your every day tasks.

Child users have restricted access to apps. Child user accounts are also monitored, allowing an adult user to check up on websites visited or apps used.

Adding a New User with Microsoft Account

To add a new user, click the start menu, and select the settings app icon.

Then select 'accounts' from the settings app home page. Select 'Family & other users'.

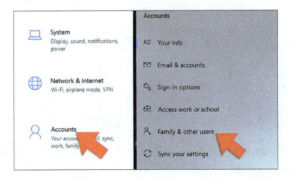

Click 'Add someone else to this PC'.

Enter the new user's Microsoft Account email address and password.

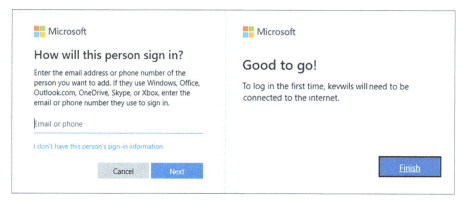

The new user will be able to log into Windows with their own account and can select it from the login screen.

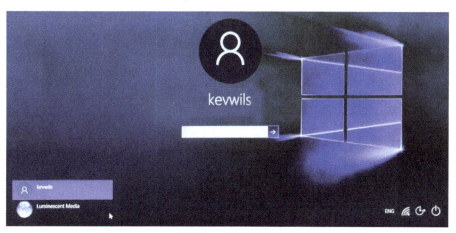

Adding a New User with Local Account

A local account is an account you can log into your computer without having to sign up for a Microsoft Account email address and password.

To add a local user, click the start menu, and select the settings app icon.

Then select 'accounts' from the settings app home page. Select 'Family & other users'.

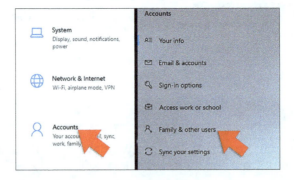

Click 'Add someone else to this PC'.

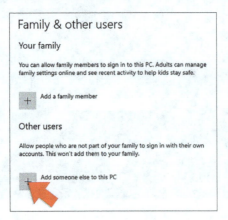

From 'how will this person sign in' screen, select 'I con't have this person's sign-in information. On the 'create account' screen, select 'add user without microsoft account'.

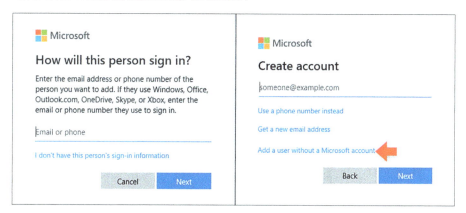

Enter the username and password for this user. Select three security questions - this is to verify your identity should you need to reset your password.

Click 'next'.

The new user will be able to log into Windows with their own account and can select it from the login screen.

Change an Account Type

As we mentioned earlier, you can change an account to either a standard user or an administrator.

To add a local user, click the start menu, and select the settings app icon.

Then select 'accounts' from the settings app home page. Select 'Family & other users'.

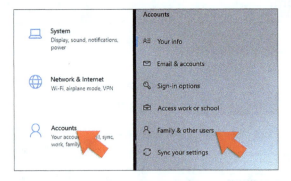

Under 'other users' select the user you want to change. From the options select 'change account type'.

From the popup dialog box, select either 'administrator' or 'standard user'.

Set up OneDrive

OneDrive comes with Windows 10 and is probably the safest place to store all your files as they are backed up in case your PC crashes.

If you signed into Windows 10 with your Microsoft Account, then OneDrive is usually installed.

To set it up, click the OneDrive's icon in the system tray on the bottom right hand side of the screen.

Enter your Microsoft Account email address then click 'sign in'.

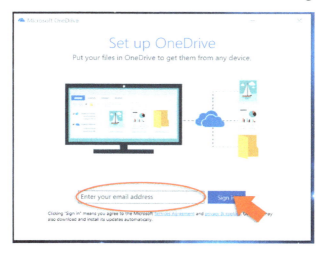

Enter your password, then click 'sign in'.

71

OneDrive will ask you where you want to store your OneDrive files on your computer while you work on them. Most of the time you can just leave it in it's default location. Click next.

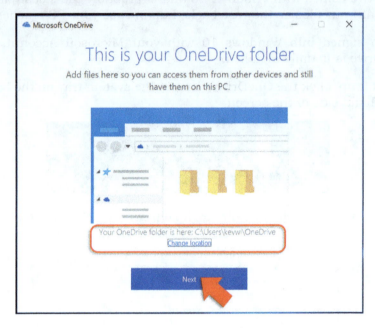

OneDrive will scan for directories and files on your OneDrive account and synchronise them with your local machine.

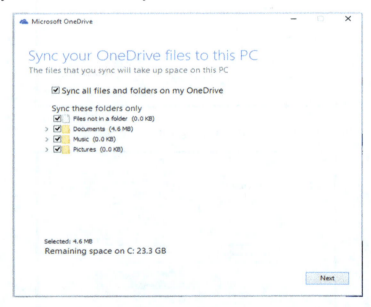

I usually select all of them. Click 'next'.

The theory is, you work on the files on your local machine - you edit, update, create, save, and do the things you need to do. OneDrive automatically copies these updates onto your OneDrive Account in the Cloud. This is called synchronisation. This means you can access your files from any of your devices whether it is a tablet, phone, laptop, or on the web.

You'll find your OneDrive files in File Explorer. To open File Explorer, click the icon on your taskbar.

You'll find your OneDrive listed in the left hand pane, as shown in the example below.

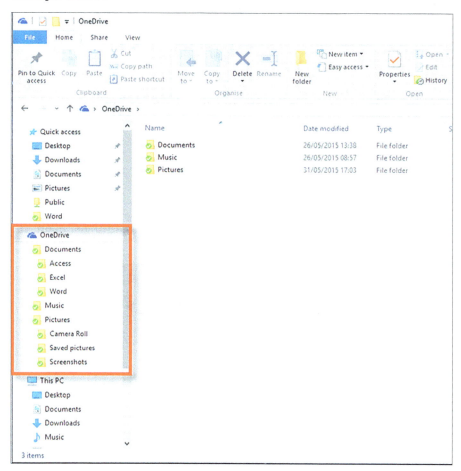

This is where you should save all your files you work on, in your apps.

Setting up Printers

You can connect a printer to your computer with a USB cable as well as using WiFi.

Using USB

Using a USB cable, plug the square end into the back of the printer, then plug the other end into a USB port on your computer.

Turn on your printer, then open the start menu and click on the settings app icon.

From the settings app, click 'devices'.

Select 'printers & scanners' from the panel on the left hand side, then click 'add a printer or scanner'.

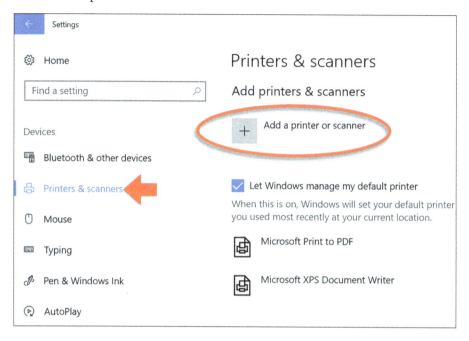

Windows will detect most modern printers. Select your printer from the list.

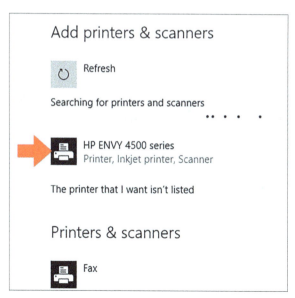

If your printer isn't listed go to page 84 to download the driver software for your printer.

HP Printers

HP have introduced a simplified setup method for their printers. To set up your printer, plug it in and turn it up. On your computer open your web browser and navigate to the following website

```
123.hp.com
```

Type your printer's model number into the search field.

Click 'download' or 'get the app'. Follow the instructions on the screen to download and install the drivers or the app.

Epson Printers

To set up your printer, plug it in and turn it up. On your computer open your web browser and navigate to the following website

```
epson.sn
```

Type your printer's model number into the search field.

Click 'lets get started'. Scroll down the page.

Follow the instructions on the screen to download and install the drivers or the app.

Canon Printers

To set up your printer, plug it in and turn it up. On your computer open your web browser and navigate to the following website

    canon.com/ijsetup

Click 'setup', then type in your printer model number.

Follow the instructions on the screen to download and install the drivers or the app.

Brother Printers

To set up your printer, plug it in and turn it up. On your computer open your web browser and navigate to the following website

    support.brother.com

Select 'downloads'.

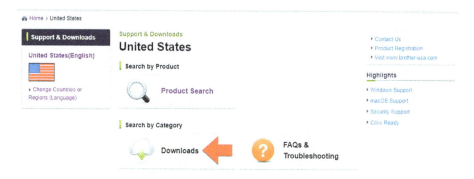

Type in your model number.

Select 'windows 10', then download the 'full driver & software package'. Follow the instructions on screen.

WPS

Wifi is definitely the way you'd want to connect to a printer if you are on a tablet or laptop. Unfortunately it is difficult to give specific instructions on printer setup as each model of printer and each manufacturer has their own method. However, I will provide some general guidelines you can use to get started.

If your printer is brand new, you'll need to connect it to your Wifi. Printers with LCD panels display step-by-step instructions for setting up the wireless connection when you first turn on the printer. So read the instructions for specifics on how to do this.

If your printer doesn't have an LCD panel, use the WPS method. You can use this method if you have a WPS button on your router - as shown in the photo below. Refer to the printer's quick start guide to find the exact procedure for your printer model. Usually you have to press and hold the WiFi button on your printer for a few seconds, then go to your router and press the WPS button.

If your router doesn't have a WPS button, you'll have to select your WiFi network (SSID) and enter your WiFi password on your printer. You'll need to refer to the printer's instructions on exactly how to do that on your particular printer.

Your printer will let you know when it's connected to your WiFi - the WiFi light usually stops flashing and lights up. Once connected, on your computer open the settings app from the start menu.

From the settings app, click 'devices'.

Select 'printers & scanners' from the panel on the left hand side, then click 'add a printer or scanner'.

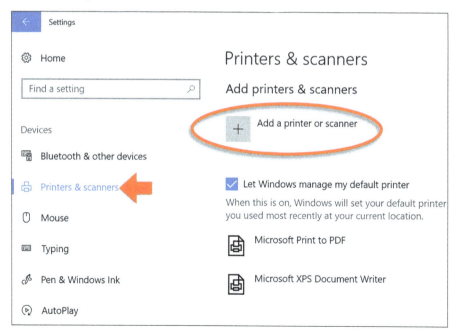

Windows will detect most modern printers. Select your printer from the list.

Select your printer from the list, then click 'add device'.

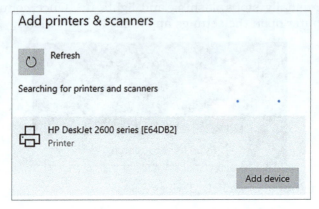

Windows will download and install the appropriate driver for your printer automatically.

To find your installed printers, type printers into the search field on the bottom left of the taskbar.

From the search results click 'printers & scanners'. In the printers & scanners page, you'll see your printers listed. Click on the printer.

Click 'open queue' to see what's printing, click 'manage' to change printer settings and preferences or click 'remove device' to un-install the printer

Older Printers

If Windows doesn't detect your printer or you have an older model, click 'the printer I want isn't listed.'

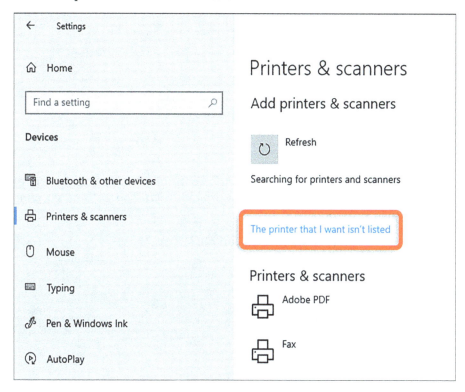

For printers connected via USB select 'my printer is a little older, help me find it.'

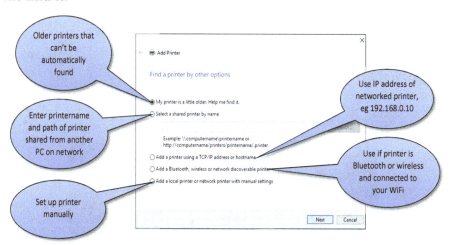

Select your printer from the results list, click 'next', then give the printer a name if required, click 'next'.

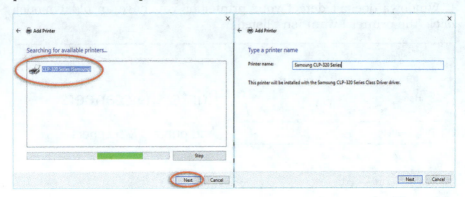

For some of the older printers, Windows may prompt you for driver software. If this is the case cancel the procedure and go to "Downloading Printer Drivers" on page 84.

Select 'do not share this printer' then click next.

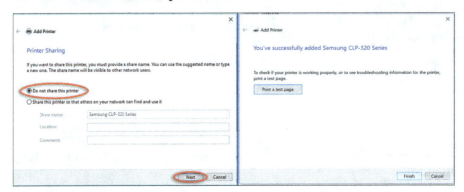

Once you're done, click 'finish'.

Managing Printers

You can get to the print queue from the Settings App on the start menu. From the Settings App, click 'devices'.

On the left hand side of the window, click 'printers & scanners', then select your printer. From the options that open up, click 'open queue'.

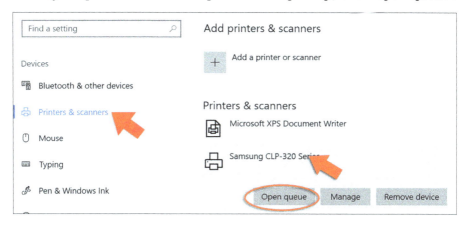

This will open up the print queue for that printer.

Document Name	Status	Owner	Pages	Size	Submitted	Port
Microsoft Word - planet earth	Spooling	kev	N/A		18:28:51 20/03/2019	
Microsoft Word - Payment Req...		kev	1	13.9 KB	18:28:18 20/03/2019	
Microsoft Word - Author Bio		kev	1	28.6 KB	18:27:06 20/03/2019	

3 document(s) in queue

Here you can see a list of documents that are queued for printing. If you right click on the print job in the list, you can cancel or pause the document. You can also change global printer settings and preferences here too.

Have a look at the 'installing printers' video demos in the 'using windows 10' section of the resources. Go to the following website:

videos.tips/using-win-10

Downloading Printer Drivers

If Windows 10 has trouble installing your printer, you'll need to download and install the printer software.

To do this, you'll need to go to the manufacturer's website and download the software.

For HP & Samsung printers go to

```
support.hp.com/drivers
```

For Canon printers go to

```
www.usa.canon.com/support
```

For Brother printers go to

```
support.brother.com
```

For Epson printers go to

```
support.epson.com
```

Somewhere on the manufacturer's website, there will be a product search field. Type in the model name of your printer. Click 'OK' or 'find'

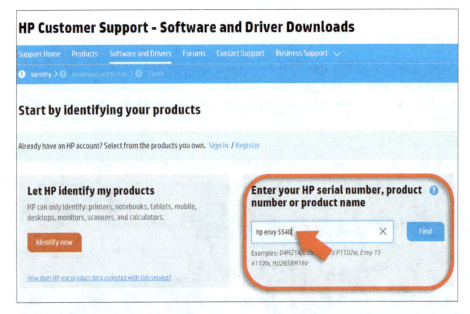

In the example above, I'm installing an HP printer. In most cases you'll need to download the driver software from the manufacturer's website.

From the search results, select your Operating System if required, usually "Windows 10 (64bit)".

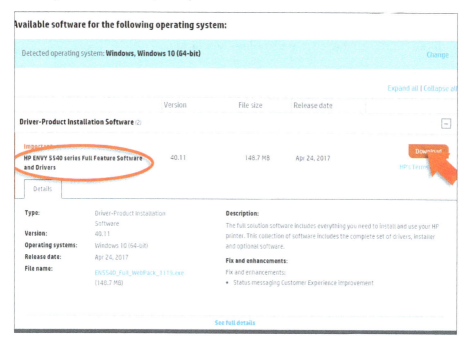

Click on the prompt at the bottom of your browser.

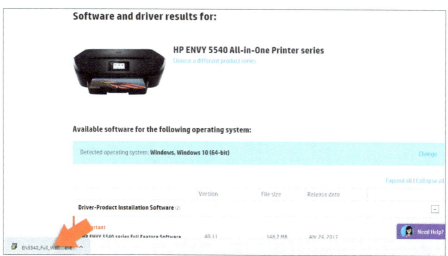

This will run the installation software. Click 'OK' or 'Yes' to the security prompt. If you don't see a prompt, go to your downloads folder in file explorer and double click on the EXE file you just downloaded. Follow the on screen instructions to connect to your printer.

Setting up Windows Hello

Windows Hello is Microsoft's biometric security feature built into some Windows 10 devices. Not all tablets and PCs support this, however this is likely to change as the technology develops.

Windows Hello allows you to sign into your device and certain services and websites, using a finger print or face scan instead of a password. You will need a compatible web cam or finger print scanner on your device/PC to do this.

Currently the only devices that support this feature are

- Surface Book Laptops

- Surface Pro Tablets

- Any PC or Laptop with a 'RealSense' camera or a finger print scanner

Windows Hello gives you some extra sign in options. Tap your settings icon, then choose Accounts. From Accounts tap 'sign in options'

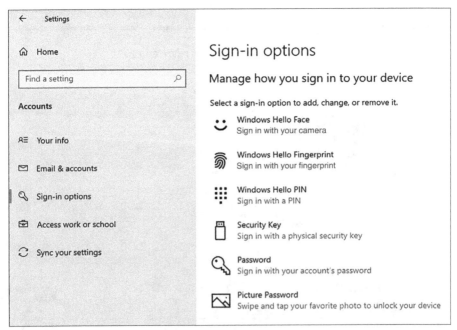

Here, you can choose 'windows hello face' for facial recognition, 'windows hello fingerprint' if you have a finger print scanner, or 'windows hello pin' if you want to sign in with a PIN code. You can also use a security key fob, password or picture password.

Finger Print Scanner

To use the finger print scanner, select 'windows hello fingerprint' from the sign in options. Then select 'set up' under the fingerprint section of the 'sign in' options under 'fingerprint'.

Scan your finger using the fingerprint reader. Most people use their index finger You may need to do this a few times. Keep going until Windows informs you the process is complete.

Select close on the bottom right.

You should now be able to sign in with your fingerprint from the lock screen. You might have to tap 'sign in options' if the feature isn't automatically selected.

So instead of typing in a password, I can now just swipe my finger on the scanner to sign into my account.

Facial Recognition

To use this feature you will however need a webcam that supports this technology. Something like the "windows hello camera", shown below.

If you have a Microsoft device such as a surface studio, surface tablet or surface book, the web cam is built in.

Tap your settings icon, then choose 'accounts'. From the accounts page, tap 'sign in options', then select 'windows hello face'

Under 'windows hello face' select 'set up'.

On your screen you'll see an image from your webcam. Make sure you can see your whole face and head in the image. Keep looking at the screen, until Windows has completed the scan. It will usually take a few seconds.

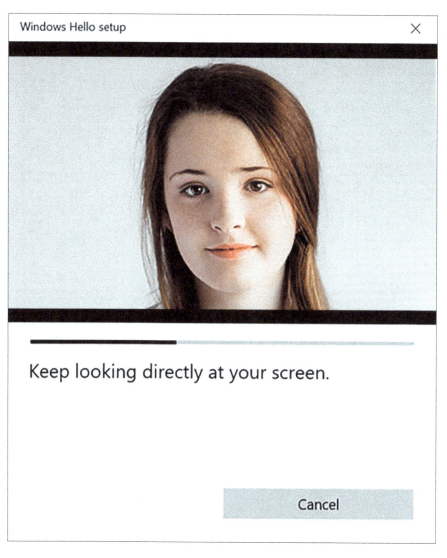

Make sure you turn on 'automatically unlock the screen if we recognise your face'.

Close the settings app.

Now when you turn on your computer, you won't need to sign in with a password, you just look at your screen and Windows will unlock your account for you.

Sign in with a PIN

A PIN is usually 4 - 8 numbers you can use to sign into windows instead of a password. To create a PIN, tap your settings icon, then choose Accounts. From Accounts tap 'sign in options. Select 'windows hello PIN' from the sign in options.

Tap 'add', then tap 'next'.

Enter your microsoft account password if prompted. Enter your new PIN. Click 'ok'.

You can now sign in with a PIN instead of typing in your password.

90

Pairing Bluetooth Devices

You can pair any bluetooth device such as a mouse, keyboard, headphones, pens and so on. To do this go to the settings icon on the start menu, select 'devices', then click 'bluetooth & other devices'.

Shift the bluetooth slider to 'on'. Then click 'add bluetooth or other device'. From the 'add a device' menu, select the type of device you're adding. In this example bluetooth.

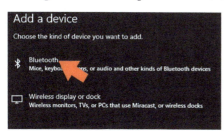

Put your device into discover mode. How you do this depends on the device, so you'll need to read the instructions that came with it to find out. In this example, I'm going to pair a bluetooth mouse. To put the mouse into pairing mode, press and hold the button on the bottom of the mouse until the light underneath starts flashing.

Your laptop or PC will start scanning for bluetooth devices, and list them in this window.

Select your device from the list. Windows will add and setup the device automatically. You'll be able to use it in a few moments. Click 'done'.

Check out the video demo in the 'using windows 10' section on pairing bluetooth devices. Open your browser and go to the following website:

```
videos.tips/using-win-10
```

Dynamic Lock

Dynamic lock allows you to automatically lock and unlock your PC using a paired bluetooth device - usually a smartphone. For this to work, you first need to pair your phone with your PC using bluetooth.

Pair your Phone

Before activating the dynamic lock, you will first need to pair your device or phone with your PC or laptop via Bluetooth. To do this open your settings app and select 'devices'.

From the left hand panel, select 'bluetooth & other devices. Then in the right hand pane, turn bluetooth to 'on' and click the '+' icon to pair a device.

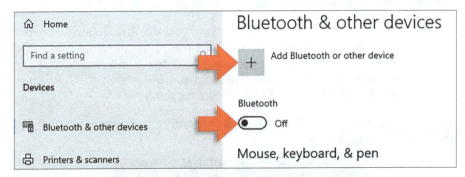

From the 'add a device' dialog box, select 'bluetooth'.

Windows will generate a code once your phone has been detected. Enter this code into your phone and tap 'pair'.

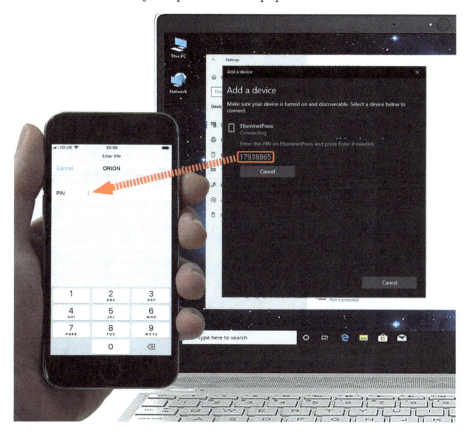

Enable Dynamic Lock

To enable dynamic lock go to: settings, select 'accounts', then click 'sign-in options'. Scroll down to 'dynamic lock'

Tick the box next to 'Allow Windows to detect when you're away and automatically lock the device.'

Focus Assist

Formerly known as Quiet Hours, Focus Assist allows you to silence notifications during a period of time, so you can focus on your work without distraction.

Change Focus Assist Mode

You can change focus assist from action center. To do this, click on the action center icon on the bottom right of your screen.

 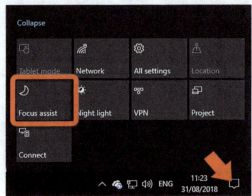

Click the 'focus assist' icon. When you click the icon, you can toggle between three different settings. Click once to set it to 'priority only', click again to show alarms only, click again to turn off completely.

Priority only mode, silences all notifications except those from the apps in your priority list, or messages from people in your priority list.

Alarms only mode, ie do not disturb mode, silences all notifications except for an alarm from the Alarms & Clock app.

Open Priority List

Open settings app and select 'system'. Then select 'focus assist' from the list down the left hand side of the window.

Now, select 'customise your priority only', then click 'customise your priority list.

Add People & Apps to Priority List

Open your priority list, Scroll down to 'people', click 'add contacts'. Select the contacts from the list, or search for them using the search bar at the top of the dialog box. You'll receive notifications when these people send you a message using email, skype, or messaging.

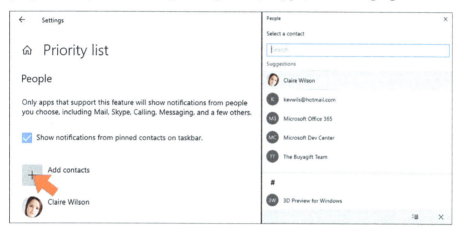

Scroll down to 'apps', click 'add app'. Then select the apps you want to receive notifications from.

Click the back arrow on the top left of the screen to return to the focus assist settings.

Select 'priority only' to enable.

Configure Automatic Rules

Open settings app and select 'system'. Then select 'focus assist' from the list down the left hand side of the window. Scroll down to 'automatic rules'. Click the slider next to 'during these times' to turn it on, if it isn't already.

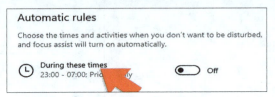

Here, you can configure the hours you don't want to be disturbed. You can set a start time and an end time.

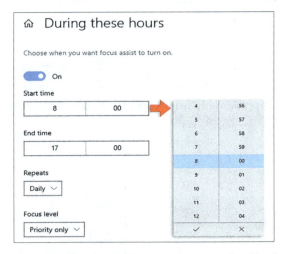

For example, you could set the start time to the beginning of your working hours, and the end time to the time you finish. Click the times, then select the time you want from the popup menu. Set 'repeats' to daily, this repeat setting every day. Set focus level to 'priority only' if you want to receive notifications from apps or people on your priority list. Select 'alarms only' if you don't want to be disturbed by any notifications during this time.

Click the back arrow on the top left of the screen to return to the focus assist settings.

Turn on 'when I'm duplicating my display', 'when I'm playing a game', and 'when I'm using an app in full screen mode' to stop notifications during these events.

96

Storage Sense

Over time, temporary files, caches and files in the recycle bin start to accumulate. Storage sense monitors and deletes these files, keeping your system running smoothly. To find storage sense, open the settings app and select system. On the left hand panel select 'storage'. Under the 'storage' section, switch the slider to 'on'.

Scroll further down the page and you'll see your hard disk drive and various categories. This is a breakdown of how your storage is being used. You'll see space allocated to 'system & reserved' such as system files. You'll also see space allocated to 'apps & features', temp files and so on. For example, click 'temporary files'

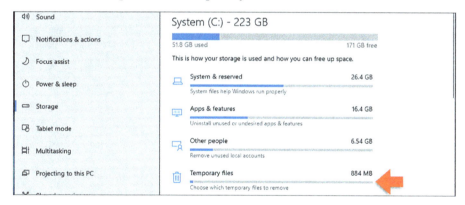

From here, you can clear out any temp files. Click 'remove files'.

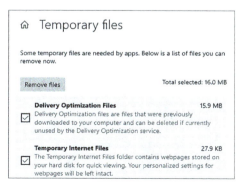

Configure Storage Sense

Open the settings app and select system. On the left hand panel select 'storage'. Click 'configure storage sense or run it now'.

Set 'run storage sense' to 'weekly'. This will allow Windows to automatically manage disk space by deleting cached and temporary files once a week.

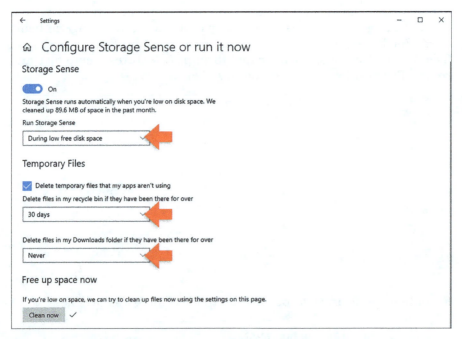

Under the 'temporary files' section, set 'delete files in my recycle bin...' to '30 days'. I don't usually allow Windows to delete files in my downloads folder, as sometimes I like to reuse or keep things I have downloaded from the web. However if you don't do this, then you can allow Windows to delete files in your downloads folder after a certain number of days - usually 30 days is a good setting.

Once you're done, hit 'clean now'. Windows will automatically clear temporary files.

Blue Light Reduction

This feature is designed to reduce the amount of blue light emitted from your device's screen in the evenings, which is said to suppress the secretion of melatonin in the brain affecting your ability to sleep.

To turn it on, click the start menu and select the settings app icon

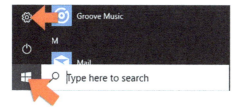

Select the 'system' icon on the settings app home page. Then select 'display' from the list on the left hand side of the screen.

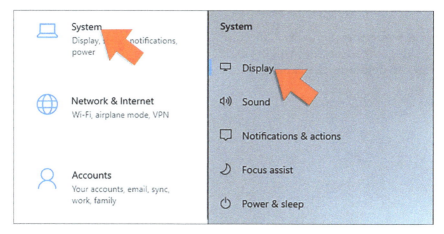

Under 'color', switch the 'night light' slider to 'on' then click 'night light settings'.

Click 'turn on now'. You can adjust the level of the night light using the 'colour temperature at night' slider.

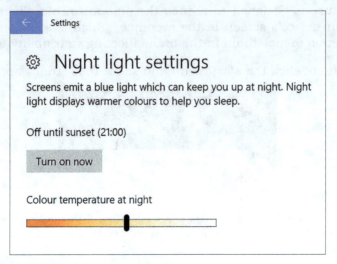

If you want the night light to come on at a specific time each night, shift the 'schedule night light' slider to 'on' and enter the time in the 'turn on' field and the time to turn it off in the 'turn off' field.

You'll see the screen turn an orange colour. Any work you produce, such as printing, editing, or photos, will not have the orange tint.

Dark Mode

Dark mode makes looking at your screen a bit easier on the eyes. It replaces the bright white backgrounds in Windows Apps with a dark acrylic background. This only works with Windows Apps such as explorer, photos, news, groove music, mail, or calendar, and not with applications such as Word, Chrome, or Photoshop. Below you can see dark mode vs light mode.

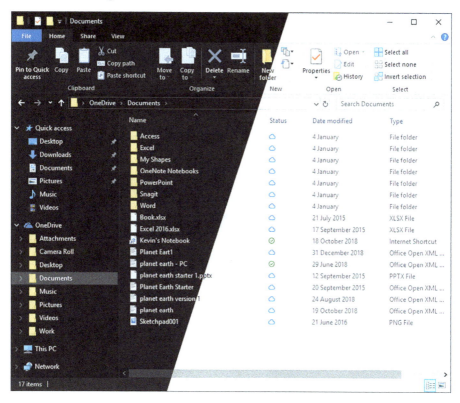

You can change between dark and light mode in the settings app. Open settings app

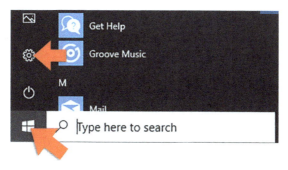

From the settings app home page select 'personalisation'. Then select 'colors' from the list on the left hand side.

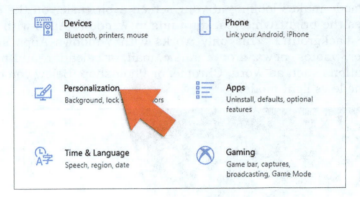

Scroll down until you see 'choose your color'. Select 'custom' from the drop down.

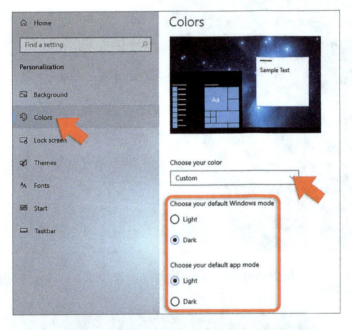

Now you can choose between dark and light mode. 'Windows Mode' sets the colour mode for the start menu, taskbar, search, system tray, and action center.

'App Mode' sets the colour mode for all windows apps including, mail, calendar, file explorer, news, weather, app store, and so on.

As an example, I prefer leaving windows mode on 'dark', and app mode on 'light'.

Light Mode

Light mode has been extended to include the start menu, taskbar, and action center. Here below, you can see windows running in light mode.

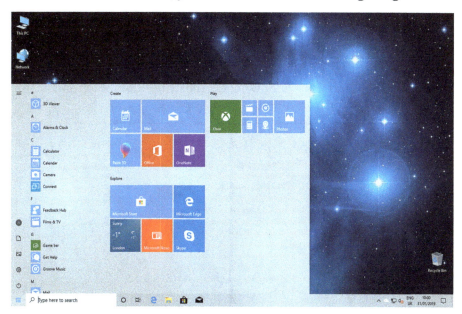

You can also see, action center, and search have a light mode look as well.

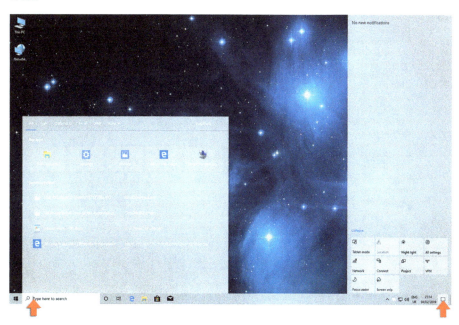

Cortana Settings

You can customise Cortana, click on the Cortana icon on the bottom left of the taskbar.

Then from the Cortana window, click the three dots icon on the top left. Select 'settings' from the drop down menu.

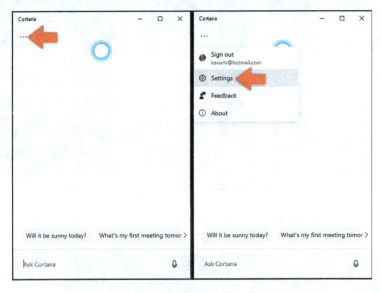

Here, you can adjust settings such as microphone, and voice activation settings.

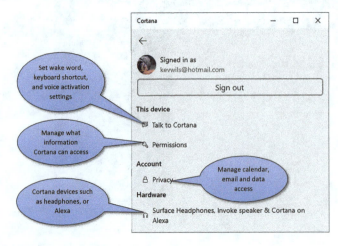

Voice Activation Settings

Open cortana settings as in the previous section, select 'talk to cortana', then click 'wake word' at the top of the window.

Here you can configure your voice activation settings. Turn all the settings 'on'.

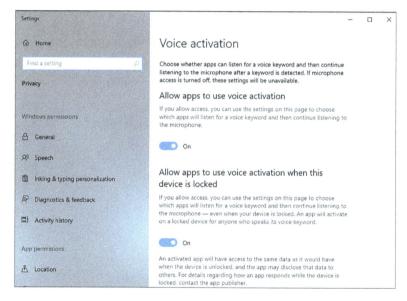

Scroll down to the bottom. Turn 'on' 'cortana'. This allows you to wake up cortana just by saying "Hey Cortana!".

If you want to be able to use cortana from the lock screen, turn on 'use cortana when your device is locked'.

Microphone Settings

To configure your microphone, make sure it's plugged into the pink 3.5mm jack on the back of your computer, or in the microphone jack.

Right-click the volume icon on the bottom right of your window, then select 'sounds' from the popup menu.

From the 'sounds' dialog box, select the 'recording' tab. Select your microphone, then click 'configure'.

From the setup wizard, select the type of microphone you have, then click 'next'.

106

Click 'next' again. Now, read the sentence displayed on your screen. Read the paragraph into the microphone using your normal speaking voice. You'll see the green bar move as you speak. You want the bar to peak in the middle of the green section of the meter. Click 'next', then 'finish'.

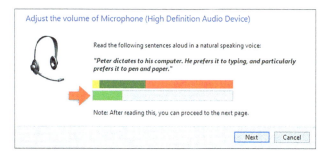

Adjust Microphone Recording Volume

Right-click the volume icon on the bottom right of your window, then select 'sounds' from the popup menu.

From the 'sounds' dialog box, select the 'recording' tab. Select your microphone, then click 'properties'.

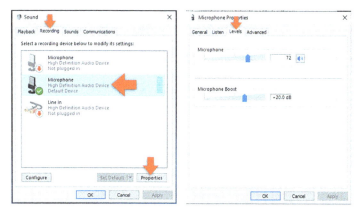

From the 'properties' window, select 'levels'. From here, set the microphone levels. Use the top slider to increase the recording levels of the microphone. Use the bottom slider to boost the microphone sensitivity.

Windows Subsystem for Linux

Windows Subsystem for Linux (WSL) allows you to run native Linux command-line tools natively on Windows, alongside your Windows apps and is primarily aimed at developers.

Enable WSL

To enable this feature, type 'turn windows features on or off' into the search bar on the bottom left of your screen, then click 'turn windows features on or off'

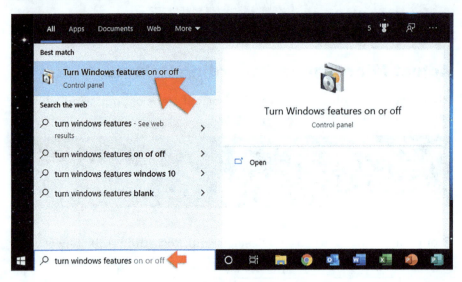

Scroll down the list, select 'windows subsystem for linux.

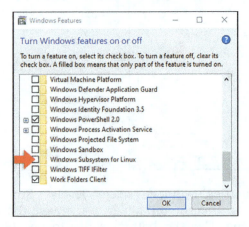

Click ok. Restart your machine when prompted.

108

Installing a Linux Distribution

Now that you have the system enabled, you need to install a linux distribution. To do this, open up your Microsoft Store app and search for linux.

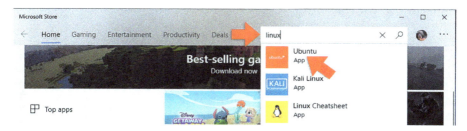

Click 'get', on the distribution's info page.

Now, find the distribution on your start menu, and run the app. It will take a few minutes to install. Run through the setup wizard, enter a username and a password

```
user@insider: ~                                                    –   □   ×

Installing, this may take a few minutes...
Please create a default UNIX user account. The username does not need to match your Windows username.
For more information visit: https://aka.ms/wslusers
Enter new UNIX username: user
New password:
Retype new password:
passwd: password updated successfully
Installation successful!
To run a command as administrator (user "root"), use "sudo <command>".
See "man sudo_root" for details.

Welcome to Ubuntu 20.04 LTS (GNU/Linux 4.4.0-19628-Microsoft x86_64)

 * Documentation:  https://help.ubuntu.com
 * Management:      https://landscape.canonical.com
 * Support:         https://ubuntu.com/advantage

0 updates can be installed immediately.
0 of these updates are security updates.

This message is shown once once a day. To disable it please create the
/home/user/.hushlogin file.
user@insider:~$
```

Family Safety

You can create child accounts for your children either on your devices or their own devices. These are special, restricted accounts you can monitor and tailor to your child. It is not a good idea to allow a young child to use your account.

Child Accounts

On your child's computer or tablet, sign in as an administrator (your own account). Open the Settings App and click 'accounts'. Select 'family & other people' on the left hand side, click 'add a family member'.

Select 'add a child' and enter their email address.

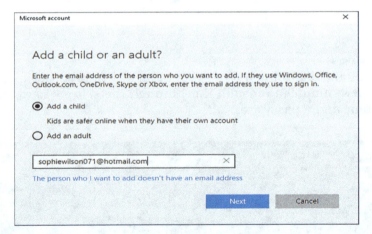

Click 'next', then 'confirm'. This will send an invitation to join to the child's email address.

If they don't have an email address, click 'the person who I want to add doesn't have an email address' and create them a Microsoft Account email address and password.

110

Children's accounts give parents the ability to block certain services or monitor their child's online activity.

Sign out of your account, then sign in with the Microsoft Account username and password you just added/created for your child.

A confirmation email will be sent to the child's email address inviting them to sign in.

Open the email app. You'll see an email from 'Microsoft Family'. Open the email and click 'accept invitation'.

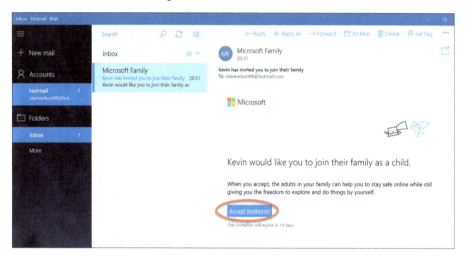

On the page that appears, click 'sign in and join'.

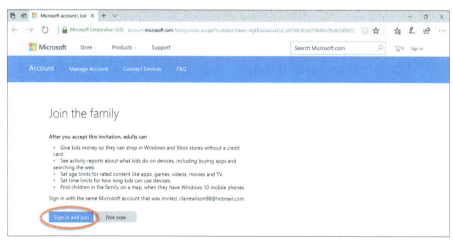

The child account will now be in the family settings on your own account.

Monitoring Family Activity

You can log on to your family safety website by opening your web browser and navigating to the following address. Click 'sign in' and enter your Microsoft Account email address and password.

```
account.microsoft.com/family
```

On the main family screen you'll see a list of child accounts.

Under their name you'll see 'activity'. This shows web activity and apps used. Screen Time, allows you to set limits and curfews to control how long your child uses the computer and times they are allowed access. Content restrictions allows you to block types of apps, and restrict content according to age. You can also see what device they are using as well as add some money for your child to spend in the store.

Web Activity

Click 'activity' to view the child's computer activity. Scroll down the list and you'll see web browsing activity.

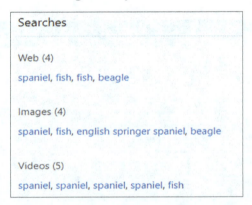

At the top you'll see web searches and the keywords they've typed in. You can click these keywords to see what search results they found.

Underneath that, websites visited are listed along with the address so you can click them to check them out.

If you feel the site is inappropriate for your child to be looking at, click 'block' next to the website in the list.

Any attempts to visit blocked sites will appear at the top of this section.

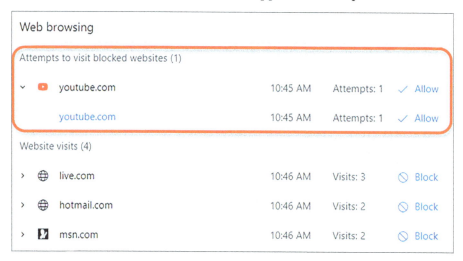

If you want to allow your child to use the website again click 'allow'.

If you don't see any activity go to this website on their device, make sure you have verified the account on the device. Check out page 57.

App Usage

Click 'activity' to view the child's computer activity. Scroll down the list and you'll see web browsing activity. Underneath the web activity you'll see 'apps and games'

At the bottom of the page, you'll see a summary chart of the screen time spend on the computer for each day.

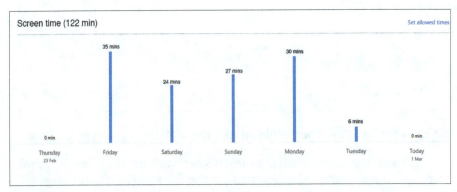

Screen Time & Curfews

You can set curfews and limits to the amount of time your children can use their devices. To do this click 'screen time'.

Screen time allows you to set curfews so you can prevent your children using their tablets or computers except in the designated hours.

For example, you could set a time limit so your child can only use their tablet or computer between certain times of the day. Click on each day.

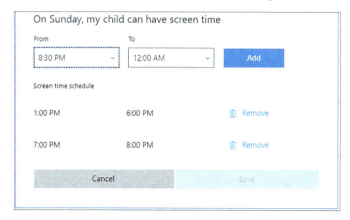

In the dialog box that appears, enter the times using the 'from' and 'to' fields. Click 'add' to add the times.

115

Navigating Windows 10

In this chapter we will take a look at the different parts of Windows 10 such as the start menu, desktop, taskbar, action center, file explorer, activity history, and clipboard.

We'll have a look at the navigational features that allow you to start apps, find files, and interact with Windows.

We'll also cover external drives such as flash drives, external hard drives and memory cards.

Take a look at the start menu section of the video resources. Open your web browser and navigate to the following website:

`videos.tips/win-10-start`

Lets begin by looking at the start menu.

Start Menu

The start menu is the central launch point for apps, changing settings, as well as system shut down, reset, hibernate, and sleep. To open the start menu, click the start button on the bottom left of the screen. Lets take a closer look at the different parts of the menu.

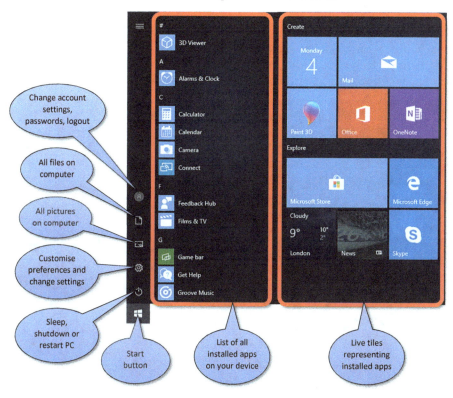

Change account settings, passwords, logout

All files on computer

All pictures on computer

Customise preferences and change settings

Sleep, shutdown or restart PC

Start button

List of all installed apps on your device

Live tiles representing installed apps

Listed down the far left hand side of your menu you'll see five little icons. From top to bottom, these icons allow you to change your account password or log out, view all files & pictures using file explorer, system settings, and shut down.

Also down the left is a list of your most frequently used applications. Underneath this list is an alphabetical list of all apps installed on your system.

On the right hand side of the menu, you'll see coloured tiles representing apps. This is the tile area and these tiles are sometimes called live tiles. Live tiles graphically represent apps and can also display basic notifications such as latest messages, or emails from your mail app, information such as weather, latest news headlines and so on, even when the app isn't running. To run the app you just click on the tile.

Tile Folders

Windows 10 allows you to group tiles into folders. This can be useful if you have a lot of apps installed on your device. You can start to group your tiles into logical folders, meaning you can group all your communication apps such as facebook, web browser, or email, into one folder, group all your office apps into another folder, and so on.

In this example, I am going to drag all my communication apps into one folder - email, edge, facebook and twitter apps. First, choose one of the apps to be the folder, eg edge browser. Then drag the other apps: email, facebook and twitter to this app, as illustrated below.

Now all these apps will be grouped into a folder, shown below left. Clicking on the folder will open up your app tiles, shown below right.

Customising your Start Menu

It is a good idea to customise Windows 10's start menu to your personal preferences and needs. We can do this by arranging, adding, grouping, and removing the tiles on the start menu.

Take a look at the demos in the 'start menu' section of the accompanying video resources. Open your browser and navigate to:

```
videos.tips/win-10-start
```

Add Tiles to Start Menu

To add tiles to the start menu, click and drag the icon off the list of apps on the left hand side, to the live tile section as shown below.

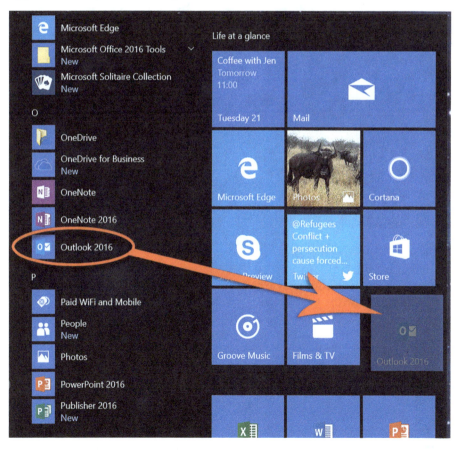

Do this with all the apps you want to appear as tiles in the live tile area of the start menu.

This way, you can maximise the use of your start menu by removing tiles you don't use, adding tiles for the apps you use the most, and grouping them into sections. This allows you quick access to your apps.

As you can see in the example below, all my Microsoft Office apps are together, and all my Creative Cloud apps are grouped underneath. Also I have access to my calendar and email, as well as photos. I like to keep up with the news so I've added the news app, and the local weather forecasts which I find useful.

If the app you want to add to your start menu isn't listed, you can search for it using the search field on the bottom left of the taskbar. In this example I want to add the app called 'notepad' to the start menu.

To pin the app to the start menu, click 'pin to start' in the search results window.

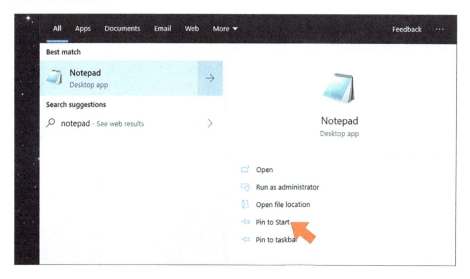

Here you can see, the icon has been pinned as a tile on the start menu. You may have to drag the tile into position.

Move Tiles on the Start Menu

To move tiles, click and drag them to the new position on the start menu. The tiles will scroll automatically as you drag your tile up and down the menu.

In the example below, I want to put Outlook 2016 with the rest of the Office Apps on my start menu. To do this, just click Outlook 2016 icon, then drag it down to the position where the rest of the Office Apps are.

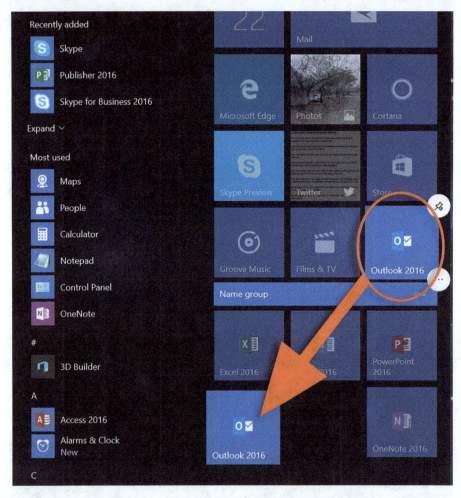

If you are on a touch screen device, tap and hold your finger on the tile for a second, then drag your finger down the screen to the position you want your tile.

Arranging and grouping your tiles like this helps to keep everything organised and easy to find.

122

Naming Groups of Tiles

You can give groups of tiles titles. To do this move your mouse to the top of the groups of tiles. You'll see 'name group' appear. Click 'name group' then type in the name you want.

Remove Tiles from Start Menu

To remove a tile, right click on it. If you are on a touch screen device, tap and hold your finger on the tile until the menu appears.

From the popup menu, select 'unpin from start'.

Resize Tiles on Start Menu

To resize a tile, right click on it. If you are on a touch screen device, tap and hold your finger on the icon.

From the popup menu that appears, click resize.

From the slide out menu, click the size you want. You will see that each tile as a number of pre-set sizes.

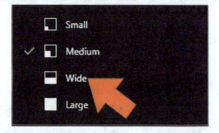

There are usually four sizes to choose from: small, medium, wide and large. You can see the differences below.

Some app tiles may not have all the sizes available.

124

Resize Start Menu

You can resize the start menu quite easily. You can resize your menu horizontally to make it wider, or vertically to make it longer.

To resize your start menu, move your mouse pointer to the edge of the start menu. Your mouse pointer will turn into a double sided arrow. Click and drag the edge of the menu left or right to resize.

To resize the height, click and drag the top edge.

If you're on a touch screen device, tap and hold the edge of the menu, then drag your finger left or right to resize.

The Desktop

The desktop is the basic working area on your PC. It's the equivalent of your workbench or office desk, hence why it is called a desktop.

Desktop Anatomy

On the desktop itself you can save files such as documents or photos - these will appear as file icons. On some devices you may see other icons such as the trash can for deleted files or network connections.

Along the bottom of the desktop, you'll find the start button on the left, windows search - to search for files or apps, cortana, as well as pinned and running apps. Over on the right hand side of the task bar you'll see status icons, the clock/calendar, and the action centre.

Themes

Desktop themes are presets that change the look and feel of Windows. Some have different styles of mouse pointer, various background images, icons, and menu colours. To change the desktop theme, click in the search field and type themes

Select 'themes and related settings' from the search results. From the themes page, edit the theme according to your preferences:-

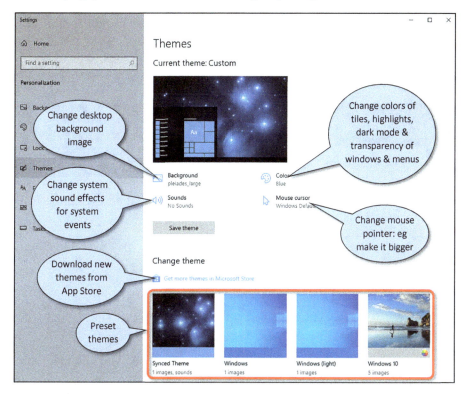

Organise Icons

You can sort the icons on your desktop by name or date modified and change the size. To do this, right click on the desktop. From the popup menu select 'sort by' and select what you want to sort the icons by. Eg by name.

You can also change the sizes of the icons. Right click on the desktop and from the popup menu select 'view'.

Changing the Background

Also known as wallpaper, the desktop background can be any image or photo you like. Some people use photos of their children or family members, others put pictures of their favourite hobby, some use photos of their favourite places. It's up to you what picture you use.

To change the desktop background, open file explorer.

Navigate to your 'pictures' folder. If you've downloaded an image from the internet navigate to your 'downloads' folder.

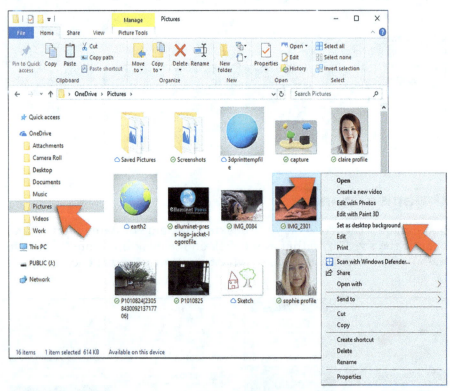

Find the picture you want to use, then right click on it. Select 'set as desktop background' from the popup menu.

You can also change the background image from the 'themes and related settings' section of the settings app, as in the previous section.

Task Bar

The taskbar shows which programs are currently running. As you open apps, the app's icons appear along the taskbar with a line underneath indicating that the app is running. The taskbar also serves as a shortcut bar so you can pin apps you use most often and switch to other apps running in the background.

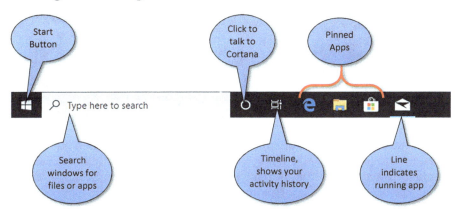

You'll also see the start button, icons for windows search, cortana and your timeline activity history.

On the far right you will see the notification area or status area, sometimes incorrectly called the system tray. This has icons representing battery, wifi networks, volume control, pen/ink, onscreen keyboard, clock, and action center. Click on these icons to view their details. Eg, click on the clock to view your calendar and upcoming events, or click on the volume control to adjust your audio volume.

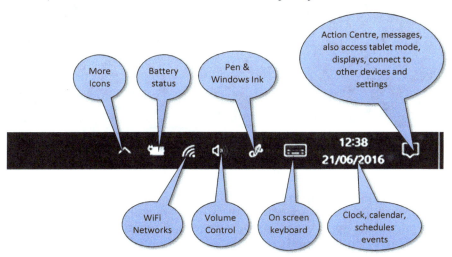

System Icons

Over on the right hand side of the taskbar you'll see your system icons in the system area. The icons that appear here will depend on what device you're using and what apps you have installed.

With these icons, you can adjust the volume using the audio icon, connect to WiFi using the WiFi icon, open OneDrive settings and so on. Some of the icons will be hidden, to reveal all the icons, click the small up arrow on the far left of the system icons.

Jump Lists

Apps that appear on the taskbar have a recent files list called a jump list.

To open the app's jump list, right click on the app's icon on the taskbar. Here, you'll be able to re-open any of your recently accessed files for that particular app. As well as pin the icon to the taskbar so it doesn't disappear when the app is closed.

Pin Icons to your Task Bar

For more convenience, you can pin all your favourite apps to your task bar along the bottom of your screen.

To do this, right click on an app in the list on the left hand side of the start menu, or on a live tile. From the menu that appears, select 'more'.

From the slide out menu select 'pin to taskbar'

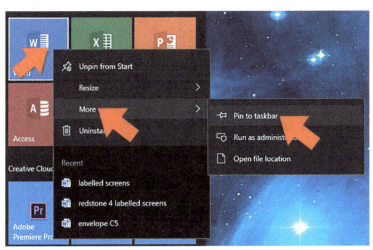

You'll see the icon has been added to your taskbar. If you right click on the icon on your taskbar, you can see a list of recently opened files. Click the little pin icon on the right hand side of the file name to pin the file to the list permanently, if you use that file all the time.

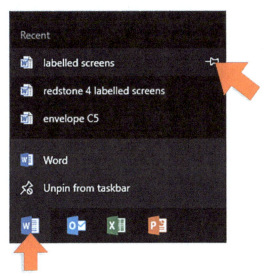

Taskbar Tools

The taskbar has a few tools and options you can use. To access these, right click on the taskbar.

Here you can show/hide Cortana and the Task View icons that appear on the left hand side of the toolbar. You can also show/hide the People App icon, Windows Ink icon, as well as the on screen keyboard on touch screen devices. Just click the option on the pop up menu to show or hide the icons.

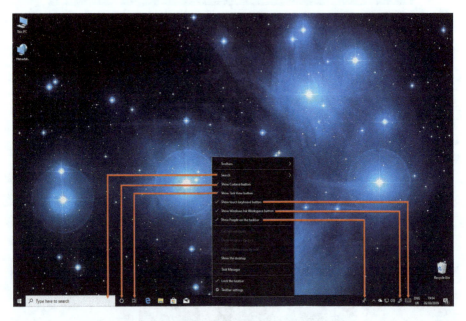

You can also open up the task manager to see what apps are running, as well as arrange open windows on the desktop.

Action Centre

The action centre shows alerts and messages from different applications, as well as some shortcut controls. To open action center, click the notifications icon on the bottom right of the screen. If you're using a touch screen, swipe inwards from the right edge of the screen.

At the top of action center, you'll see notifications and messages. These could be email message that have just arrived, system messages or status alerts from applications.

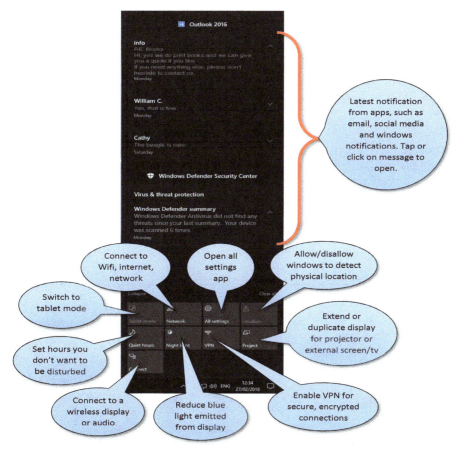

Along the bottom of the notifications window you will see your 'quick actions' such as tablet mode, display settings, media connect for connecting to projectors, second screens etc. Click on these to adjust the settings. Click 'expand' if you don't see all of the icons.

133

Select What Notifications you See

To select which apps you want to receive notifications for, type `notifications` into the search field on the bottom left of the taskbar. Click 'notification & action settings' from the search results.

Scroll down to 'notifications & actions', here you can turn off notifications, show/hide notifications from appearing on your lock screen. Scroll

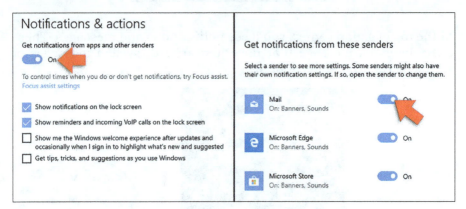

Scroll further down to 'get notifications from these senders'. Here you can turn on/off notifications from specific apps. Just set the on/off switch to 'off' to turn off notifications from an app in the list.

Edit the Quick Actions

To edit the quick action buttons on the action centre sidebar, type `notifications` into the search field on the bottom left of the taskbar. Click 'notification & action settings' from the search results. At the top of the screen select 'edit your quick actions'.

You'll see action center open up on the right hand side with a small pin icon on the top left of each button. Click the pin icon to remove the icon then click 'done'. To add an icon back to action center, click 'add' at the bottom and select the button from the popup list.

134

Quick Configure Notifications

In Action Center, on each notification you have options to configure and turn off notifications from an app and website right. To do this click the small settings icon on the right hand side of the notification.

From here, you can turn off all notifications for that particular app, or you can configure them. To configure them, select 'go to notification settings' from the popup menu.

Here, you can turn the notifications on or off, select whether you want banners to show up on the desktop or in the notification center, show on lock screen and whether or not you want a sound to play when a notification arrives. You can also set priority.

Timeline Activity History

You'll find the timeline icon on your task bar on the bottom left of your screen, next to Windows search and Cortana. Click the icon to open timeline.

When timeline opens, you'll see a history of apps, websites and files you've used, organised in reverse chronological order.

Files and apps you are currently running, will appear at the top. You can click or tap on these to switch to them.

Along the right hand side you'll see the timeline. You can drag this down to browse through your activity history.

You'll see apps and files you've had open listed according to the date you last used them. Click or tap on any of these files to go back to where you left off.

On the top right of the screen, you'll see a magnifying glass.

This allows you to search for activities, files you've used and so on. Type the name of the file in the search field. Click any of the documents in the search results to open them up.

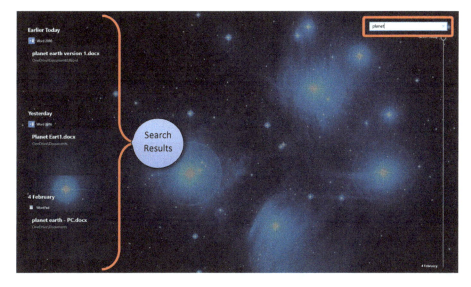

To remove an activity, right click on the thumbnail preview of the activity you want to delete, then select 'remove'.

To clear all the history for a particular day, select 'clear all...' from the popup menu.

Using Multiple Desktops

Using 'Multiple desktops' is almost like having two or more desks in your office, where you can do your work. You could have a desktop for your web browsing and email, another desktop for your word processing, another desktop for your photo editing and sharing and so on. Multiple desktops help to organise your tasks, so you can keep things you are working on together.

To create a new desktop, click the timeline icon on your taskbar.

Click on 'new desktop' to open a new desktop, then open the apps you want to run.

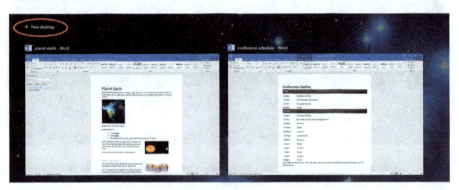

In this example, open Word and Edge. Click the timeline button on the task bar, then click 'new desktop'. Now open Email and Calendar. Hit the task view button again and click 'new desktop'. Now open Groove Music and TV & Videos app.

So now I have a desktop for my word processing and internet research with Microsoft Word and Edge Browser, a second desktop for email & calendar, and a third desktop for entertainment with Groove Music and TV.

To switch between the desktops, click on the thumbnails listed across the top of the screen (Desktop 1, Desktop 2, Desktop 3 and so on). You'll see it's easier to flick between the apps when they are grouped into different desktops for similar tasks and projects. This is like having a different desk in your office for each project you're working on.

To get a preview of what is running on a particular desktop, hover your mouse over the thumbnails listed across the top of the screen. You will see previews of the apps running underneath. To switch to an app click on its thumbnail.

You can also rename your desktops. Click the name (eg 'Desktop 1'), type in a meaningful name.

File Explorer

File explorer can be used to find your files on your computer, access your OneDrive, network resources, and external hard drives or flash drives. You'll find file explorer on your taskbar, or on your start menu.

Down the left hand side of the main window, you will find a list of all the libraries of files on your computer, ie documents, photographs, music and videos, as well as external drives, and network resources.

In the right hand pane at the top, Windows will start to list the most used folders you have accessed. If you click on 'quick access' on the top left, you will see a list of your most recently accessed files.

You can select any of the folders in the left hand pane. When you do this, the contents of those folders will appear in the right hand pane.

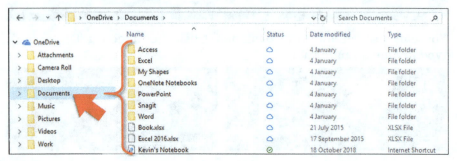

Along the top of the explorer window you will see the ribbon menus. This is where you'll find tools to create new folders, copy or move files, share files, sort files, and so on. You can select the different ribbons using the tabs along the top of the screen.

Home Ribbon

On the home ribbon, you'll find all your most common tools, such as copy and paste files, create folders, move files, delete files and show file properties.

Share Ribbon

On the share ribbon you can burn files to a CD, print them, zip them up into a compressed file - useful if you want to email a few documents together. Or you can share files with other computers on your home network, email, or near share.

View Ribbon

With the view ribbon you can display your files as a list, as icons and as thumbnails. Icons and thumbnail views can be useful for browsing photographs. To do this click on the layout options in the middle of the ribbon (large icons, medium sized icons, list or details).

You can also sort files by date added, alphabetically or by size. To do this click 'sort by'. From the menu, select 'name' to list your files alphabetically by name, or click 'date...' to sort by 'date edited' or 'date created'.

Sharing Files from File Explorer

Share option on right click context menu. Right click on the file you want to share, then from the popup menu, select 'share'.

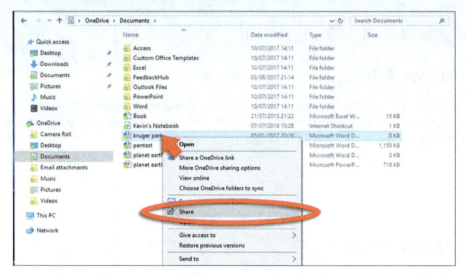

From the popup dialog box, select the person you want to share the document with. Contacts that you have added to the people app or pinned to your taskbar will appear at the top. If the contact is not in the list, you can send via email or skype at the bottom.

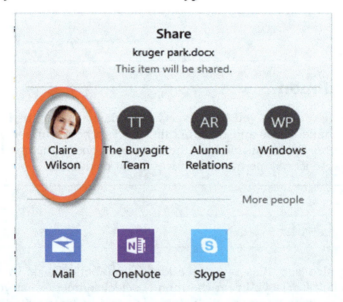

The options will depend on what apps you have installed.

In this example, I am going to email the document. An integrated email will appear in the window allowing you to type a message.

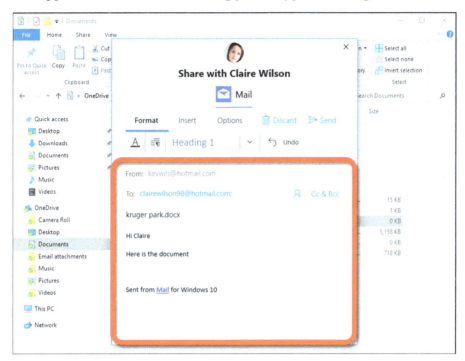

Click 'send' when you're ready to send your email.

Take a look at the file explorer demos in the 'using windows 10' section of the video resources.

Open your browser and navigate to the following website:

```
videos.tips/using-win-10
```

Basic File Management

There are many different types of file types; files for photos, videos, documents, speadsheets, presentations and so on. These files are identified by a file extension.

`filename.extension`

So for example...

A photograph is usually saved as a JPEG or JPG. Eg **photo-of-sophie.jpg**. This could be from a graphics package or a camera.

A document is usually saved as a DOC or DOCX. Eg: **production-resume.docx**. This is usually from a word processor such as Microsoft Word.

The 3 or 4 letters after the period is called a file extension and it is what Windows uses to identify the application needed to open the file.

It's best to save all your files into your OneDrive.

Windows stores your files in a hierarchical tree like structure.

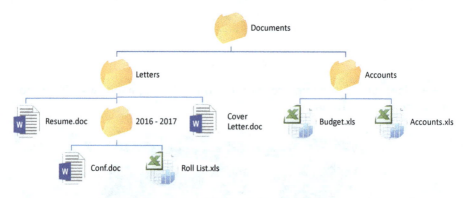

You can create yellow folders to store files of the same type or for the same purpose.

In the example above, letters to various recipients are stored in a 'letters' folder. This can be further divided into year folders, so you have one for each year.

Similarly, all files to do with the accounts are stored in an 'accounts' folder.

Storing files in this fashion keeps them organised and makes them easier to find.

Creating Folders

It's a good idea to create folders to help organise all your files. You could have a folder for your personal documents, work documents, presentations, vacation/holiday photos, college work and so on. To do this open your File Explorer.

On the left hand side of your screen, navigate to the place you want to create a folder. In this example, I'm going to create a folder in my 'OneDrive'.

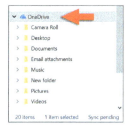

From the home ribbon along the top of your screen, click 'new folder'.

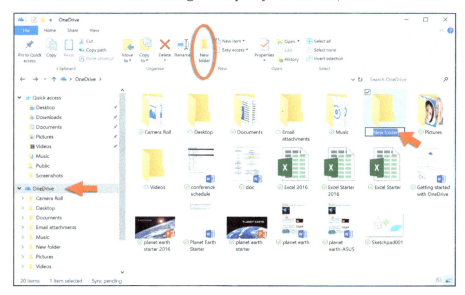

On the right hand side of your screen, you'll see a new folder appear called 'new folder'.

Delete the text 'new folder' and type in a meaningful name - ideally the name of the group of documents you are saving into this folder.

Moving Files

Moving files is a bit like cut and paste. To move files, open your File Explorer.

In the left hand pane, click the folder where the file you want to move, is saved, eg documents. Then click on the file(s) you want to move to select them. Hold down the ctrl key while you click to select multiple files.

From the home ribbon select 'cut'.

Using the left hand pane, navigate to the folder you want to move the file to, eg documents > excel. Click the small down arrows to open the folders. Click the folder you want to move the files to.

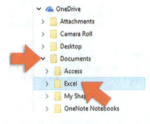

Select 'paste' from the home ribbon.

Copying Files

Copying files is a bit like copy and paste. To copy files, open your File Explorer

In the left hand pane, click the folder where the file you want to copy, is saved, eg documents. Then click on the file(s) you want to copy to select them. Hold down the ctrl key while you click to select multiple files.

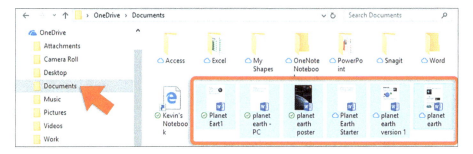

From the home ribbon select 'copy'.

Using the left hand pane, navigate to the folder you want to move the file to, eg documents > word. Click the small down arrows to open the folders. Click the folder you want to move the files to.

Select 'paste' from the home ribbon.

Renaming Files

To rename a file, open up your File Explorer and find the file you want to rename.

Navigate to the folder your file is saved in. In this demo it's in the OneDrive > documents folder. Click on the file to select it.

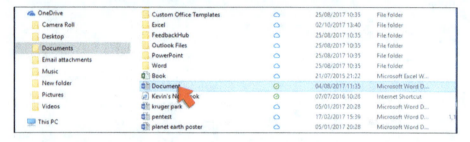

From the home ribbon click 'rename'.

You'll see the name of the file highlighted in blue.

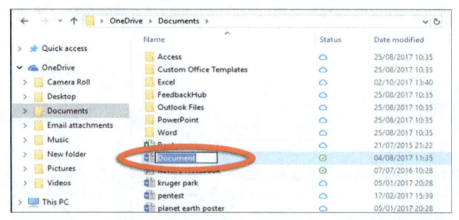

Now type in a name for the file. Press 'enter' on your keyboard when you're done.

Sorting Files

Within File Explorer, you can sort files alphabetically by name, or by size and date created. This makes it easier to find files especially when you have a lot of them in one folder. To sort your files, select the folder from the left hand side of File Explorer, eg, 'documents'.

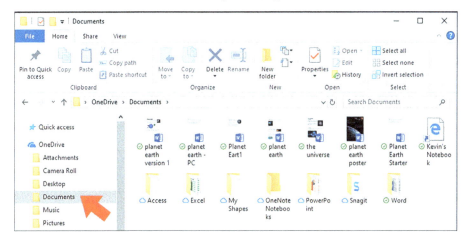

Select the 'view' ribbon. From here you can view your files as a list or as icons, just select from the layout options. I'm going to choose icons for this example.

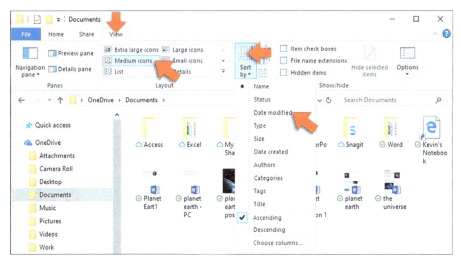

To sort the files, select 'sort by', then select what you want to sort your files by. This could be date modified - so the latest files appear at the top. Or by name - so your files appear in alphabetical order by file name.

At the bottom of the menu, select ascending or descending order.

Deleting Files

Deleting files is fairly straight forward. In File Explorer, click on the files you want to delete. Hold down the CTRL key on your keyboard while you click to select multiple files.

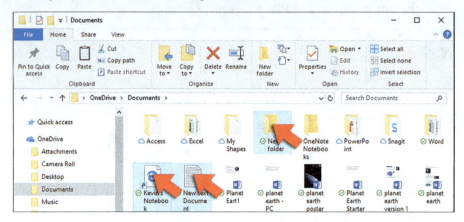

Press the DEL or DELETE key on your keyboard. You can also click the 'delete' icon on the home ribbon in File Explorer. These files will be moved to the trash (or recycle bin).

Restoring Files

When you delete a file, Windows moves the file to the trash (or recycle bin). You'll find the recycle bin icon on your desktop - double click the icon to open it up.

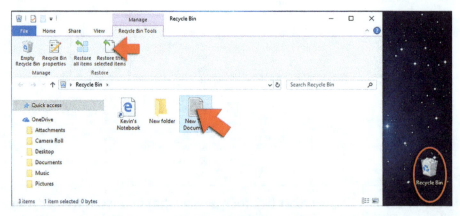

Click 'empty recycle bin' to permanently delete all files in recycle bin. Click 'restore all items' to put all the files back where they were deleted from. Or select a file and click 'restore the selected items' to restore individual files.

150

Searching for Files

You can search for files within File Explorer using the search field on the top right of the window. First, select the location to search from, eg OneDrive, This PC. Then type your search keywords into the search field. You'll see a list of suggestions appear, to select, click on one in the list.

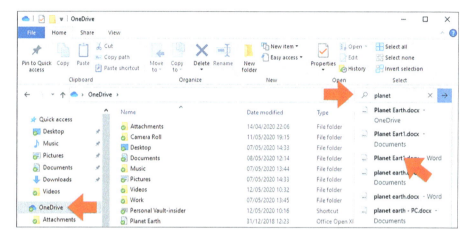

To perform a full search, click the blue arrow icon to the right.

A list of matching files will be listed.

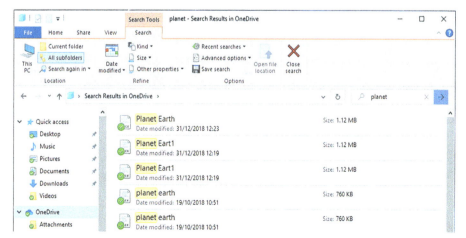

You'll also see a new 'search' ribbon tab appear along the top of the window.

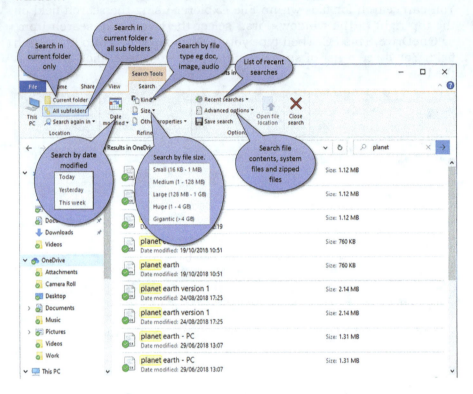

From here, you can refine your search. You can search by date modified (eg files you've used today, yesterday, or in the last week).

You can search by file type (kind), so you can search through all documents, or images. Just select the options from the sections labelled above.

You can also save the searches, so you can find the files again without performing another search.

Take a look at the file explorer demos in the 'using windows 10' section of the video resources.

Open your browser and navigate to the following website:

`videos.tips/using-win-10`

External Drives

You can attach storage devices to your computer. The most common ones are memory sticks - also called usb keys, usb sticks, flash drives or thumb drives. The other type is the portable hard drive.

Memory sticks are usually smaller in capacity ranging from 1GB all the way up to 256GB. Portable hard drives can be larger than 1TB.

To read the drive, plug the device into a USB port on your computer, then select file explorer from the task bar.

The device will show up in File Explorer, under 'This PC' section.

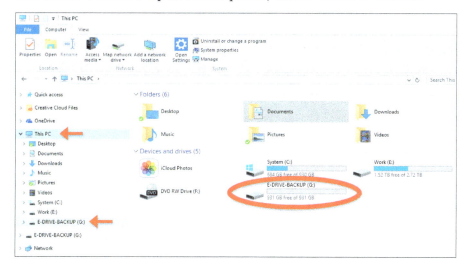

Double click the drive icon, circled above, to open the contents of the drive.

To copy files to the drive, just drag and drop them from file explorer. To do this, select the folder from the left hand side of file explorer, where the files you want to copy are saved - this could be on OneDrive or 'This PC'. In this example, I'm copying a file from the 'documents' folder in the 'this pc' section.

From the pane on the right hand side, click and drag the file you want to the external drive, as shown below.

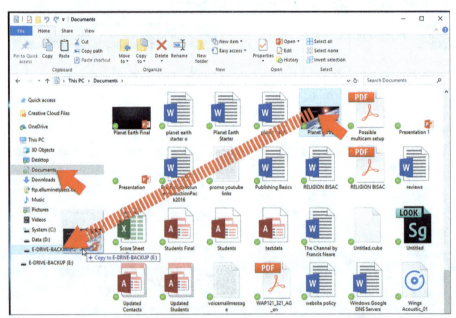

Take a look at the 'file explorer' demos in the 'using windows 10' section of the video resources. Open your browser and navigate to the following website:

`videos.tips/using-win-10`

Memory Cards

Many laptops and tablets now have memory card readers built in. The most common memory card being the SD Card. This can be a full sized SD card or a Micro SD card.

Standard SD   Micro SD   SD Card Adapter

Standard SD cards are commonly used in digital cameras, and many laptops have standard size SD card readers built in. Tablets, phones, and small cameras usually use micro SD cards.

You can get an SD Card adapter if your SD card reader does not read Micro SD cards.

There are various types of SD cards available, each are marked with a speed classification symbol indicating the data transfer speed. If you are merely storing files, the data transfer speed doesn't really matter as much, however, if you are using the card in a dash cam or digital camera, the faster data transfer speeds are necessary. To be safe, the higher the speed the better. You can see a summary in the table below.

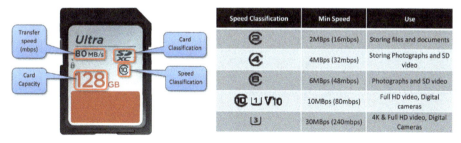

Speed Classification	Min Speed	Use
	2MBps (16mbps)	Storing files and documents
	4MBps (32mbps)	Storing Photographs and SD video
	6MBps (48mbps)	Photographs and SD video
	10MBps (80mbps)	Full HD video, Digital cameras
	30MBps (240mbps)	4K & Full HD video, Digital Cameras

SDHC stands for "Secure Digital High Capacity", and supports capacities up to 32 GB.

SDXC stands for "Secure Digital eXtended Capacity", and supports capacities up to 2 TB.

SDUC stands for "Secure Digital Ultra Capacity", and supports capacities up to 128 TB.

To read your SD Card, slide it into the card reader on your tablet or laptop. If your laptop or tablet has a built in reader, it is usually on either of the side panels or the front panel.

Select file explorer from the task bar.

The card will show up as another drive in file explorer. Click on the drive to see the contents of the card.

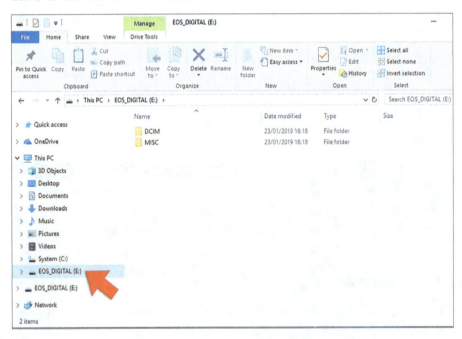

You can copy files to and from the card as you would with a normal disk drive. See copying and moving files on page 146

To release the card, press the it inwards and it will pop out. Some other cards will just slide out, depending on your card reader.

Near Share

Near Share allows you to share files between devices in the same vicinity using Bluetooth. First you'll need to turn on near share. To do this, open up your action center. You'll see an icon called 'nearby sharing'. Click this to turn it on.

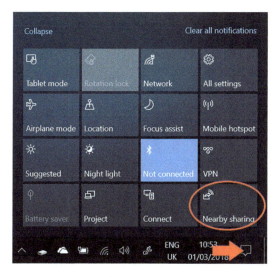

In file explorer,click the file you want to share. Select 'share' from the 'share' ribbon.

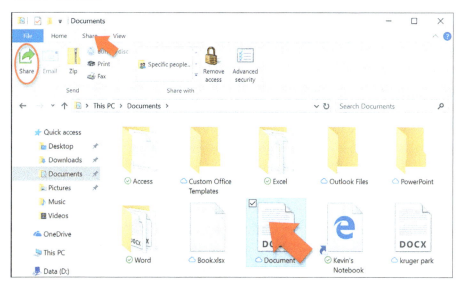

You can also share from Edge and most other apps using the share icon

157

In the share dialog box, you'll see a list of devices in the near vicinity. Click on the device you want to share the file with.

In this example, I am sharing a document from my laptop to a surface tablet. The surface tablet is named ORION.

If you're having trouble finding other devices, go to the settings app, select 'system', then 'shared experiences'. Under 'nearby sharing', change 'I can share or receive content from' to 'everyone nearby'. Do this on both devices.

On the other device, a notification will appear in Action Center asking for confirmation.

Click 'open' to receive the document. All your received files will be stored in your downloads folder.

OneDrive

OneDrive is a cloud file hosting service and synchronises your files between your device (pc, laptop, phone or tablet), and the cloud file hosting service.

You'll find OneDrive in your File Explorer window. Click the icon on your taskbar to open.

OneDrive is where you should save all your files from Microsoft Office, photographs, music, videos and so on. The advantage is, if your computer crashes, you won't lose all your files as they will still be stored on OneDrive.

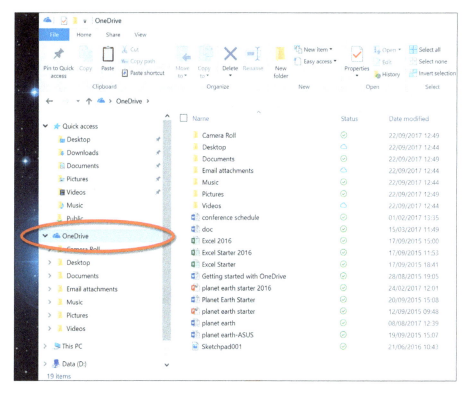

The other advantage of OneDrive, is you can access all your files on all your devices. So you can see your documents on your PC, phone, tablet or laptop, and you can access them from anywhere that has an internet connection.

Files on Demand

Files On-Demand stores all your files on OneDrive Cloud and allows you to open them from Windows File Explorer.

Once you open your file, it is then downloaded to your device. This works with devices that have limited local storage such as tablets and smart phones, that do not have enough space to hold your entire OneDrive contents.

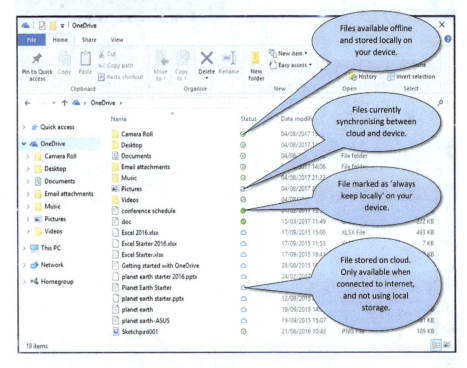

On the icons themselves or in the status column, you'll see some status indicators. Lets take a look at what they mean.

Icon	Description
⊘	Files marked with this status icon are stored online and are downloaded to your device only if you open the file.
✓	Files marked with this status icon will be download to your device, and will be available even when you are offline. Select "Always keep on this device".
☁	Files marked with this status icon indicate that the file is only available online.
☁ ዳ	Files marked with this status icon indicate that the file has been shared with someone else.
⟳	Files marked with this status icon are currently being synchronised between your device and online.

Enable and Disable Files On Demand

Right-click the OneDrive cloud icon in the notification area. From the popup menu select 'settings'.

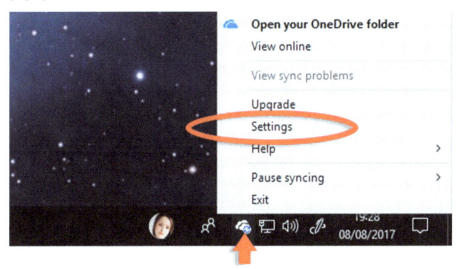

Select the 'settings' tab.

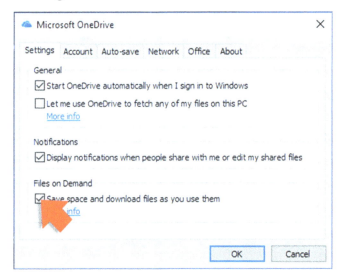

Under 'Files On-Demand', click the tick box next to 'Save space and download files as you use them' to enable the feature.

This will mark all your files as 'online', meaning they are stored on OneDrive Cloud not on your device. When you select a file to open, your file is downloaded to your device and then opened.

Making files available Offline

Having full access to all your files on OneDrive without having to download the whole contents to your device is great, but what happens if you don't always have an internet connection? Well, you can mark certain files as 'available offline', meaning OneDrive will download these files to your device.

To do this, select the files you want to make available offline - hold down control and select your files, if you want more than one.

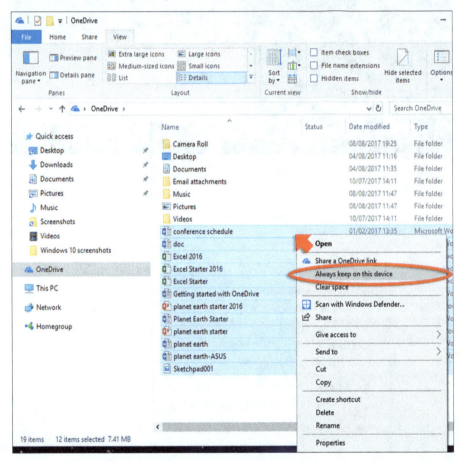

Right click on the selected files, and from the popup menu select 'always keep on this device'.

OneDrive will download the selected files to your device, so you can access them when you don't have a connection. If you change your files while offline, OneDrive will sync the changes once you re-connect to the internet.

Cloud Clipboard

Cloud clipboard allows you to copy & paste multiple items across all your devices. So for example, you could copy a paragraph off a Word document on your laptop and paste it into a document on your surface tablet.

To open cloud clipboard, hold the windows key, then tap V.

You'll see a small window appear on the right hand side of the screen.

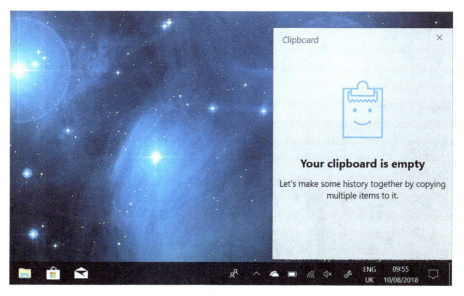

Here you'll see a list of all the images and text you've cut or copied.

Copying Multiple Items

If you are doing something that requires you to copy and paste different images or text, you'll find yourself re-copying the same piece of text or image multiple times. Cloud clipboard allows you to copy multiple images or blocks of text, so you can store them on your clipboard, then select and paste in what you need.

You can see below, as we've copied the paragraph, it has been added to the clipboard.

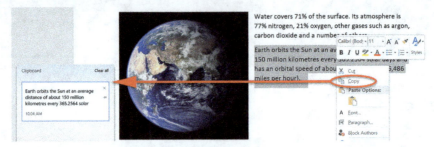

Now, lets copy something else. You can see in the cloud clipboard, there are now two items.

You can select any of the items in the clipboard and paste them in. Just position your cursor in the document and select the item in the clipboard you want to paste. Remember press windows key & V to open the cloud clipboard, if it disappears.

164

Copying Across Devices

To sync your clipboard across all your devices, first check that this feature is enabled and you are signed into your device using your Microsoft Account.

To check, open your settings app, click 'system', then select 'clipboard' from the list on the left hand side.

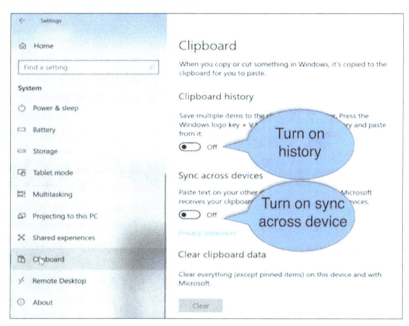

Now do this on all your devices. Now that we have set up cloud clipboard, in this demo we're going to copy a paragraph from a Word document on a laptop and paste it into another document on a surface tablet. You can see this setup in the photograph below.

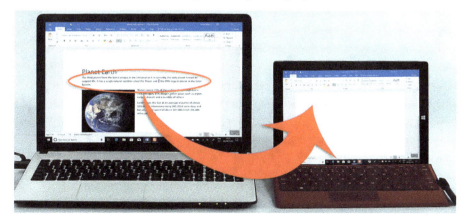

On the laptop, select and copy the text using normal copy and paste.

Now go onto the other device - the surface tablet. Hold down the windows key, then press V.

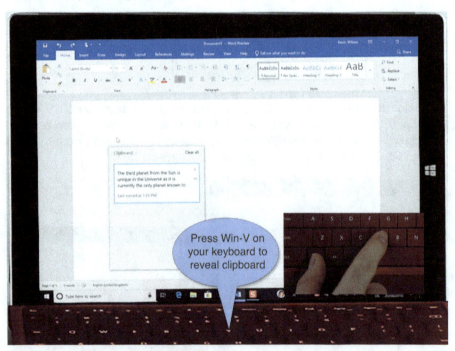

You'll see the clipboard window open up.

Click on the clipping from the clipboard window to paste it into the word document.

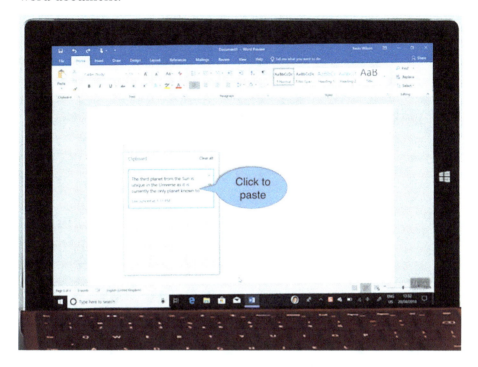

You can do this with text and images. Anything you can copy and paste, you can now paste to any device you've signed into with your Microsoft Account.

Note that all your devices must be running the October 2018 Update (1809) or later for this feature to work.

Take a look at the cloud clipboard demos in the 'using windows 10' section of the accompanying video resources. Open your browser and navigate to the following website:

```
videos.tips/using-win-10
```

Screen Snip

Screen snip allows you to take snapshot of your screen. You can use it to save and share recipes, stories, articles and so on

You'll find the screen snip tool on your action center. You can also press Windows Key, Shift and S.

Along the top of your screen you'll see a toolbar with some options.

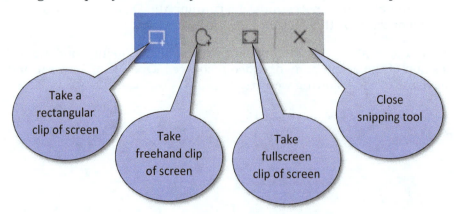

Select which type of clip you want to capture. The rectangular or fullscreen clips are the most useful. You can also take a freehand clip.

To take a rectangular clip of the screen, drag the rectangular box highlight around the area that you want.

To take a freehand clip of the screen, select the freehand slip icon, then draw around the section of the screen you want.

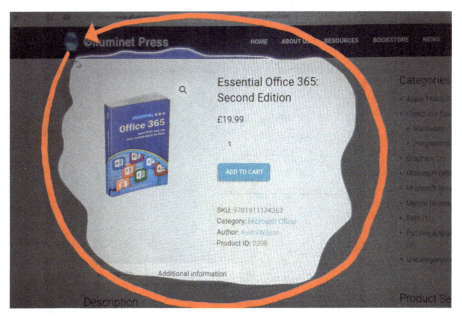

You'll be able to find the clips of the screen on your clipboard, where you'll be able to paste into a message, document, image editor or email.

Multiple Screens

You can plug in more than one screen into most modern computers or tablets if you have the correct adapters.

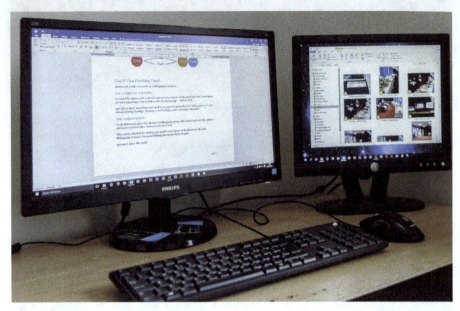

You can set up multiple screens by right clicking on your desktop and selecting 'display settings'.

Select 'extend these displays' from the 'multiple displays' drop down menu shown below.

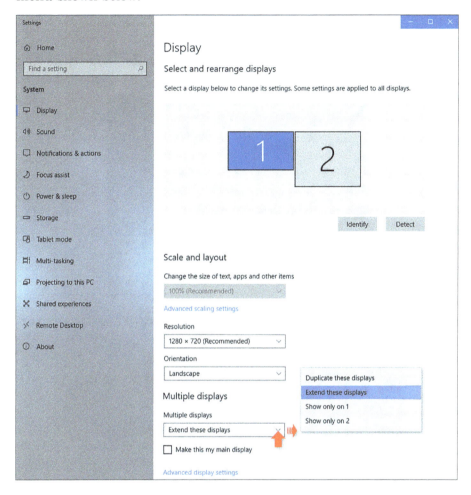

Your screens are identified by a number, shown above. To check which is which, click 'identify' and you'll see a big number appear on each screen.

Make sure you click on your main display using the numbered rectangular icons at the top of the screen. Remembering which number appeared on which screen, click the one you use to do most of your work and click 'make this my main display'. This tells apps that this 'main display' is the one where you will control windows from and do most of your work.

The other display becomes your secondary display; a second desk. This could be another monitor, tv screen or projector.

Using Projectors

Much like using multiple screens, you can also use a projector as your second display.

Open your action center. To do this, click the icon on the bottom right of your taskbar.

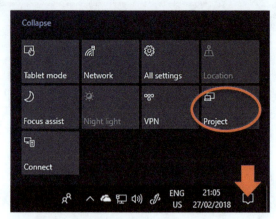

You can also press Windows-P on your keyboard. From the options, select the display you want.

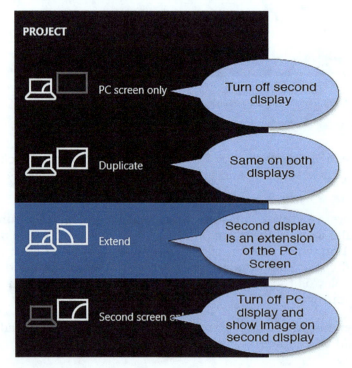

<u>Duplicate</u> PC screen onto Second Screen

Everything you do on the laptop screen (PC Screen) will be duplicated on the second screen (eg projector). So both screens will show the same image.

Second Screen Only

This disables your PC's monitor and allows the display to only appear on the second screen.

PC Screen Only

This disables the projector and allows the information to be seen only on the PC's monitor.

<u>Extend</u> PC screen onto Second Screen

The second screen (such as a projector) acts as an extension to your laptop screen (PC Screen), rather than just a duplicate. So you can have something on your laptop screen and show different images on the projector as shown below.

This allows you to move windows from the laptop's screen (PC Screen 1) to Screen 2 (eg projector) and vice versa.

Screen 2 becomes an extension of the PC Screen. Ideal for using presentation software such as Pro Presenter or PowerPoint.

Arranging Windows on Desktop

It's useful when working in Windows 10 to arrange the windows on your desktop, especially when you're using more than one application at a time. For example, you could be browsing the web and writing a Word document at the same time- perhaps you're researching something, you could have Word open and your web browser next to it on the screen.

Take a look at the 'resizing and moving windows' demo in the video resources. Open your browser and navigate to the following website:

```
videos.tips/win-10-nav
```

Moving a Window

Move your mouse pointer to the top of the window.

Now click and drag the window to your desired position on the screen.

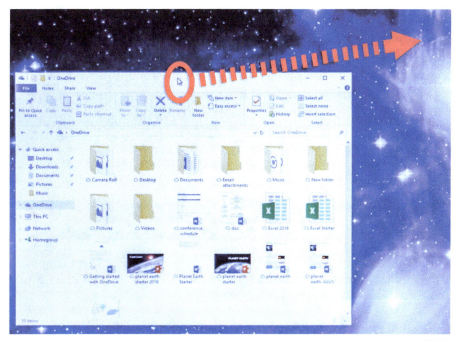

Resizing a Window

To resize a window, move your mouse pointer to the bottom right corner of the window - your pointer should turn into a double edged arrow.

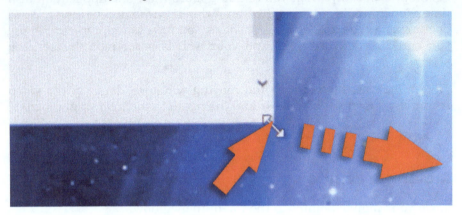

The double edged arrow means you can resize the window. Now click and drag the edge of the window until it is the size you want.

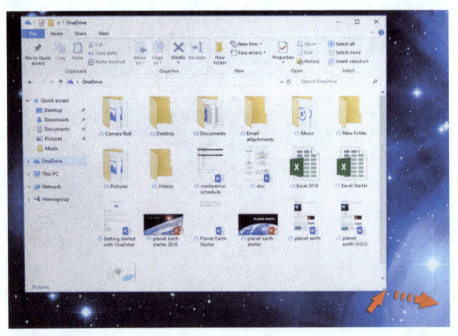

You can drag any edge of the window - left, bottom or right edge, but I find using the corner allows you to freely resize the window much more easily.

If you're on a touch screen, tap and drag the corner of the window.

Minimise, Maximise & Close a Window

On the top right hand side of every window, you'll see three icons. You can use these icons to minimise a window, ie reduce it to the taskbar essentially hiding the window from the desktop. With the second icon, you can maximise the window so it fills the entire screen, or if the window is already maximised, using the same icon, restore the window to its original size. The third icon you can use to close a window completely.

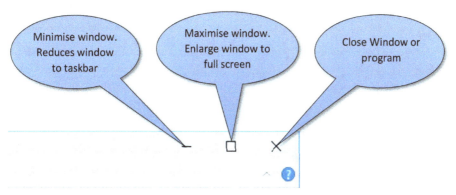

Window Snap Feature

The snap feature allows you to organize the windows on your screen. You can 'snap' them into place allowing you to put two app windows side by side. To do this, open an app, then click the title bar of the app and drag your mouse pointer to the edge of your screen.

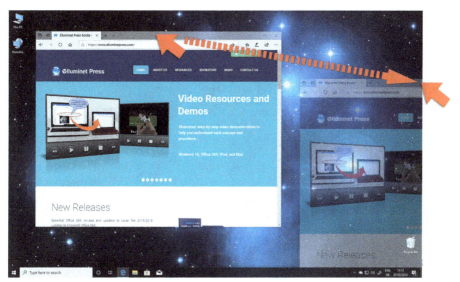

An highlight box will appear to show you where the window will snap to once you release your mouse button.

Once you let go of your mouse button, the window will snap into position.

Now you can open another app, click the title bar and drag your mouse pointer to the left edge, and you'll have two apps running side by side.

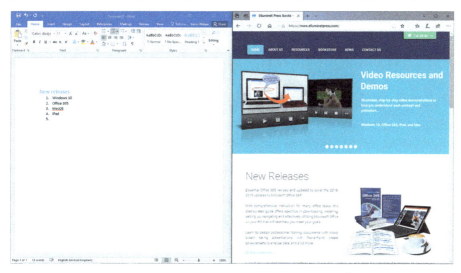

You can also have a window in each corner of the screen. To do this just click the title bar of the window and drag your mouse pointer to one of the corners of the screen instead of the edge.

Drag each window to a corner of the screen: left, right, bottom left, bottom right.

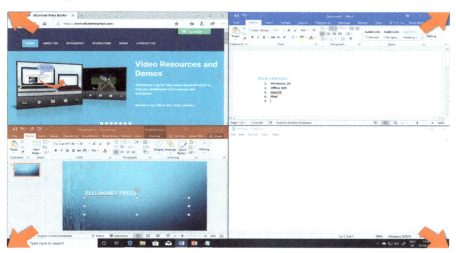

Keyboard Shortcuts

Keyboard shortcuts are performed using 3 main function keys: the control key, the windows key and the alt key.

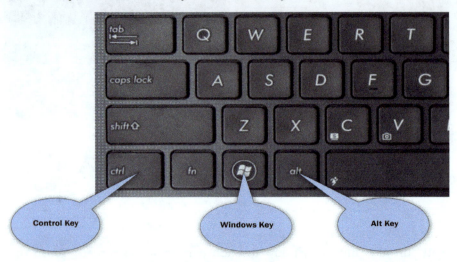

To execute a command using a keyboard shortcut. Hold down the appropriate function key and tap the key for the function you want shown in the table below.

Windows + Tab	Opens thumbnail list of open applications
Windows + A	Open Windows 10 notification centre
Windows + D	Show Windows desktop
Windows + E	Open Windows Explorer
Windows + K	Connect to wireless displays and audio devices
Windows + P	Project a screen
Windows + R	Run a command
Windows + X	Open Start button context menu
Windows key + Arrow key	Snap app windows left, right, corners, maximize, or minimize
Windows key + Comma	Temporarily peek at the desktop
Windows Key	Show windows start menu
Alt + Tab	Switch to previous window
Alt + Space	Reveals drop down menu on current window: Restore, move, size, minimize, maximize or close.
Alt + F4	Close current app
Ctrl + Shift + Esc	Open Task Manager
Ctrl + Z	Undo Command
Ctrl + X	Cut selected text
Ctrl + C	Copy selected text
Ctrl + V	Paste selected text at cursor position
Ctrl + P	Print

Windows Search

Windows search has now been separated from Cortana. You'll find the search field on the bottom left of the taskbar. With Windows search you can search for files, apps, email, music, people, and settings on your PC, as well as a web search. To do this, click in the search field on the bottom left of your taskbar.

When the search window opens, you'll see media you can search for along the top: apps, documents, email, web, more. This is useful if you want to search only for documents, email, or apps, rather than your whole PC. This helps to narrow down your search.

Underneath, you'll see icons representing the most used apps on your PC. These could be anything such Microsoft Word, File Explorer, or even your favourite games. Windows keeps track of the applications you use and displays them here. Click the icons to open the apps.

Further down the window, you'll see your most recently opened files, emails, and websites. Click a file or website in the list to open it.

Searching for Files

To search for something, type it into the search field on the taskbar. This could be the name of an app, a document, email, or website.

On the left hand side of the search results, you'll see a list of files, apps, and web search suggestions.

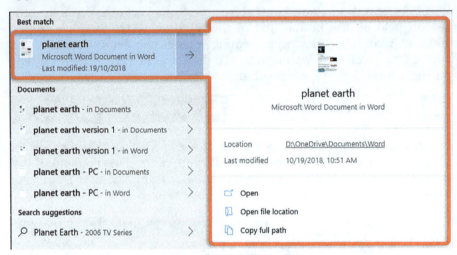

Press the down arrow key on your keyboard to scroll down the list to see some details about the search result. These details will appear in the right hand half of the window. Click on the search suggestion in the list on the left hand side to open it up.

Searching for Apps

You can also search for apps, just type the name of the app into the search field on the bottom left of the taskbar. Click the app to open it.

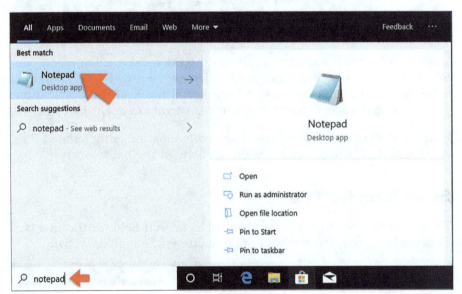

Searching for Windows Settings

You can also search for settings. For example, you can search for printer settings, WiFi, BlueTooth, display settings and so on. Just type the setting you're looking for into the search field on the bottom left of the taskbar. Click the setting you want to open it up.

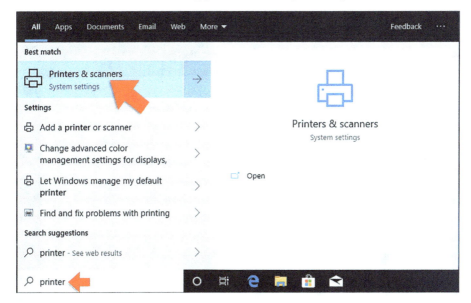

Narrowing Down the Search

Along the top of the window, you'll see a bar with some options. These allow you to restrict your search to apps, documents, email, web, folders, music, people, photos, settings, or videos (click 'more' to see the rest of the options).

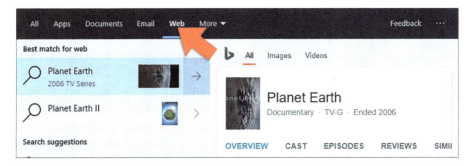

So, if I was searching for 'planet earth' on the web, I'd select 'web' from the options on the bar. If I just wanted to search my email, I'd select 'email' from the options.

Cortana Personal Assistant

Cortana is Microsoft's voice activated, personal assistant. You can use Cortana to perform various tasks using your natural voice, rather than typing or clicking an icon.

When you click the Cortana icon on the taskbar, you'll see this window pop up. You can move the window to any position on the screen.

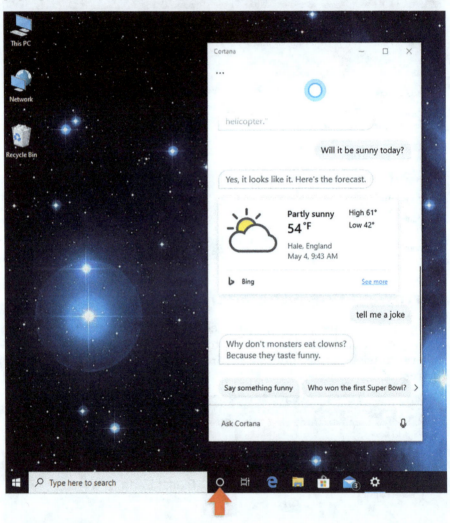

You can ask Cortana questions about current weather and traffic conditions, local points of interest such as closest or popular places to eat, you can find sports scores and biographies. You can talk to Cortana using a text based chat, or using voice commands.

Using the Chat Feature

Tap/Click the Cortana icon, located on the bottom left hand side of the task bar.

At the bottom of the Cortana window, you'll see a text field. Type your question or command

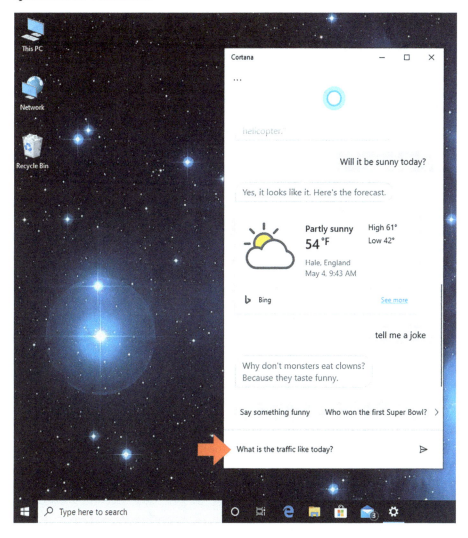

Try it, see what Cortana says.

Using Voice Commands

Tap/Click the Cortana icon, located on the bottom left hand side of the task bar.

You'll see Cortana's window pop up with the words 'listening...' at the bottom. This means Cortana is waiting for a voice command.

Try some of the following voice commands. You may need to change some of the names.

- *"Call Sister at home"*
- *"Send text to Sophie: When are you coming to play?"*
- *"Create a meeting with Claire at 2pm tomorrow"*
- *"Make Note: Pick up kids, take dog for walk, feed kids, buy milk and ice-cream on way home"*
- *"Show me restaurants nearby"*
- *"What's the forecast for this weekend?"*
- *"How do I get to Liverpool One?"* or *"Show me directions to Liverpool One."*
- *How many pints are there in a litre?*
- *What's 20 pounds in dollars?*
- *Add milk to shopping list.*
- *Hey Cortana! Tell me a joke.*

Voice Reminders

You can add reminders using Cortana, just ask her to remind you of something. To do this tap the Cortana icon on the taskbar and say it using your voice.

Try something like: "Remind me to pick up Claire today at 10:30pm."

Cortana will ask if she should remind you... Say 'yes' to confirm the reminder.

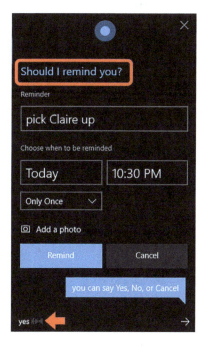

Click 'see all reminders' to view the reminders you have set, or to delete any.

Windows 10 Tablet Mode

Windows 10 is designed to run on a tablet computer, and has a mode called 'tablet mode' that enables Windows to optimise the user interface for touch screens.

This means that the start menu takes up the whole screen, and apps run full screen to make them clearer and easier to use on a small touch sensitive screen, rather than using a mouse.

You won't see the desktop in tablet mode but you can still use your desktop apps such as Word, it will just run full screen instead of in a window.

Take a look at the navigation section of the accompanying video demos. Open your browser and navigate to the following website:

```
videos.tips/win-10-nav
```

Using a Tablet

You can easily switch to tablet mode, where apps show up full screen and are a bit larger to make it easier to navigate using touch. Tap action center icon on the bottom right, then tap 'tablet mode'.

You can see that in tablet mode everything opens up in full screen. The start menu becomes the start screen allowing you to tap directly on the tiles rather than using the mouse.

In desktop mode, you see the start menu and everything runs in a window which is easier with a point and click keyboard and mouse interface.

This is what you'll see if you are running Windows 10 on a tablet in tablet mode.

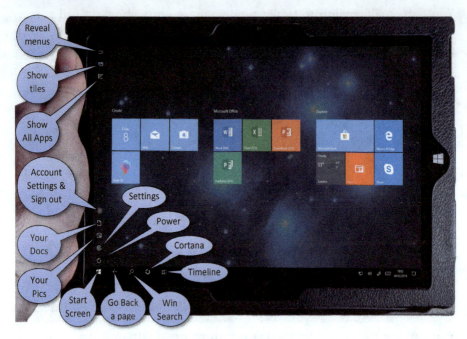

On the top left of the screen, you'll see three icons. The top one reveals the side menu, the second icon shows your tiles, and the third icon shows an alphabetical list of all the apps installed on your device.

On the bottom left, you'll see five icons. The top icon is your Microsoft Account, here you can change your account settings, lock the screen, and sign out. The next icon down shows all your files in file explorer, the icon below that shows all your photos in file explorer. The next icon down allows you to change system settings, and the last icon allows you to shut down or restart your device.

On the right hand side of the start screen you will see an array or coloured tiles. These represent your apps. You can tap these to start them up.

Along the bottom of the start screen, you'll see a black bar, this is the task bar.

From here you can tap the start screen icon, go back a page, search windows, open Cortana, and view your timeline/activity history. On the right hand side of the taskbar, you'll see your notification area.

Gestures for Touch Screens

On your tablet's touch screen, you can use various gestures using your forefinger and thumb.

One Finger Tap

Tapping with one finger is equivalent to clicking with your mouse, usually to select something. Tapping twice with your finger is the same as double clicking with the mouse and is usually used to start an app.

Tap and Hold

Tapping on the screen with your finger and holding it there for a second or two, is equivalent to using the right click with the mouse and usually invokes a context menu.

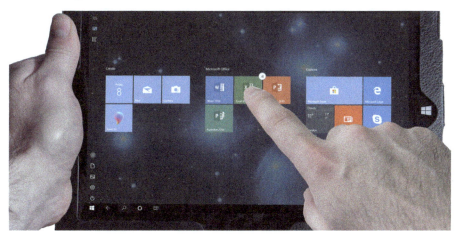

One Finger Slide

Use this to move objects such as windows and icons around the screen. Tap on an object, then without lifting your finger, slide your finger across the screen. This is the same as click and drag with the mouse.

Two Finger Pinch & Spread

Use your forefinger and thumb to zoom in and out. Spread your finger and thumb apart to zoom in, pinch your thumb and finger closer together to zoom out. Use this gesture on maps or when viewing photos.

Two Finger Rotate

Use your forefinger and thumb to rotate images or maps on the screen. You can rotate clockwise or counter-clockwise.

Scroll

Slide your finger over the screen to scroll up & down documents and web pages.

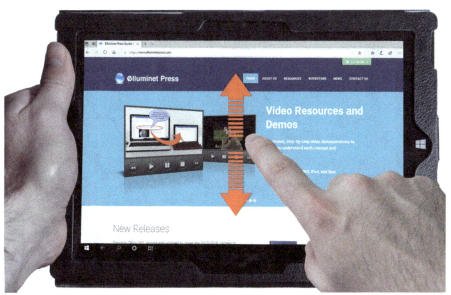

Swipe from the Left Edge

Swipe from the left edge of the screen gives you your timeline/taskview; a thumbnail list of open apps. Tap on the thumbnail to switch to the app.

Swipe from the Right Edge

Swipe from the right edge of the screen opens your action centre.

Three Finger Tap

Tapping on the screen with three fingers at the same time will call up Cortana personal assistant. This doesn't work on all tablets.

Three Finger Swipe Left/Right

Swiping three fingers left and right across the screen will flick through open applications running on your device.

Customising your Start Screen

You can customise your start screen by resizing or moving tiles around to suite your needs.

Move Tiles

Just tap on the tile and slide your finger across the screen to where you want to place the tile.

Add Tiles

To add tiles, first you need to reveal all your apps. To do this, tap the 'all apps' icon on the top left of the screen..

From the list, tap and hold your finger on the icon you want to add.

From the popup menu, tap 'pin to start'.

196

Resize Tiles

You can also resize tiles. To do this, tap on the tile with your finger, and hold until the little icons appear.

Tap the icon with the three little dots.

From the pop up menu tap resize.

From the slide out menu tap the size you want: small, medium, wide or large.

197

On-screen Keyboard

Your on-screen keyboard will appear whenever you tap inside a text field. To bring up the keyboard at any other time, tap the icon on the right hand side of the task bar. Note this icon wont appear if you have a keyboard plugged into your tablet.

Your keyboard will open up on the bottom third of the screen.

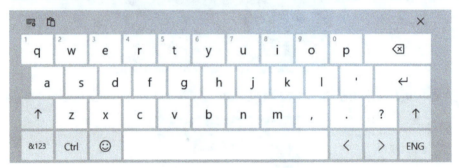

You can type normally using the keys. To quickly type in a number, use the keys on the top row, you'll notice a small number in the top left hand side of the key. To do this, tap and hold your finger on the key with the number you want to type, eg press and hold 'r' for the number 4. Tap the number in the popup.

If you're typing in more than one number, tap the '&123' icon on the bottom left of the screen and use the keypad. Tap 'abc" to get back to the standard keyboard.

Changing Keyboards

You can also select different keyboards: a split keyboard, or a floating keyboard. The standard keyboard is the default and the one that's used for normal typing. To change the keyboard, tap the icon on the top left of the keyboard.

On a split keyboard, half appears on the left and the other half appears on the right. This can be more comfortable to type.

A floating keyboard is useful if the standard keyboard gets in the way.

You can drag a floating keyboard anywhere on the screen.

The on-screen keyboard also has a hand writing recognition feature that instead of typing, you can actually write words and sentences using your pen or finger.

To do this, tap the small icon on the top left of the keyboard, then select handwriting from the drop down.

You'll see a panel open up. Tap in the field you want to enter text into. Write the text you want to 'type' in on the line. For example, when saving a file, you can write the file name instead of typing it, and the text appears in the text field.

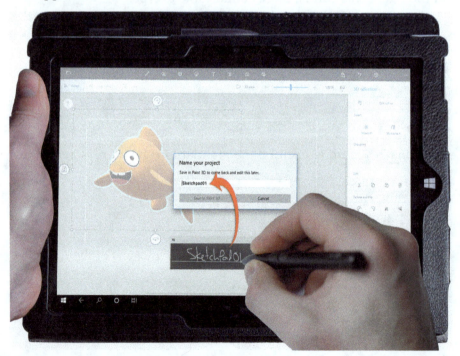

You can even use this feature in Word processing apps; write instead of typing.

Cases

A case is a must for any tablet. A case helps to protect your tablet from scratches. Some cases double as a stand to allow you to prop your tablet up which is useful if you want to watch a movie. Some also come with pockets and a place to keep your pen.

External Keyboards

Some cases come with built in keyboards. Most of these types connect to your tablet using bluetooth. You can pair them in the usual way - see pairing bluetooth devices on page 91.

When you plug a keyboard in, Windows 10 goes into desktop mode.

Hybrid Devices

Hybrid devices are a combination of a tablet and a laptop. They often have detachable keyboards such as the surface tablet...

...or keyboards that flip back behind the screen such as the lenovo yoga.

When you attach your keyboard, the display is optimised for point and click desktop use. When you detach the keyboard, the icons become larger and further apart making it easier to use on a touch screen.

Change Between Desktop & Tablet Mode

You can also manually change between the two. To do this, open up your action centre.

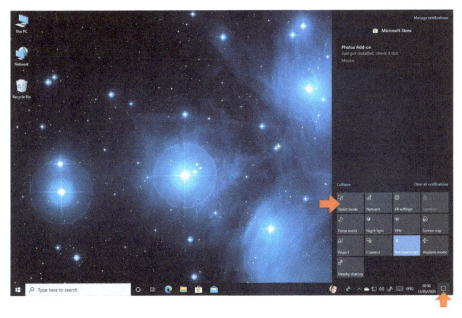

Tap or click on 'tablet mode', or if you're already in tablet mode, tap or click 'desktop mode'.

Pens

You can buy pens and styluses to use with your tablet. These come in useful for Windows Ink & OneNote, as well as any art apps out there that you can find in the App Store.

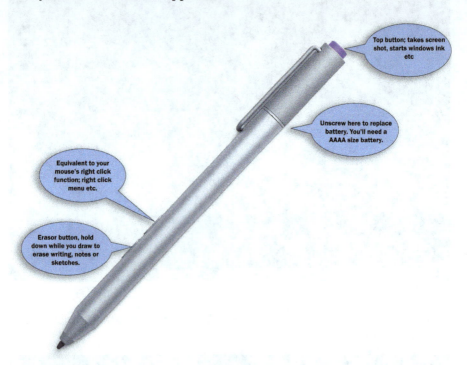

These come in various types but the ones that work best have bluetooth capability, meaning you can pair the pen with your tablet giving you extra features such as shortcut buttons, mouse button equivalents and so on.

First put your pen into 'pairing mode'. To do this, hold down the top button for about 10 seconds, until the little green light on the side of the pen starts flashing.

On your tablet, go to:

Settings -> Devices -> Bluetooth

Turn bluetooth on if you need to. Select your pen from the list.

Click 'pair'.

Your pen will automatically pair itself with your tablet.

Other Accessories

You can buy little USB adapters that plug into the side of your tablet. This allows you to plug in standard USB devices such as a mouse, digital camera, card reader, printer, etc.

Internet, Email & Communication

In this chapter, we'll take a look at the browser Microsoft Edge. We'll also take a brief look at Google Chrome as it is a good alternative to Microsoft Edge.

Windows 10 also has mail and calendar apps, where you can add all your email accounts, whether it's Google, Yahoo, Microsoft account or any other account, you can have them all in one place. We'll take a look at these later in this chapter.

Also we'll take a look at how to get started using Skype for making calls.

For this chapter, take a look at the communication section of the video resources. Open your browser and navigate to the following website

`videos.tips/win-10-comms`

Lets begin by taking a look at Microsoft's browser, Edge.

Microsoft Edge Browser

There is a completely new version of Edge available. This version has been rebuilt and now includes more features, is faster and more secure. You should receive the update in the usual Windows Update channels, if not navigate to the following website and download it.

`www.microsoft.com/edge`

Click the 'download' button in the middle of the screen.

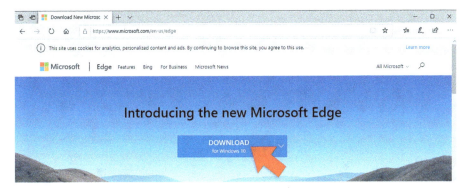

Click 'accept and download'.

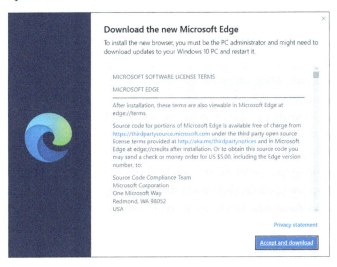

Click 'run' when prompted.

If not, go to your downloads folder and double click 'MicrosoftEdgeSetup. exe'.

Chapter 5: Internet, Email & Communication

You'll find Edge on your taskbar (note the new app icon). You'll also find it on your start menu. Click the icon to start the app.

When Edge starts, you'll see the main screen. Lets take a look at the different parts of Edge.

Along the top of the window you will find your address bar where you can enter search keywords, or website addresses (called URLs). You can add websites to favourites, make website collections, and annotate pages.

You can open websites in tabs instead of new windows. This helps to keep things organised when you have more than one website open at a time.

You can also access your Microsoft Account profile settings so you can sync your favourites, passwords etc across all your devices.

Take a look at the demos in the communication section of the video resources. Open your web browser and navigate to the following website:

```
videos.tips/win-10-comms
```

Set your Home Page

Setting a home page allows you to set a page to show when you first start Edge or when you click the home icon on the toolbar. Ideally you should set the home page to a website you use most often such as Google search.

To set your home page, click the 'three dots icon' on the top right of the screen, then from the menu select 'settings'.

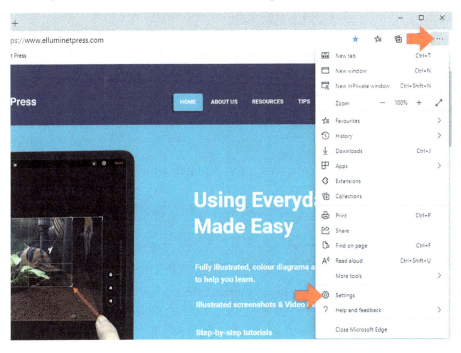

On the left hand panel click 'on startup'.

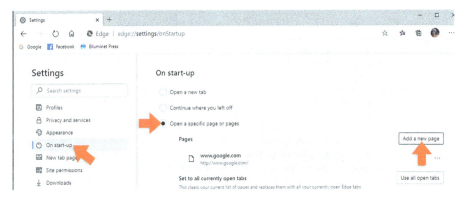

Select 'open a specific page or pages', then click 'add new page'

Enter the website address (URL) into the field (eg www.google.com).

Click 'add'.

Favourites Bar

The favourites bar is where you can save websites. The bar shows up just below the address bar at the top of the screen. I'd advise you to only pin the websites you use most often to this bar, otherwise it can get a bit cluttered.

To enable the favourites bar, click the 'three dots icon' on the top right of the screen, and select 'favourites' from the menu.

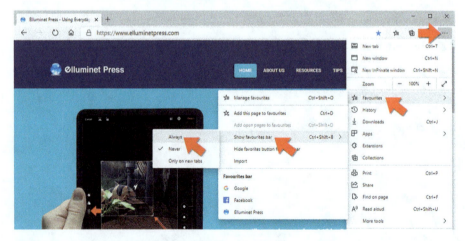

Go down to 'show the favourites bar'. From the slide-out menu select 'always' to turn it on.

Add Website to Favourites Bar

To add a website, first navigate to the page you want to add, then click the star icon on the top right of the address bar.

In the dialog box that appears, type in a meaningful name for the website.

Click on the drop down box next to 'folder'. Select 'favourites bar' to add the website to the favourites bar, or select the folder you want to save the website into.

Click 'done' at the bottom of the dialog box.

Organising the Favourites Bar

You can organise your favourites into folders. This helps keep sites of the same genre together. For example, you could have a folder called 'work' for all your business sites, a folder called 'social' for all your social media, or a folder for any interests you have eg gardening or photography. Create these on your favourites bar for easy access.

To create a folder, right click on the favourites bar, select 'add folder'.

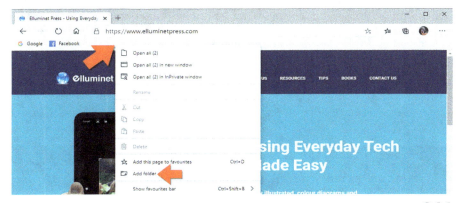

Type in a meaningful name for the folder, eg: 'work'.

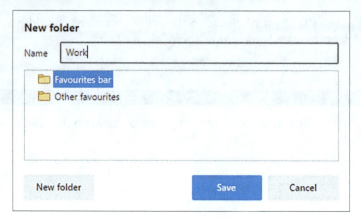

You'll see your folder appear on the favourites bar.

You can click & drag any favourite into the folder.

Click on the folder name to open it up

Revisit a Website on Favourites

To revisit your favourite sites just select them from the favourites bar.

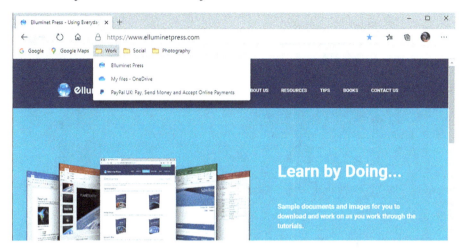

You'll also find your favourites using the 'favourites' icon on the top right of the screen.

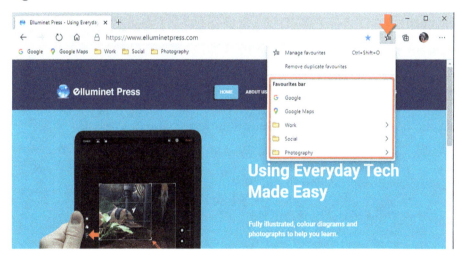

Managing Favourites

Click the 'favourites' icon on the top right of the screen. Select 'manage favourites'.

From here, you can drag sites into folders, change the order, create new folders, as well as delete favourited sites.

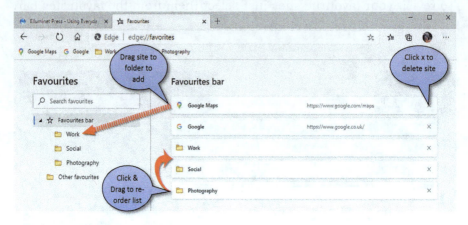

Import Favourites

You can import your favourites from other web browsers. To do this click the 'favourites' icon on the top right of the screen. Select 'manage favourites'.

At the bottom of the screen, select 'import favourites'.

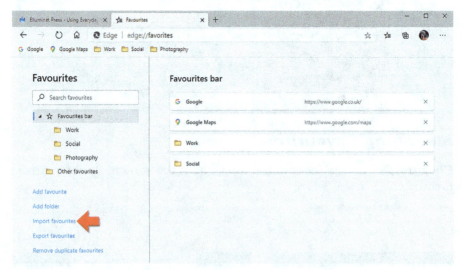

Use the 'import from' field to select which browser to import your data from, eg Chrome. *(If you want to import from a file see bottom of page).*

Select which data you want to import (favourites, passwords, etc).

Click 'import'.

If you want to import from a file, click the 'import from' field then select 'favourites or bookmarks HTML file'.

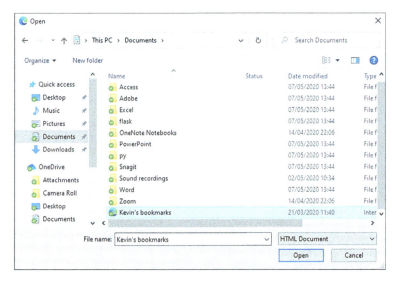

Browse to and select the HTML bookmarks file, then click ok.

215

Export Favourites

You can also export all your favourited websites to a file if you want to later import them on another machine or give them to someone else. To do this, click the 'favourites' icon on the top right of the screen. Select 'manage favourites'.

At the bottom of the screen, select 'export favourites'.

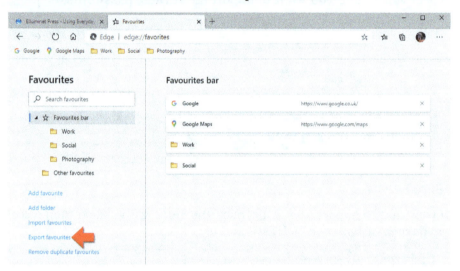

Browse to a folder to save the file, then click 'save.

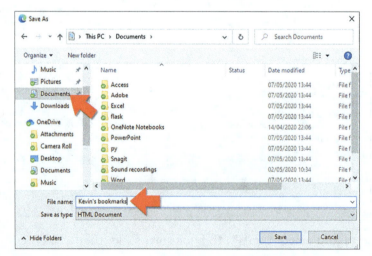

Collections

Collections allow you to organize content you browse on the web. You can gather text, images from the web and then place them inside a note page and share organized sets and export them to Office apps.

To create a collection, click the collections icon on the top right of the toolbar. Then click 'start new collection'.

Enter a meaningful name.

Highlight and drag content from webpages into the collection. You can drag paragraphs, images and videos.

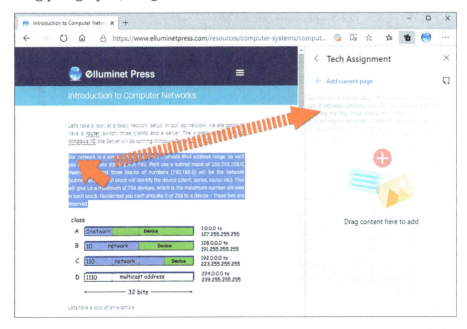

You can also add a whole page. To do this, navigate to the page you want to add, then in the collections panel, click 'add current page'.

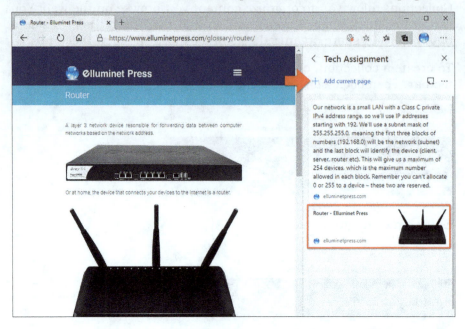

To add notes to your collection, click the notes icon on the top right of the collections panel.

Type your note. You can format your note text as well as add bullet points and lists.

You can send your collections to Word or Excel. This will open your collection in a Word or Excel document using the online versions of these apps. Sign in with your Microsoft Account email address and password if prompted.

To share your collection, click the three dots icon on the top right of the collections panel. From the drop down menu, select the app you want to send your collection to. Eg 'word'.

You'll see the collection open in the app within Edge.

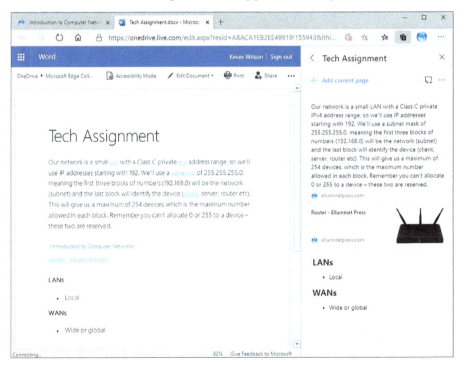

From here you can save the document, edit and share it.

Finding Files you've Downloaded

Whenever you download files from a website, you'll find the files in your downloads folder.

To open your downloads folder, click the 'three dots icon' on the top right of the screen, and select 'downloads'

Here, you'll see a history list of all the files you've downloaded. Down the left hand side, you can search for downloads, or you can use the categories in the list to find a specific type of tile such as an app, image or video.

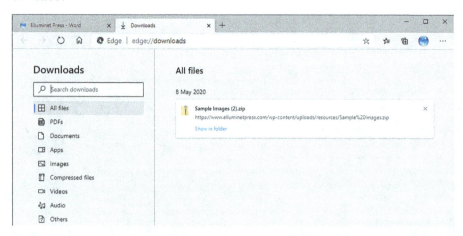

To open or run any of these downloads, double click on the link in the list.

To open your downloads folder in File Explorer, click 'show in folder'. From File Explorer, you can double click on the file to open it or run it.

Browsing History

Edge keeps a list of every website you visit. To find your browsing history, click the three dots icon on the top right. Select 'history'.

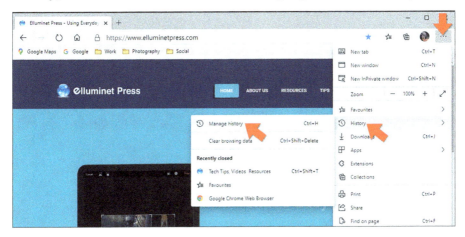

You'll see a list of the sites you've visited. Click on a site to revisit. To clear the history click 'clear browsing history on bottom left.

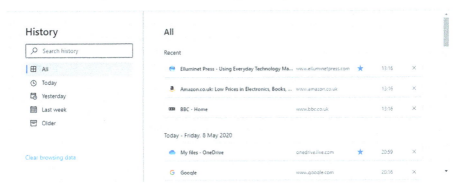

You can also see a list of sites you've visited while you've been browsing if you click and hold your mouse pointer on the back icon.

Click any of the links to return to the website.

Reading Mode

Some websites, especially those with a lot of text can be difficult to print or read on screen. You can use the immersive reader feature. To use this feature, click the reader icon to the right of the address bar. Or press F9.

From here, you can read the main text without adverts or any other distracting parts of a website.

You can get Edge to read the document aloud - click 'read aloud'. You can change the size of the text or the background colour - click 'text preferences'. You can enable 'line focus' that allows you to concentrate on each line as you read - click 'reading preferences'. You can also highlight syllables, verbs, nouns and adjectives in the text using the grammar tools. Give it a try.

To exit reader mode, click the reader icon again or press F9

Page Translator

You can translate any page into another language. To do this, right click your mouse on the web page, then select 'translate to...'

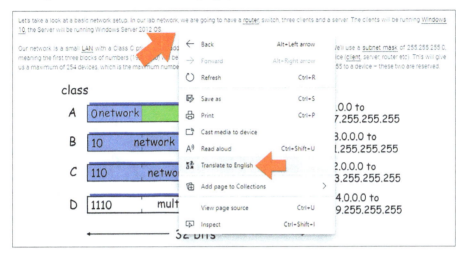

In the drop down box, select the language you want to translate the page into. Lets try Portuguese... Click 'translate', or 'try again'.

Here you can see Edge has attempted a translation. Translations aren't 100% accurate but will give you the general idea.

Print a Page

To print a web page, click the three dots icon on the top right of the screen, then select 'print' from the drop down menu.

From the panel on the left hand side, select the printer. Under 'copies', enter number of copies if needed.

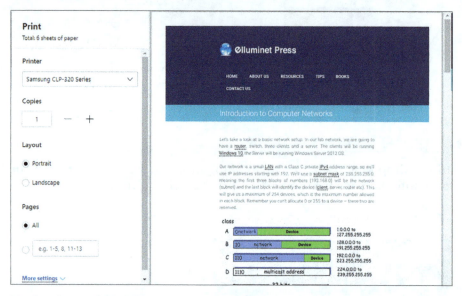

Under 'layout', select portrait or landscape. Under 'pages', enter the page numbers you want to print. You'll see the page numbers in the print preview on the right if you scroll down the page.

Click 'more settings' on the bottom left. From here you can print background graphics, add or remove headers and footers, or print more than one page to a sheet of paper, and change the paper size.

Share a Page

You can share a web page with anyone on your contact list using email, skype, messages and so on.

To share a page, click the three dots icon on the top right of the screen. From the drop down menu, select 'share'.

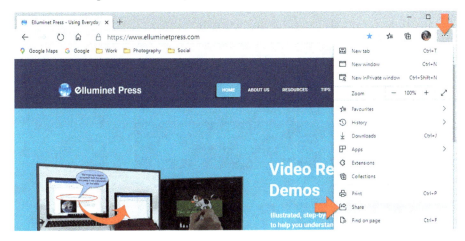

From the dialog box, select the person you want to share the page with, or select an app to share the page. Eg, email.

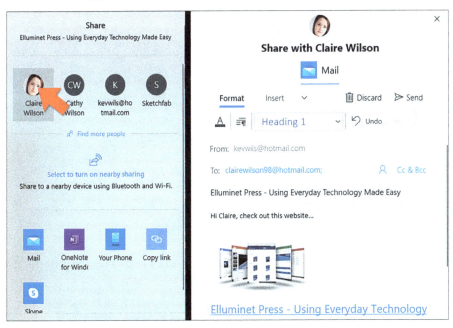

Type in a message, click 'send'.

Pin Website to TaskBar

A useful feature of Microsoft Edge is the ability to pin a website shortcut onto your taskbar. You should only really use this feature for websites you visit very often, as you can quite easily fill up your taskbar with clutter. Perhaps if you use a web based email or facebook - create a taskbar short cut.

To do this, open the website you want to pin in Microsoft Edge. Click the three dots icon on the top right, go down to 'more tools', select 'pin to taskbar' from the slide out menu.

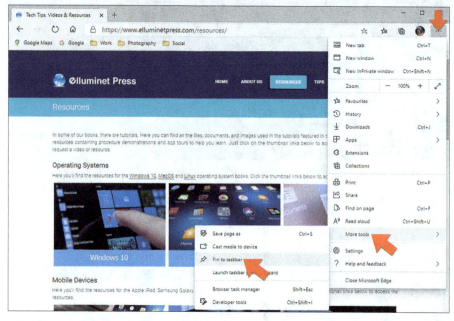

Give the site a name, then click 'pin'.

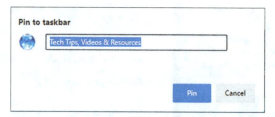

You'll see the website link appear on your task bar. The icon depends on the website's own icon.

Edge Extensions

Extensions add functionality to the Edge Browser. To add extensions to Edge, click the three dots icon on the top right of your screen and select 'extensions'.

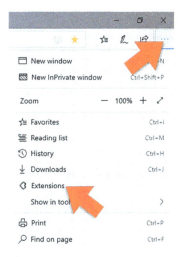

You'll see a list of any extensions that have been installed on the right. To install a new extension, click 'get extensions from microsoft store'

The Microsoft Store will open up showing the newest extensions available. In this example, I'm going to add the uBlock extension. So click 'uBlock Origin'.

From the extension details page, click 'get'.

Click 'add extension' on the confirmation dialog box.

You can access your extensions anytime, just click the three dots icon on the top right of your screen and select 'extensions' from the menu.

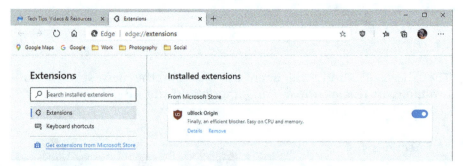

Any installed extensions will appear on the right. Click the icon to open the extensions settings.

You'll also see an icon appear on the toolbar.

Install Chrome Extensions in Edge

With the new Edge browser, you can install chrome extensions from the chrome web store. To do this, you first need to enable extensions from other stores.

Click the three dots icon on the top right, select 'extensions' from the drop down menu.

Enable 'allow extensions from other stores', on the bottom left.

Type `chrome.google.com` into the search bar in Edge.

Use the search bar on the left hand side in the chrome web store to search for apps.

Click 'add to chrome' to install any app.

Google Chrome

Google Chrome is a fast and streamlined browser that is a good alternative to Microsoft Edge. To use Google Chrome in Windows 10, you'll first need to download it.

You can download Google Chrome from

`www.google.com/chrome`

Hit the 'download chrome' button. Click 'accept and install'. Go to your downloads folder and double click 'chromesetup.exe'

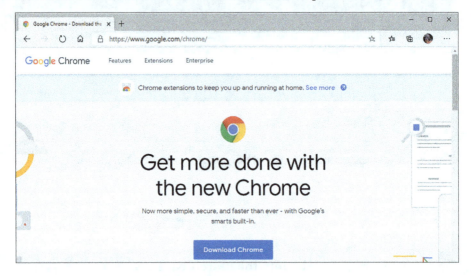

Follow the on screen instructions to install the browser. You'll find Chrome on your start menu and on your desktop.

Once Chrome has loaded, click the profile icon on the top right and enter your Google account username and password.

This is the same account that you use for Gmail if you have one.

You can use Chrome without a Google account, but you won't get any of the personalised features or be able to add apps to Chrome from the Chrome Store.

You can use Google Chrome in a similar way to Edge. This is Chrome's Start screen. You can type in your Google Search or type a URL if you know it into the search bar. Along the bottom you'll also see your most visited websites.

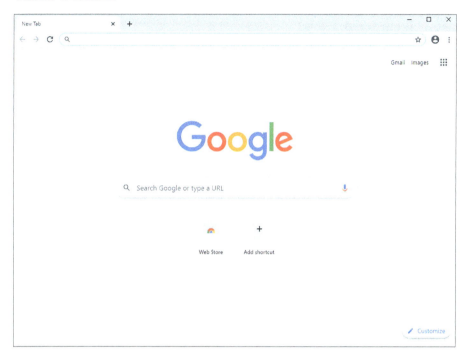

Let's take a closer look at Chrome's interface.

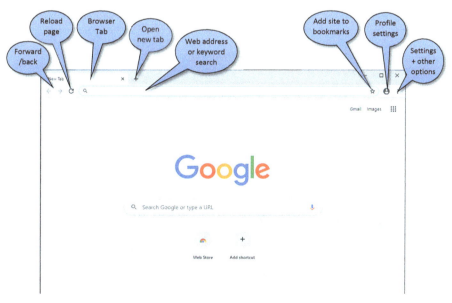

Bookmarks Bar

The bookmarks bar is where you can save websites. The bar shows up just below the address bar at the top of the screen. I'd advise you to only pin the websites you use most often to this bar, otherwise it can get a bit cluttered.

To enable the bookmarks bar, click the 'three dots icon' on the top right of the screen, and select 'bookmarks' from the menu.

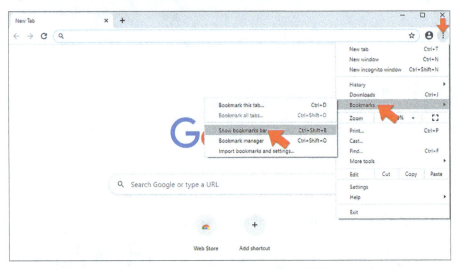

Click 'show bookmarks bar' to enable it.

Add Website to Bookmarks Bar

To add a website, first navigate to the page you want to add, then click the star icon on the top right of the address bar.

In the dialog box that appears, type in a meaningful name for the website.

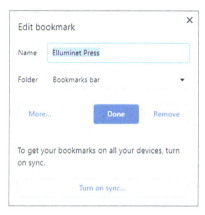

Click on the drop down box next to 'folder'. Select 'bookmarks bar' to add the website to the bookmarks bar, or select the folder you want to save the website into.

Click 'done' at the bottom of the dialog box.

Organising the Bookmarks Bar

You can organise your bookmarks into folders. This helps keep sites of the same genre together. For example, you could have a folder called 'work' for all your business sites, a folder called 'social' for all your social media, or a folder for any interests you have eg gardening or photography. Create these on your bookmarks bar for easy access.

To create a folder, right click on the bookmarks bar, select 'add folder'.

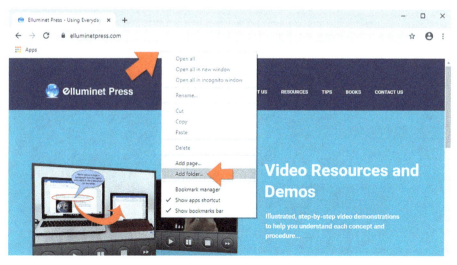

Type in a meaningful name for the folder, eg: 'work'.

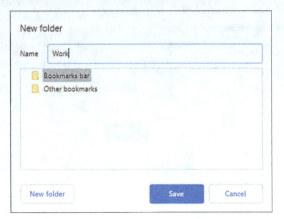

You'll see your folder appear on the bookmarks bar.

You can click & drag any bookmarks into the folder.

Click on the folder name to open it up

Browsing History

Chrome keeps a list of every website you visit. To find your browsing history, click the three dots icon on the top right. Select 'history', then click 'history' on the slide out menu.

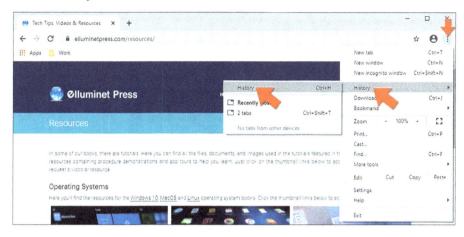

You'll see a list of the sites you've visited. Click on a site to revisit.

You can also see a list of sites you've visited while you've been browsing if you click and hold your mouse pointer on the back icon.

Click any of the links to return to the website.

Finding Files you've Downloaded

Whenever you download files from a website, you'll find the files in your downloads folder.

To open your downloads folder, click the 'three dots icon' on the top right of the screen, and select 'downloads'

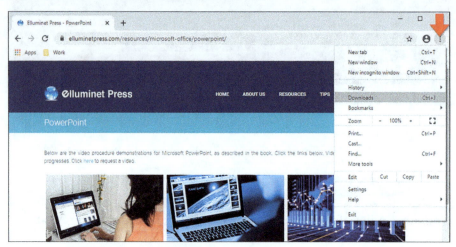

Here, you'll see a history list of all the files you've downloaded. To open or run any of these downloads, double click on the link in the list.

To open your downloads folder in File Explorer, click 'show in folder'. From File Explorer, you can double click on the file to open it or run it.

To delete the download from your list, click the x on the right hand side of the download item in the list.

Printing Pages

To print a web page, click the three dots icon on the top right of the screen, then select 'print' from the drop down menu.

From the panel on the right hand side, select the printer. Under 'copies', enter number of copies if needed.

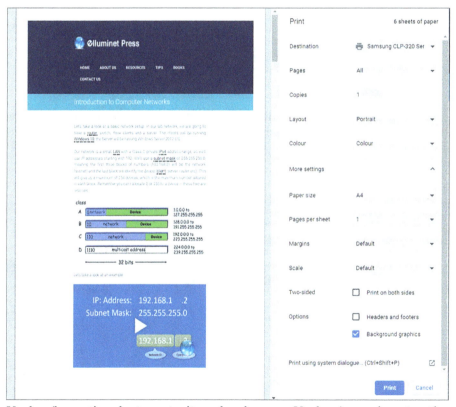

Under 'layout', select portrait or landscape. Under 'pages', enter the page numbers you want to print. You'll see the page numbers in the print preview on the left if you scroll down the page.

Click 'more settings' on the bottom left. From here you can print background graphics, add or remove headers and footers, or print more than one page to a sheet of paper, and change the paper size.

Extending Chrome

Extensions are small apps that add functionality to the chrome browser. To see what extensions are installed on your chrome browser, click the three dots icon on the top right. Select 'more tools', then click 'extensions' from the slide out menu.

You'll see a list of any extensions that are installed. To add new extensions, click the hamburger icon on the top right.

Select 'open chrome web store' on the bottom left.

In the web store, you can search for an app.

Click 'add to chrome' to install the extension

Mail App

You can start the Mail App by tapping or clicking on the mail icon on your start menu.

If this is the first time you are using this app, you may be asked to add your email account.

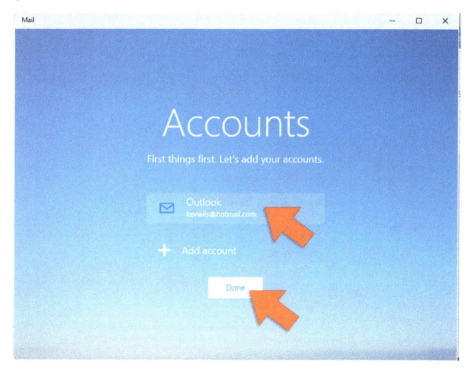

If you are using your Microsoft Account, mail app usually finds it as shown above.

Select this email account then click 'done'.

Take a look at the demos in the communication section of the video resources. Open your web browser and navigate to the following website:

videos.tips/win-10-comms

239

Adding Other Email Accounts

If you have another email account such as Gmail or Yahoo you can add these too.

To do this click the settings icon on the bottom left of the screen.

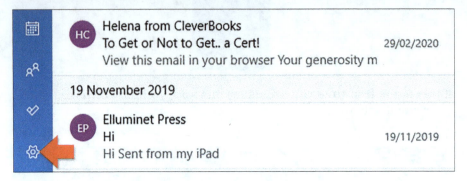

Click 'manage accounts' on the side panel on the right hand side of the screen.

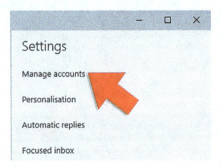

Click 'add account'.

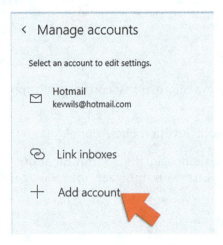

Select the account provider. Eg if you are adding a GMail or Google account, click 'Google', if it's Yahoo, click 'Yahoo', or Apple, click 'iCloud'.... If your provider isn't in the list above click 'other account'.

In this example, I want to add my Gmail account. So I'd select Google.

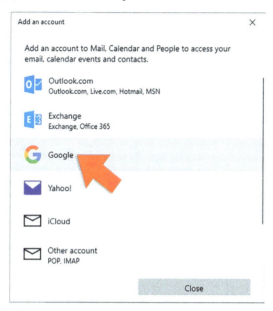

In the 'connecting to a service' dialog box, type in your email address for the email account you're adding. Click 'next'.

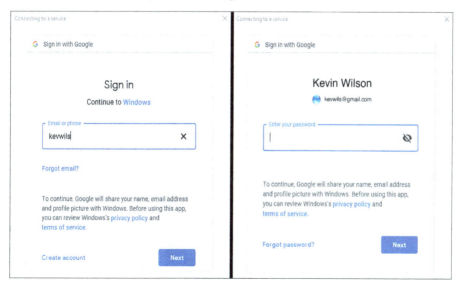

Enter your password on the next screen, click 'next'.

Chapter 5: Internet, Email & Communication

In the next window, scroll down and select 'allow' to give Windows permission to access your account. Then click 'done'.

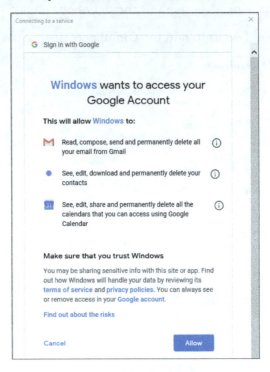

All your email accounts will appear under the accounts section on the left hand side of the screen. Click the hamburger icon on the top left of the screen to reveal the full sidebar.

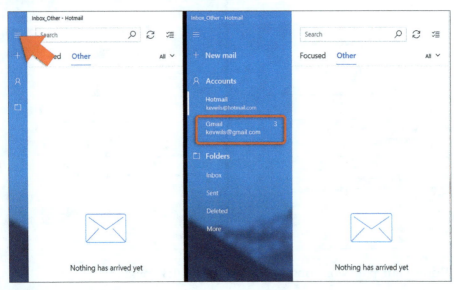

Reading Mail

When you open mail app it will check for email, any new messages will appear in your inbox.

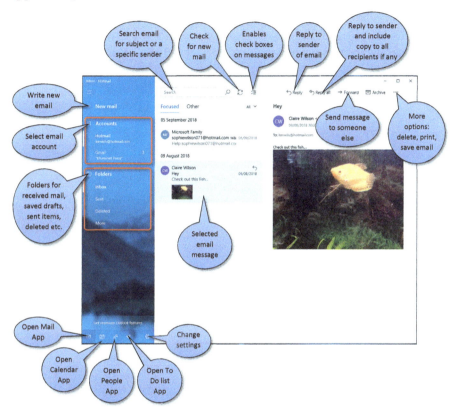

Click on the message in your inbox. The contents will be displayed in the reading pane on the right hand side.

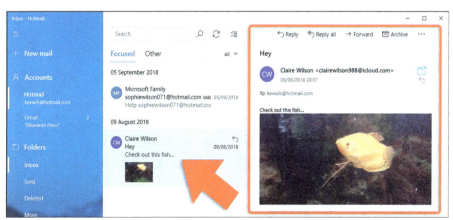

Writing a New Message

To start a new message, click 'new mail' on the top left hand side of the main screen.

First you need to enter the person's email address in the 'To' field. Click the people icon on the far right to open up your contacts. Scroll down and select the person you want to send the email to.

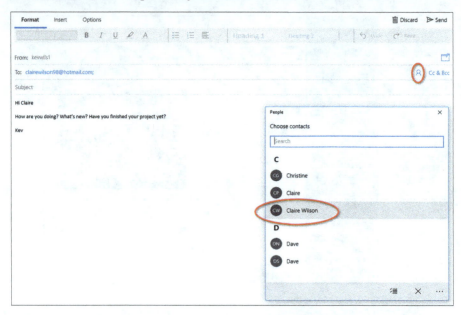

Add a subject, then type your email in the body section. In the body section, you can use the normal text formatting tools such as bold, change the font colour or size and so on, using the format tool bar as you can see below.

For example, select the text, click bold icon. Change text size, select text, click font size. Change font, select text, click on font name in toolbar.

Hit 'send' on the top right to send your email message.

Reply to a Message

To reply to the message, click the reply icon at the top of the screen.

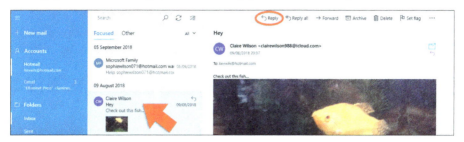

You'll see a screen that looks a bit like a word processor. Here you can type in your message. Your message will appear at the top. The original message will be appended to the end of the email.

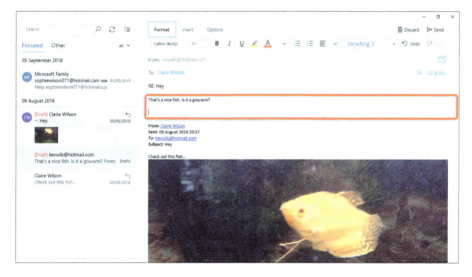

You can use the basic formatting tools. You can make text bold - select the text and click the 'B' icon on the toolbar. Or you can make text into a list. Select the text and click the list icon, then select a number style.

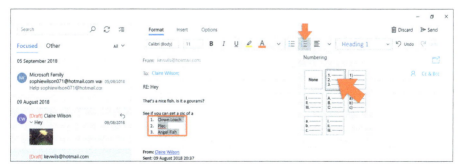

Adding Attachments

To attach a file, click 'insert' then select 'files'. Select the file you want to attach. Use this option to attach files such as documents, videos, music or photos.

Select your file from the dialog box. Hold down the control key to select multiple files. Click 'open' when you're done.

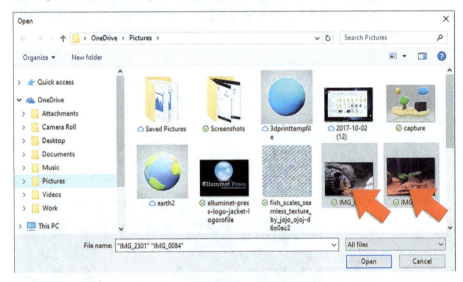

These attachments will be added to the end of the email.

Once you are done, click 'send' on the top right.

Inserting Images

Inserting images is a little different from adding an attachment. When you insert an image, you insert it into the body of the email message so it appears inline with the text.

In your email message, click 'insert'. From the options, select 'pictures'.

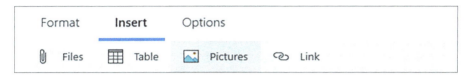

Select your picture from the dialog box. Hold down the control key if you're selecting more than one picture. Click 'insert'.

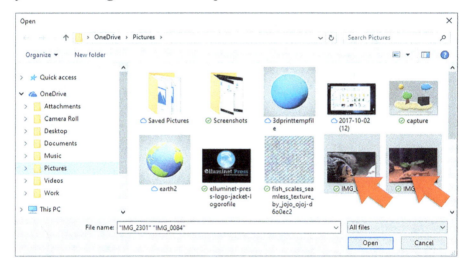

Click the 'send' icon on the top right when you're done.

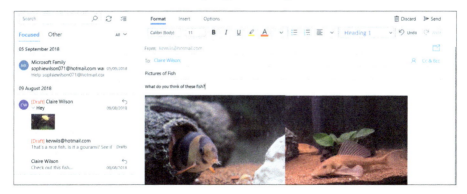

Images are inserted in the body of the email message.

Calendar App

The calendar app links in with the mail app, you can find it on your start menu. It will either have a calendar icon or it will be displaying the current date.

If this is the first time you are using this app, you may be asked to add your email account.

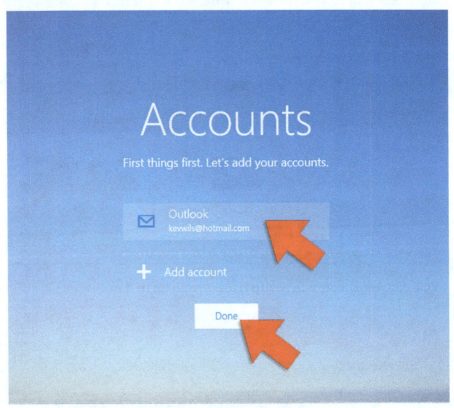

If you are using a Microsoft account, calendar app usually finds it for you. If this is the case select the account and click done.

If you use another email account click 'add account' then enter your username/email and password details given to you by the account provider.

Once you have done that, you will see your main screen.

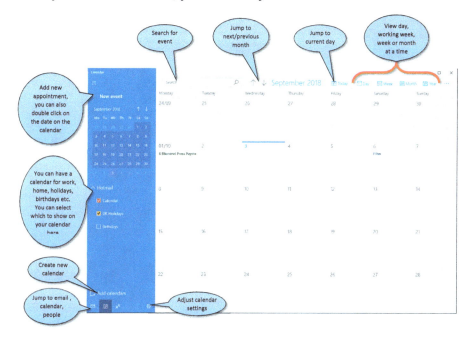

Add an Event

You can add events and appointments by clicking on the 'new event' button or click on the date in the calendar.

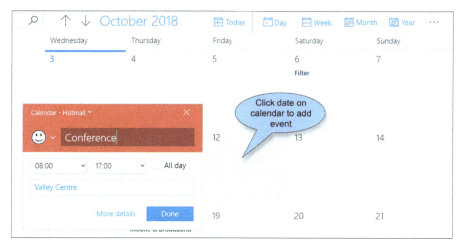

Type the location where you are meeting. Un-tick 'all day' and enter start and estimated finishing times. Unless it's an all day event.

Hit 'more details'.

You can add notes and any details about the event in the large text box at the bottom of the screen.

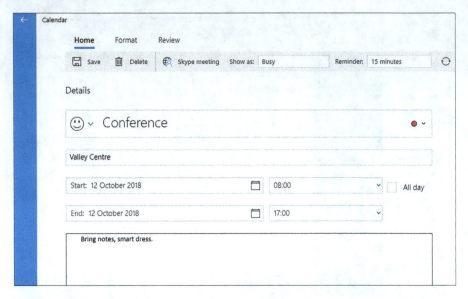

You can add a reminder too, by changing the reminder field. You can set it from none, 5 mins before, 15 mins before, a day before and so on. Reminders will pop up in your action centre as they occur.

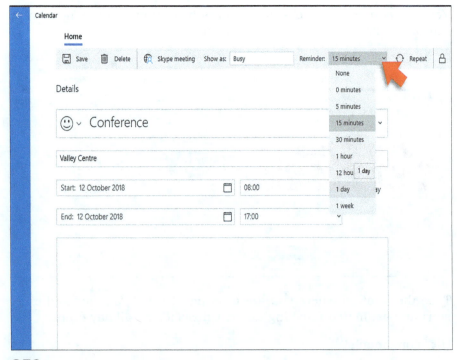

If the event is recurring, eg happens once a week or once a month, you can set this by clicking 'repeat'.

Under the 'repeat' section, you can set the event to occur on a daily, weekly, monthly and yearly basis. This saves you having to enter it for every occurrence.

Next, change any specifics such as what day a week/month the event occurs. In this example, the event occurs every week on a Tuesday.

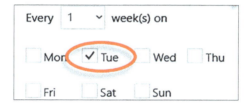

If the event ran every two weeks on Tuesday, we would change the top line to every 2 weeks.

In the next bit, you can set the date your recurring event ends. Eg if it is a course it might be weekly for 6 months or a year.

Hit 'save and close' on the top left of the screen when you're done.

Add Calendar Event From Taskbar

You can quickly add an event or appointment to your calendar from the task bar. To do this click the click/calendar on the bottom right of the task bar.

Click the day on the calendar

Then below, enter the name of the event or appointment,

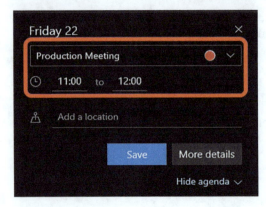

Click on the start time and select a time from the popup menu. Do the same for end time.

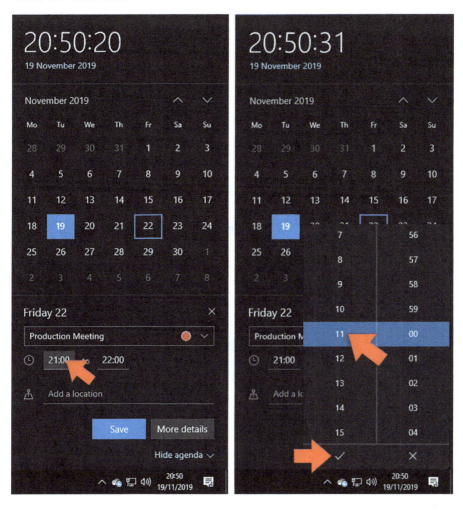

In the 'add a location' field, enter a location - place name, meeting place, address, etc.

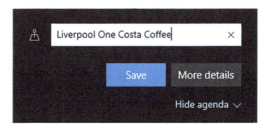

Click 'save'.

People App

The People App brings communication to the forefront of Windows 10. You can pin the people you communicate with the most, directly to your task bar. You can find the People App on your start menu

When the People App opens up, you'll see a list of your contacts on the left hand side. Any contact you click on, their contact details will appear in the right hand pane.

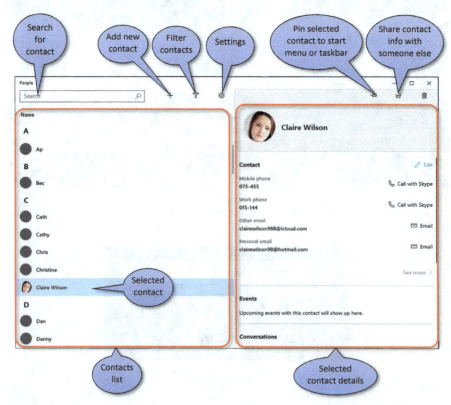

Edit Contact

You can click on any of the contacts in your list to view or edit their contact information.

Here I've clicked on Claire in the contacts list. In the right hand pane, you'll see her contact details, plus upcoming calendar events she's been invited to or involved in and recent messages. Click 'see more' to see all of these.

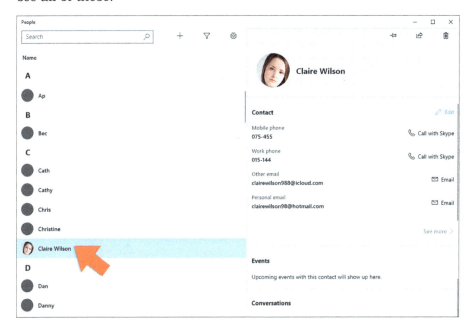

To edit her contact details, click 'edit'. In the new window you can edit her name, add phone, email addresses and physical address.

Click the plus sign next to the one you want to add. For example 'address'.

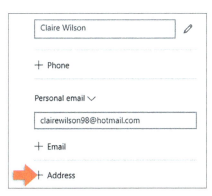

Select whether the address is 'home' or 'work'.

Enter the details into the fields that appear.

Click 'save' when you're done.

Pin Contacts

To pin a contact to your task bar, right click on the contact's name and select 'pin to taskbar' from the popup menu.

Select 'pin' from the conformation box that appears.

Select the person's icon from the bottom right of the taskbar

Click the app you want to use to communicate with this person, from the selections. Eg 'mail'.

Here, you'll be able to use this shortcut on the taskbar to communicate using the app you selected in the previous step, as well as see a conversation history and options to start a new message.

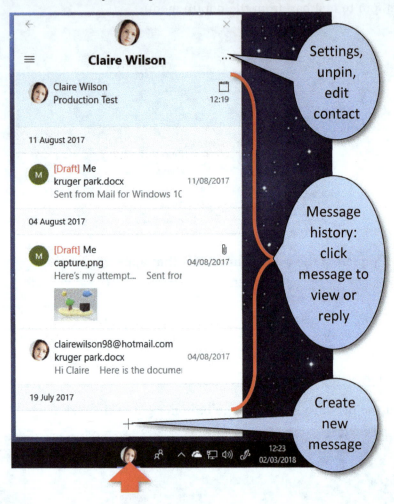

To remove a contact, right click on their icon on the taskbar, then select 'unpin from taskbar'.

If you want to go back and select another app, eg Skype, then click the back arrow on the top left of the pop up box

Share Files with Contacts

You can drag files to the person's icon on the task bar if you want to share with them. If I wanted to share this file with Claire, I can drag and drop the file from file explorer onto her icon on the taskbar.

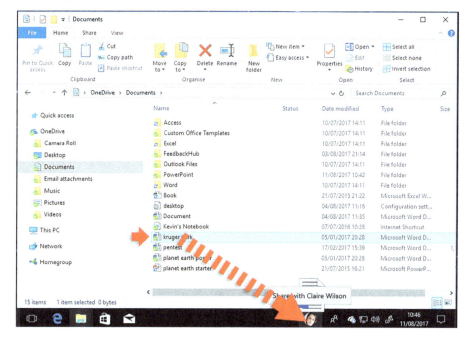

The People App will open a contact window using your default method of contact - in this example, email.

Add a message if you wish, then click 'send' to send the message.

Skype

Skype has now been redesigned, and is a little easier to use than before. You can use it along with your Microsoft Account and your mobile/cell phone number. You'll find the skype icon on your start menu.

Once you start skype, you'll see the main screen which will look something like this.

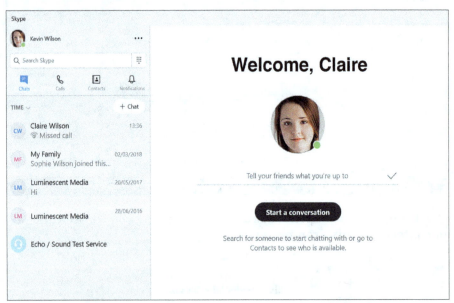

On the left hand side of the main screen, you'll see a new contact panel. Here you can see your chat/contact history, call history, contacts list and notifications. You can also search for skype contacts here too.

Chats lists all your recent chats/conversations and displays them in the main window as a transcript.

Calls lists all the contacts you have recently placed a video or voice call to.

Contacts lists all the contacts in the people app or your contacts list.

Notifications lists all the alerts such as incoming call or app notifications.

Making a New Call

To make a new call, tap 'calls' on the top left of your screen, then tap '+call' to place a new call.

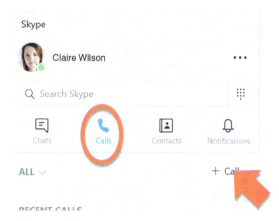

You can also select a name from the recent call history

From the 'new call' dialog box, type the person's name into the search field at the top.

Select the contact's name, the click 'call' on the top right of the dialog box. From the drop down, select 'video call'. Select 'call' for just voice.

Chapter 5: Internet, Email & Communication

Now wait for the other person to answer. You'll see a preview of your camera until the other person answers, use the time to make sure you are squarely in the frame and your camera is clear. Once the other person answers you'll see an image of them on your main screen. In the demo below, Claire is on her tablet skyping with Sophie.

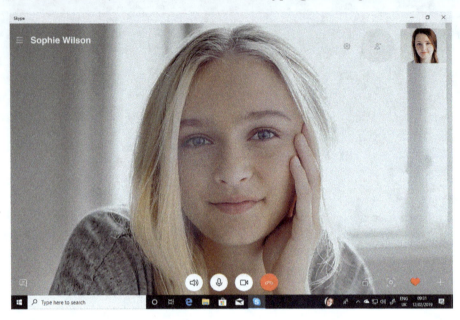

On the top right of your screen you'll see a thumbnail preview of your own camera. With two icons to the left.

Along the bottom of the screen you'll see some more icons. Tap the screen to reveal these icons if they disappear during the call.

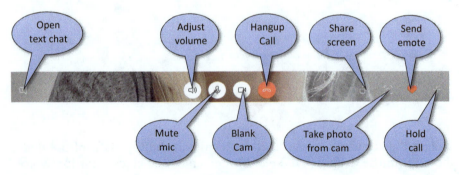

Calling Someone on your Contact List

To call someone on your contact list, click the contacts icon on the left hand side.

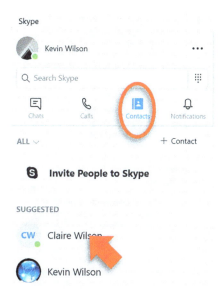

If you have corresponded with this person before, a contact transcript will open up. At the bottom of the screen, you can type a message. If you want to place a video/voice call, tap the icon on the top right of the screen.

Sending Files

To send someone a file, you can simply drag and drop the file from file explorer directly into the person's call window.

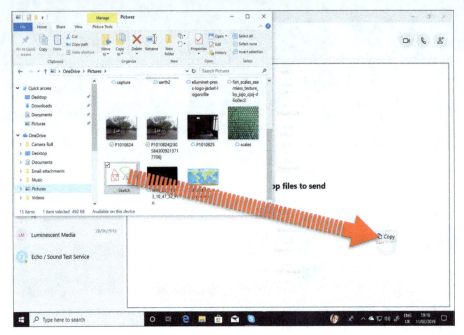

Answering Calls

Any incoming calls will display an alert along the top of your screen when skype is running. Tap the green cam icon on the far right to accept video call. To just accept as voice call, select the green phone icon. To decline the call click the red phone icon.

If the person's profile is pinned to your taskbar, then you'll see a popup similar to this one.

Screen Sharing

Another cool feature of Skype is the ability to share your desktop with the user you are having a skype call with.

This is a great way to keep in touch with people you don't see very often, as well as friends and family. It makes a great collaboration tool for business users too and enables you to share your screen to show photos, word documents, presentations etc.

In the demo below, the tablet on the right, is sharing its screen with the user logged onto the laptop. The tablet user is then able to launch any app, in this example, photos. Then the tablet user can open photos to show the other user.

The user on the laptop can see everything the tablet user is displaying on their screen.

Both users can still talk and see one another as if they were still in conversation. You'll see a thumbnail view of them in the bottom right hand corner of your screen.

To share your screen, make your video call as normal, then from the in call screen, tap the screen share icon..

From the dialog box that appears, set 'share computer sound' to on so your friend can hear sound to any videos etc, then click 'share screen and sounds'.

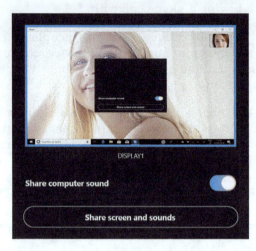

The other user will now be able to see everything on your screen. So you can minimise skype and open other apps such as the photos app and show your pictures.

Your Phone App

This app works best with an Android phone running Android 7 or later. This app has limited use on an iPhone.

You'll find the app on the start menu on your PC. Click on the icon to open it up.

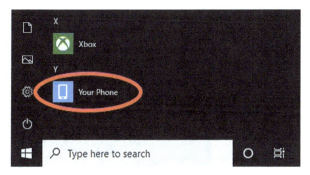

One the app starts, you'll see your phone in the top left corner. Listed below that you'll see the apps you can currently sync with your phone. In this case photos and messages.

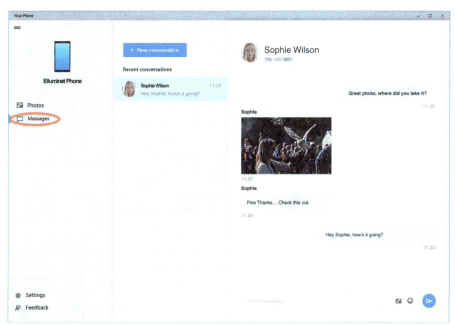

Select 'messages' to view messages you've sent and received on your phone. You can also respond using this app, just select the person's name from the 'recent conversations' list and you'll see the conversation.

You can also access photographs and videos you've taken with your phone. Click 'refresh' or 'update' at the top of the screen to sync the latest photos from your phone.

From the 'Your Phone' app, you can drag and drop photographs into any of your Windows Applications. Either use a photo from your library, or quickly snap one with the camera app on your phone.

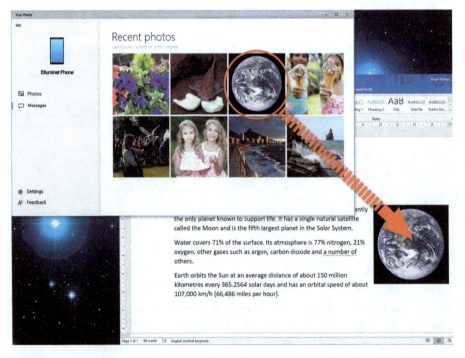

Mobile Hotspot

Also known as tethering, this feature allows you to share your internet connection with your other devices and does this by creating a temporary WiFi hotspot. This can be useful if you have a 4G data connection on your phone but no WiFi available and need to access the internet on a tablet or laptop.

Enable the mobile hotspot on your phone. On Android phones go to settings, select 'network & connection', then 'mobile hotspot'. Turn on 'bluetooth tethering'. On iPhone go to settings app and tap 'personal hotspot', turn on 'personal hotspot'.

On your laptop or tablet, tap on the WiFi icon on the right hand side of your taskbar to reveal the available networks.

The network name is usually the name of your phone. Look at the personal hotspot settings. You'll find the network name and password.

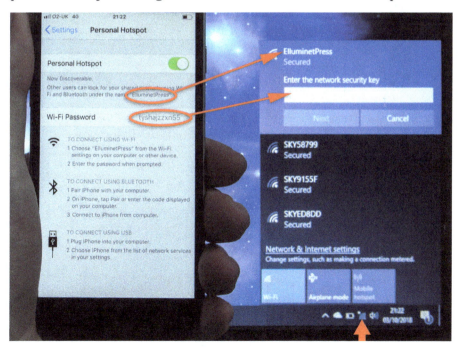

On your laptop or tablet, select the network name from the list and enter the password. Click 'next'.

Remote Desktop

Remote Desktop, also known as terminal services allows you to connect to another machine remotely over a network connection. The user interface is displayed from remote machine onto the local machine and input from the local machine is transmitted to the remote machine – where software execution takes place. Only Windows 10 Pro allows remote access and isn't available in the home edition. To enable remote connections type 'remote desktop settings' into the search field on the bottom left of your screen.

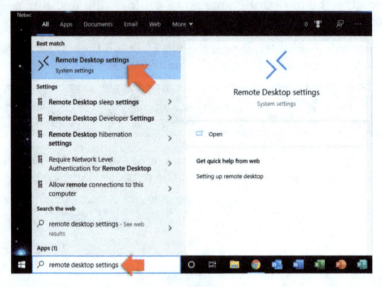

Set the 'enable remote desktop' switch to on. This allows other machines to connect to this PC. Click 'confirm' on the blue dialog box.

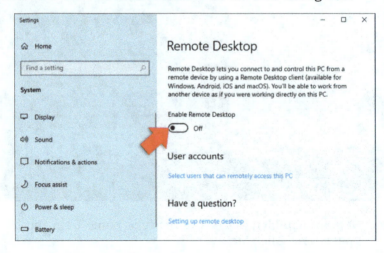

Now you need to find out the IP address of the machine. To do this open the command prompt. Type 'cmd' into the search field on the bottom left of your screen. Click 'command prompt'

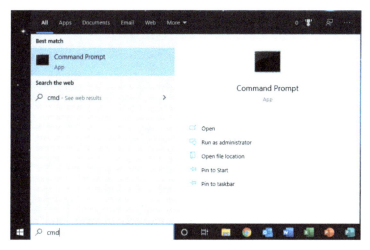

Now, type ipconfig and find the IPv4 address. In this case 192.168.1.13. Note down this IP address, you'll need it later.

Now you can connect from another machine on the LAN. To do this, on another machine, open the remote desktop connection app. Type 'remote desktop connection' into the search field on the bottom left.

Type the IP address you noted earlier into the app. Click 'connect'.

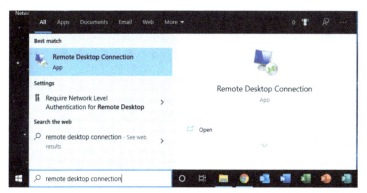

Enter your windows 10 username and password when prompted.

You'll see your desktop appear in the remote desktop window.

Multimedia

Windows 10 has a several multimedia applications available.

There is an app to organise and enhance your digital photos whether it be from your phone or digital camera.

There is an app to take photographs using your phone/tablet.

There is an app to organise your music collection and a store for you to buy new music.

You can download and watch movies and television programmes which are available from the store.

Windows 10 doesn't come with the ability to play DVDs but you can download some software that will allow you to still enjoy your DVD collection.

For this section have a look at the multimedia resources. Open your web browser and navigate to the following website:

`videos.tips/win-10-mm`

Photos App

The photos app is a nice little way to organise your photos and works whether you are on a tablet, phone, or desktop PC.

You can find the photos app on the start menu.

Photos app will import photos directly from your digital camera or on-board camera if you are using a tablet or phone.

You can also perform minor corrections and enhancements such as removing red-eye, lightening up a dark photograph or apply some simple effects such as sepia or black and white.

View a Photo

To view a photo, tap or click on the image thumbnail, this will open the image in view mode.

In view mode, you'll see the photo you selected appear full screen. Along the top of the photo you'll see a toolbar with some options

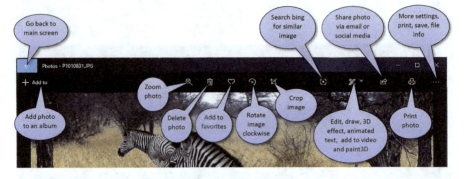

Crop a Photo

Open your photo in 'view mode' as shown in the previous section, then select the crop icon from the toolbar.

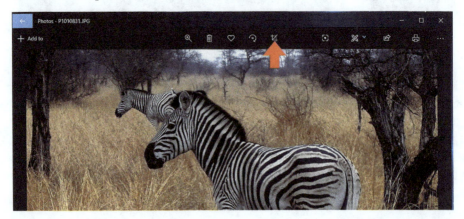

If I wanted to crop my zebra photo, you'll see a box around the photo with four white dots on each corner. These are called crop handles.. Click and drag the white dots to resize the box so it surrounds the part of the photo you want to keep, as shown below.

Straighten a Photo

Open your photo in 'view mode' as shown in the 'view a photo' section, then select the 'edit & create' icon. From the drop down menu, select 'edit'. This enters edit mode.

Select the 'crop & rotate' icon at the top. Drag the control handle on the right hand side, to level up the photo.

Click 'save a copy' at the bottom when you're finished.

Adjusting Brightness & Colour

Open your photo in 'view mode' as shown as shown in the 'view a photo' section, then select the 'edit & create' icon. From the drop down menu, select 'edit'. This enters edit mode.

Select the 'adjustments' on the top of your screen. On the right hand panel, click 'light' to reveal the brightness, exposure and contrast settings. You'll see four sliders appear. Drag the sliders left or right to adjust the contrast, the overall brightness (or exposure), highlights (ie the bright parts of the image such as the sky), and the shadows (ie the dark parts of the image).

Now click 'color'. This will allow you to correct the white balance of the photograph (the warmth). Drag the slider to the left to make the image cooler (more blue), or to the right to make the image warmer (more orange).

Click 'save a copy', when you're done.

Spot Fix

The spot fix brush allows you to correct small blemishes on your photograph. To use the spot fix brush, open your photo in view mode 'view a photo' section. From the drop down menu, select 'edit'. This enters edit mode.

Select the 'adjustments' on the top of your screen, then click 'spot fix' on the bottom right.

With the brush, click on the area of the image you want to fix.

Click 'save a copy' when you're done

277

Annotating Photos

Open your photo in 'view mode' as shown in the 'view a photo' section, then select the 'edit & create' icon. From the drop down menu, select 'draw'

Draw with your pen or finger to annotate your photograph.

Along the top of your screen you'll see a tool bar. You can select from three different writing tools: a pen, a pencil, and a calligraphy pen.

The next icon along is an eraser. This allows you to use your pen or finger to rub out parts of your drawing.

You can also save photos with your annotations using save icon.

Use the last icon on the toolbar to close drawing mode.

Animated Text

Open your photo in 'view mode' as shown in the 'view a photo' section, then select the 'edit & create' icon. From the drop down menu, select 'add animated text'

On the right hand panel, type your text into the field at the top, select a text effect from the list. Select a layout - where you want the text to appear.

Drag the two markers, to indicate the start, end and length of the effect.

Click 'save a copy' when you're done.

3D Effect

Open your photo in 'view mode' as shown in the 'view a photo' section, then select the 'edit & create' icon. From the drop down menu, select 'add animated text'

On the right hand panel, select the effect you want to add

Drag the two markers, to indicate the start, end and length of the effect.

Click 'save a copy' when you're done.

Creating Videos

The Photos App allows you to quickly blend 3D effects, photos, and videos together into a video clip that you can share on social media, send to a friend, or use to promote an idea.

Creating Videos Automatically

Click the photos/videos you want to include in your video. Hover your mouse over the top right corner of the image and click the tick box. Do this on all the images/videos you want to include.

Click 'new video' on the toolbar at the top of the screen, then select 'automatic video' from the drop down menu.

Type in a name for your video.

Click 'ok'

When it's finished, you'll be able to see a preview of the video remix has created..

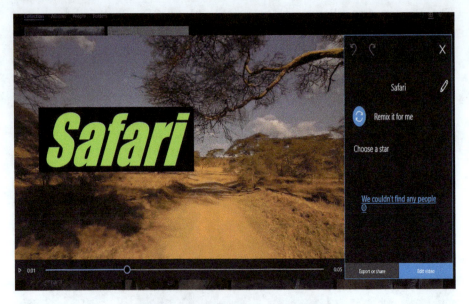

If you don't like the style, you can click the 'remix it for me' button and Photos App will generate a new video.

If you have any people in your video, an image of them will appear for you to select. Click 'choose a star' and select the main people in the video. This highlights them in the video.

To make any custom changes just click 'edit video' on the bottom right. This will take you to the custom edit screen where you can make changes to your video. See page 255.

If you're happy with the results, click 'export or share'.

Creating Custom Videos

To create a video, click the photos/videos you want to include in your video.

Click 'new video' on the toolbar at the top of the screen, then select 'new video project' from the drop down menu that appears.

Type in a name for your video.

Click 'ok'

283

Chapter 6: Multimedia

You'll see the main editing screen. Lets take a look at the different parts.

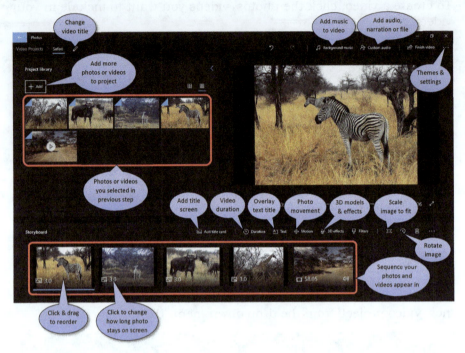

Top left, you'll see all the photos and videos you selected in the previous step. On the top right you'll see some icons to add themes, music, audio files, narrations, as well as an export feature so you can share your creations.

Underneath that on the right hand side you'll see a large preview screen. This is a preview of your video. You can scrub through it using the progress bar underneath.

Along the bottom is your storyboard or timeline. This is the sequence of photos and videos that will make up your video.

Along the top of the storyboard are some icons that allow you to add a title screen, photo filters, add text overlay titles, motion effects and some 3D effects. These help to make your video more interesting for viewers to watch.

Take a look at the demos in the multimedia section of the video resources. Open your web browser and navigate to the following website:

```
videos.tips/win-10-mm
```

Add and Arrange your Media

On the top left, you'll see all the photographs and videos you added at the beginning. You can drag and drop these onto the storyboard along the bottom of the screen.

Along the bottom, you'll see the order of photos/videos you have added. To reorder these, drag them across to the position in the sequence you want them.

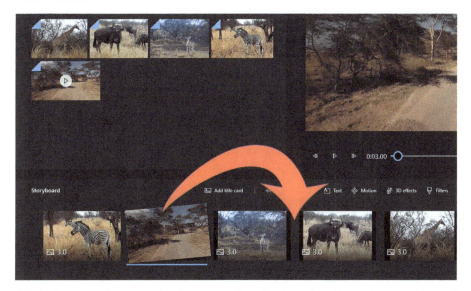

Click the numbers on the bottom of each thumbnail on the storyboard to change the duration of each photo/video

Add Text Titles

You can add text to your video. First, select the photo or video you want the text to appear. Then select 'text' from the bar along the top of the storyboard.

Select a template from the bottom right (I'm going to choose 'adventure'). Type your title into the text field on the top right.

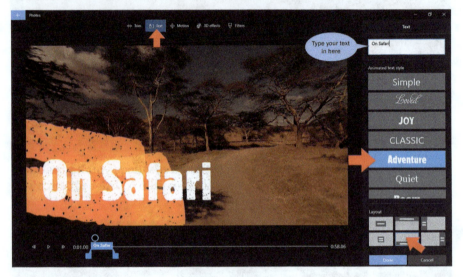

Under layout on the bottom right, select where you want the text to appear: centre, top, left...

Move the two blue markers to indicate where you want the effect to start and finish, and how long you want the effect to stay on the screen for.

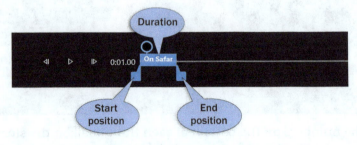

Click 'done' on the bottom right when you're finished.

Add Music

Now, how about some music. Select the 'background music' option on the top right of the screen.

I'm going to use the 'explorer' music - seems appropriate. From the popup window select 'explorer'. *To hear a preview of the music, click the small triangle icon next to the name.*

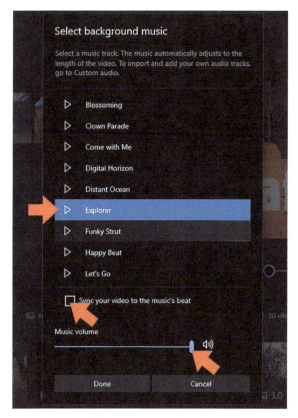

Select 'sync your video to the music beat'. This will cut your video in time with the music.

Set the music volume using the slider.

Click 'done'.

Add Audio File

You can also add your own music, narration, or audio file. Click on 'custom audio'.

Click 'add audio file' on the top right.

Navigate to your music folder on your computer - this is usually called 'music' and select a track.

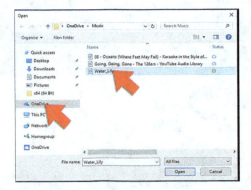

Move the blue markers to mark the beginning and end of the audio

If you want to add another file, click 'add audio file' again, and select the file.

Click 'done' when your happy.

Slideshow Motion

To change the motion of your photographs in your slideshow, select the photo slide you want to change.

Now select a motion style from the options on the right hand side of the screen

Here you can select 'zoom in right', which will slow zoom into the right hand side of the image; or 'zoom in left' zooms into the left hand side of the image. These are useful if the subject in the photograph is on the left or right hand side of the image - helps draw attention to your subject. You can also pan across the image or zoom into the centre.

3D Effects

3D effects can only be added to video clips not still photographs. If you select a still photograph, the 3D effects button will be greyed out.

Click '3D Effects'.

Scrub to the part of the footage you want the effect to appear, using the progress bar underneath your video preview.

Select the 'effects' icon on the top right to reveal the effects panel, if they are not visible.

Browse through the effects listed down the right hand side of the screen.

Drag and drop the effect onto the position you want the effect to appear in the video.

In this example, I want the "impact on sand" effect to appear to the right of the dirt road.

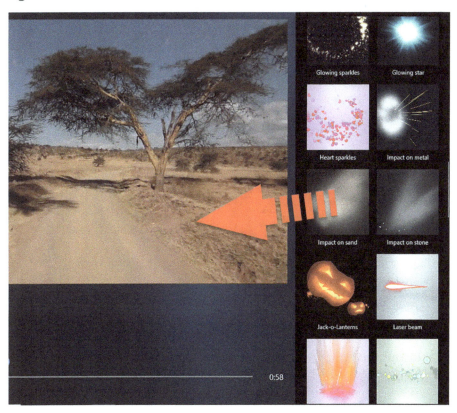

You can rotate the effect around the frame using the tree axis handles indicated with the arrows below. You can move the effect by moving the surrounding grey box and you can resize the effect using the square resize handles on the corners of the resize box.

Now to make the 3D effect more realistic, you can anchor it to a position in the video clip. Turn 'anchor to a point' to the on position.

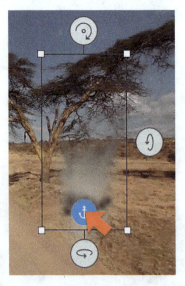

Make sure the blue anchor on the effect is in the position you want the effect anchored to. When you play the video, the effect will stay in that position even if the camera moves.

Some of the effects have sound. You can adjust this using the volume control in the panel on the right hand side

Add more effects if you want to using the drag and drop method described earlier.

You can also add effects to other parts of the clip. Scrub across your clip using the progress bar, as before. Lets add a portal.

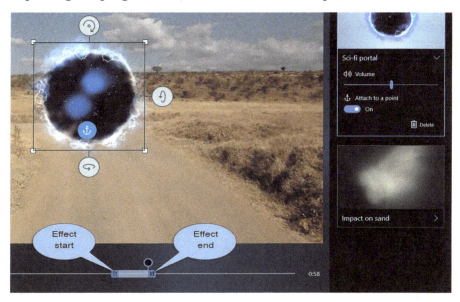

Notice below on the progress bar, you'll see a range bar appear. This will allow to adjust the duration of the effect. To adjust the range, click and drag the start and end handles, and drag them along the progress bar.

When you have added all the effects you want, click 'done' at the top right hand side of the screen.

Adding 3D Models

You can add 3D models to your videos. To do this, click '3D Effects'. You can add 3D models from Microsoft's Remix library or even your own models from Paint 3D.

Scrub to the part of the footage you want the effect to appear, using the progress bar underneath your video preview.

Select the '3D Models' icon on the top right to reveal the models panel, if they are not visible.

Browse through the models listed down the right hand side of the screen.

Drag and drop the model you want, onto the position you want it to appear in the video.

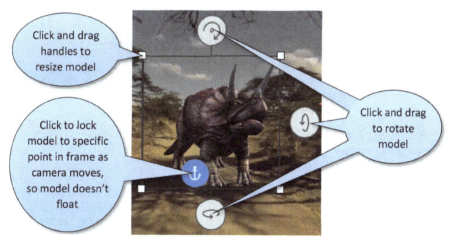

Use the handles to rotate, resize and position the model in the frame, as you would do for the effects we added earlier. Under the video preview window, adjust the length of time you want the model to remain on-screen. Use the beginning and end sliders as shown below. The black dot is where you are in the video, eg 58 seconds into the video clip.

Chapter 6: Multimedia

Export your Video

To export your finished video project, click 'finish video' on the top right of the screen.

This will allow you to save the video project as an mp4 video file. Select 'high 1080p' from the 'video quality' dialog box, then click 'export'.

Select your 'videos' folder on your computer. Give your video a meaningful name.

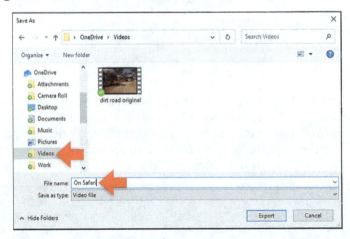

Click 'export'.

Share your Creations

You can share your creations via email or post on social media. Click on your video to open it in 'view mode'

Select 'share' from the to right hand side of the screen.

Select the person you want to share with or the app you want to use to share, eg email or skype. In this example I'm going to use skype.

In the skype window, enter a message in the box at the top of the screen. Then in the 'search' field underneath, type in the person's name.

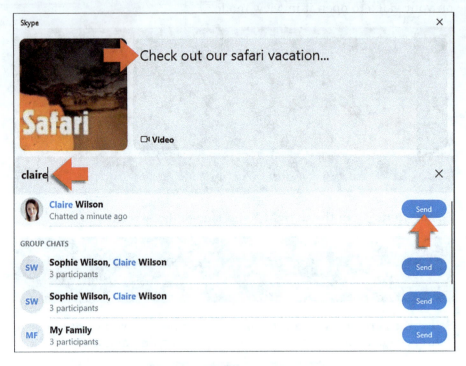

From the list of contacts, select 'send' next to the person's name. The video will be sent to this person.

If selected 'mail' from the 'share' dialog, enter the person's email address in the 'to' field, then type your message in the box at the bottom.

Click 'send' when you're done.

Camera App

The camera app makes use of the on board camera on your phone or tablet to take photographs. Tap the camera app icon on your start menu to start the app.

Your tablet or phone usually has two cameras; a front facing camera, and a rear camera. The rear camera is usually higher quality and for taking photos/videos of things, while the front facing camera is usually for skype video calls and selfies.

When you start up the camera app, you'll see an image from your camera on screen.

Tap on the small camera icon to take a photo.

Once you have taken your photo, you can view them by tapping/clicking the icon on the bottom right to view in photo app.

You can also take movies by tapping on the 'switch to video' icon, on the right hand side. This works just like a video camcorder.

You can also take panoramic photos. To do this, tap the panoramic photo icon, on the right hand side. You'll see a square box appear along the centre of the screen. Point the camera at the position in the scene you want the panoramic photo to start. Tap the large white button, on the right hand side of your screen. Now, pan the camera to your right, rotating around your hips/shoulders, until you have covered the scene. You'll see the box in the centre of the screen start to build your image.

Tap the large white button again, to finish.

You can also adjust your exposure settings such as ISO, White Balance, Shutter Speed and Brightness on your camera, as well as set a timer delay. To access these settings, tap the 'pro' icon on the top of your screen.

This will reveal the exposure settings.

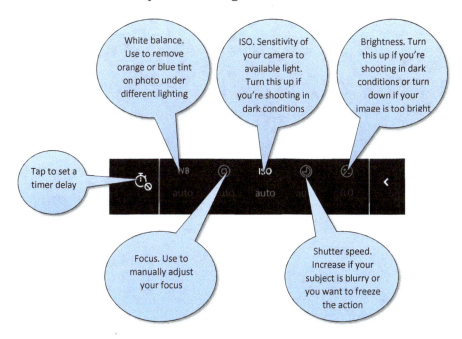

To adjust the settings, tap on one of the icons.

In this example, I am going to adjust the ISO. So tap on the ISO icon.

When you do this, you'll notice a semi-circle control appear around the 'take photo' icon, on the right hand side of your screen.

To make the adjustment, tap on 'ISO', on the right of the screen, then drag this upwards to increase the ISO, drag it downwards to decrease the ISO, as illustrated below.

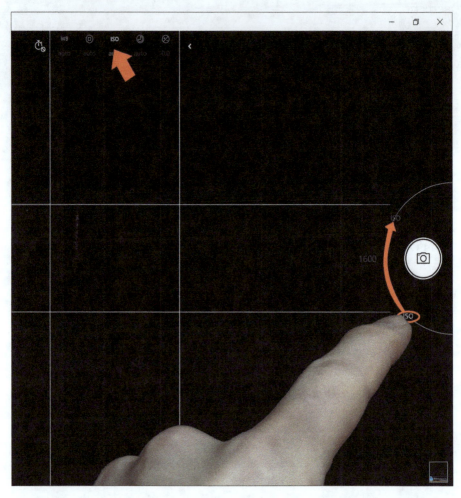

You'll see the value in the centre increase or decrease as you make your adjustment. In this example, I've set the ISO to 1600.

You can use this technique for the other settings too (white balance, focus, shutter speed and brightness).

Take a look at the demos in the multimedia section of the video resources.

Open your web browser and navigate to the following website:

```
videos.tips/win-10-mm
```

Groove Music App

You can find the music app icon on your start menu

When you start Groove Music for the first time, it will automatically scan your computer for music and add it to your library.

You'll land on Groove Music's main screen. From here you can play music stored on your PC or stream music from Spotify. Let's take a look at the main screen.

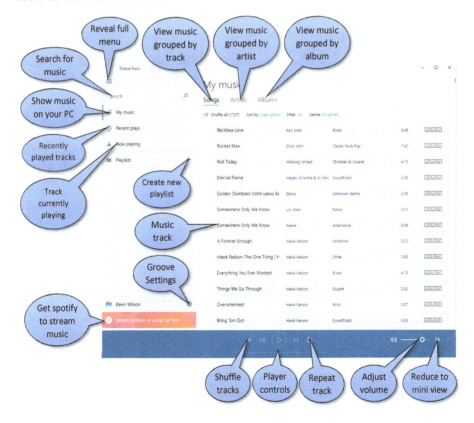

To reveal the menu, tap the hamburger icon on the top left. ☰

Music on your PC

Here you can see all the songs on this machine listed in order they were added.

Playlists

To create a playlist, select the track in the list. Click the '+' sign that appears next to the track name. From the popup menu, select the list you want to add the track to, or click 'new list' to create a new one. From the dialog box that appears, enter the playlist name, eg 'favourites', and click 'create playlist'.

Your playlists will appear down the panel on the left hand side of the screen. To remove tracks from the playlist, right click the track and from the popup menu select 'delete from playlist'.

304

Spotify

Microsoft dropped their music streaming feature 'Groove Music Pass' in favour of Spotify. To get started, click 'stream millions of songs for free' on the bottom left of the Groove Music window - it will change to 'get spotify'.

From the app store page, click 'get' to download the spotify app.

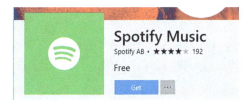

Once downloaded and installed, you can start the spotify app from your start menu. You'll need to sign up for a free account. Click 'sign up for free' and fill in your details. If you already use spotify, click 'log in'.

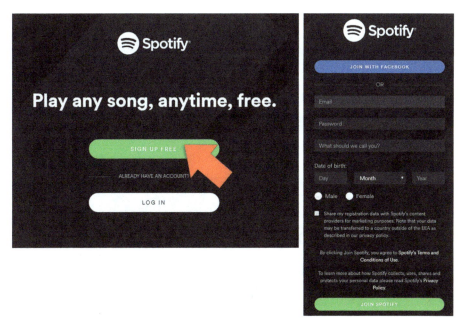

Click 'join spotify' when you're finished.

Chapter 6: Multimedia

With spotify, you can search for any song, album or artist you like. Just type it into the search field at the top of the screen.

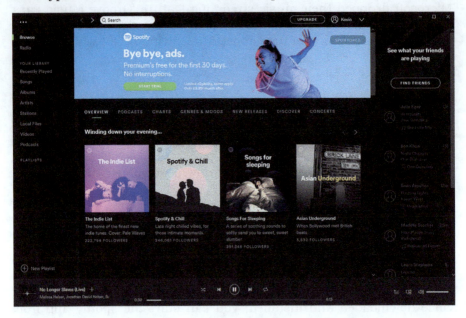

You can scroll down the main page and browse through the genres. Once you've found a song, either by searching or browsing through your favourite genres, you can add them to your library. To do this, click the '+' sign to the left of the track name.

You'll find the tracks in your library on the top left of the main screen

Click on the track to play.

Movie & TV App

You can find the Movies & TV app on your start menu.

With the Movies & TV App you can buy/rent the latest TV shows and Films, as well as your own video content you've taken with your phone or a digital camera.

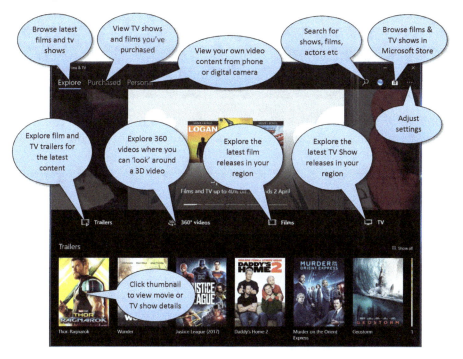

Along the top of your screen you'll see three categories: Explore, Purchased and Personal.

In the 'explore' category you'll be able to browse through the latest TV shows and Films that have been released in your region/country. You can scroll down the page and select the ones you're interested in.

In the 'purchased' category, you'll see a list of all the films and TV shows you have purchased. This is where you can select them to watch.

The 'personal' category will show you video content you have taken with your camera

Chapter 6: Multimedia

Purchasing Content

Once you have found the film or TV show you want to watch, select the thumbnail cover to view the show's details

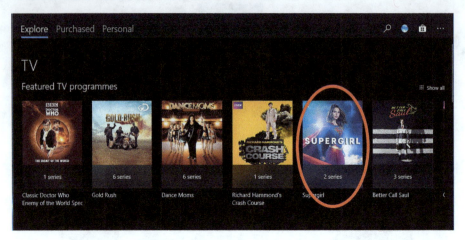

You'll be redirected to the Microsoft Store. On the store page you'll see some details about the series or film. To buy the film, or buy a whole season if it's a TV show, click the 'buy' button.

If you scroll further down the page, you'll see a description, devices you can watch the film on and in the case of TV shows different seasons.

Here you can click on the season whose episodes you want to see.

Scroll down further and you'll see a list of each episode. Here you can purchase individual episodes. To do this just click the price button next to the episode you want

Viewing Purchased Content

You'll find all the films and TV shows you have purchased in the 'purchased' section on the main screen.

Click thumbnail to play, then select an episode if you're watching a TV show.

Make sure you click the little play button next to the episode title.

Chapter 6: Multimedia

Search for New Content

To search for TV shows and films, click the magnifying glass icon on the top right of your screen. In the search field, type in the show's name or the film's title. Press enter.

By default, the search algorithm searches your purchased collection. To search for new content, you'll need to select 'search in microsoft store'

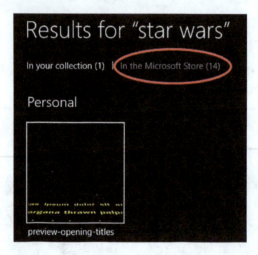

Here you'll be able to click on the thumbnails to view details and purchase the content.

Personal Content

This is where you can see the video content you have taken with your camera. Select the 'personal' category from the top of the main screen.

Along the top of the personal content window you'll see: 'video folders', 'removable storage' and 'media servers'.

Select 'video folders' to see video clips stored on your device or PC. You can also add other folders - to do this click 'add folder'.

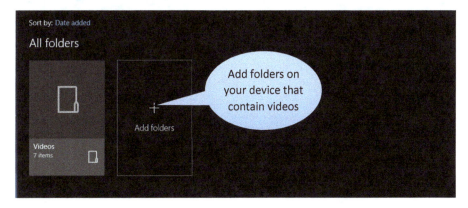

Scroll down a bit further to see all the clips in the folder.

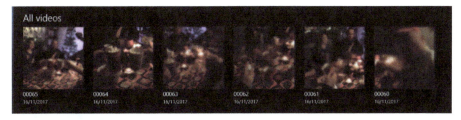

Click on one of the clips to view.

Picture-in-Picture

Also known as 'compact overlay' and allows you to watch a small video window in the corner of your screen while working in another app. In the video window, you'll see a new icon, circle below. This icon will appear in the video window on most apps as well as youtube videos in the Edge browser.

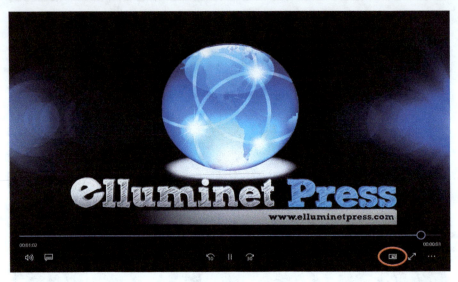

Just click this icon and the video will shrink to the top right of the screen. You can them click and drag this window to any part of your screen. I find the bottom right is a good place to put it if you're working on something else.

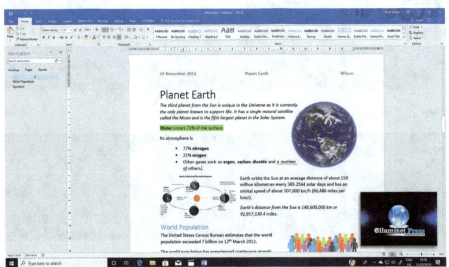

Playing DVDs & Blu-Rays

If you like watching DVDs or Blu-rays on your PC, Windows 10 can't play them out of the box, so you'll have to download a free player instead.

The best one I found is VLC Media Player, which can play DVDs, Blu-ray, CDs and a range of other file types.

Just go to the following website and download the software.

`www.videolan.org`

Click the 'Download VLC' on the homepage.

Click 'Run' when prompted by your browser and follow the instructions on screen.

DVDs & Blu-rays are becoming obsolete, thanks to high speed internet services available to most homes, video/film streaming services that allow you to access on demand films, and television programs you can access from the comfort of your favourite arm chair.

Many computers, particularly laptops and mobile devices no longer include a Blu-ray/DVD drive. You can still buy external USB DVD / Blu-ray drives if you need them.

Once you've installed VLC player, you'll find it on your start menu. Scroll down and click 'VideoLAN', then click 'VLC Media Player'

Insert the disc into the DVD/Blu-ray drive either on your computer or an external USB drive.

Click the play button on the bottom left of the VLC Media Player window.

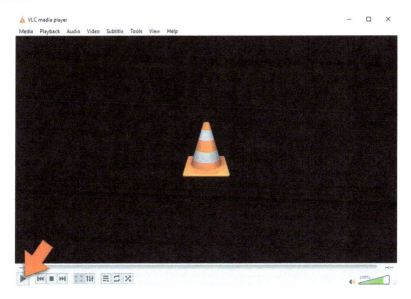

From the pop up dialog box, select the 'disc' tab along the top.

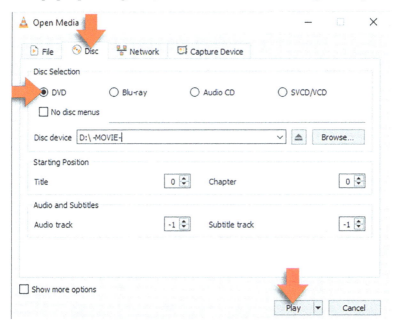

Make sure 'DVD' is selected from the 'disc selection' options for DVD movies, and 'blu-ray' for blu-ray movies. Click 'play' to start playing the movie.

Fun with 3D

The Creator's Editions of Windows 10 introduced a variety of 3D content creation tools, one of which is Paint 3D.

In this chapter, we'll take a look at creating simple 3D scenes using this app.

We'll also take a brief look at Windows Holographic using the HoloLens headset.

Take a look at the demos in the multimedia section of the video resources. Open your web browser and navigate to the following website:

videos.tips/win-10-mm

Paint 3D

Paint 3D is an app for creating 3D scenes and objects using a stylus pen, mouse and a keyboard and replaces the old paint app in Windows 10. You can find Paint 3D on your start menu.

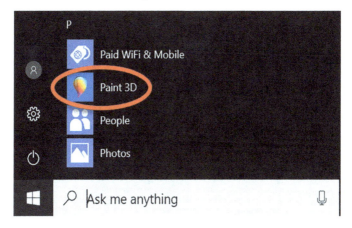

Once the app has started, you'll see the welcome screen. From here you can open a blank canvas, open a saved project, or paste the contents of the clipboard into a paint canvas.

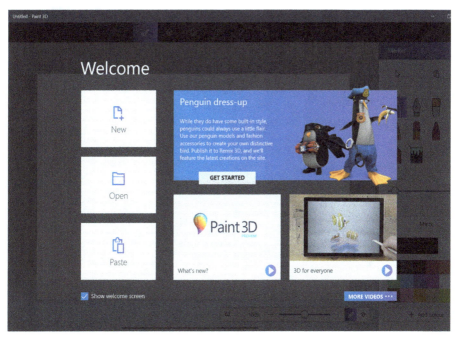

Let's create a new blank canvas. To do this click 'new'.

Chapter 7: Fun with 3D

Along the top of the window you'll find your tools. Each icon in the tool bar will open up the side panel.

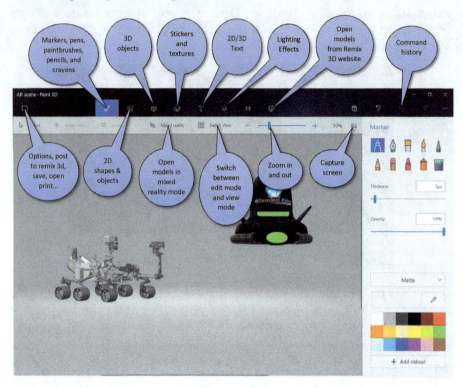

In the centre of the screen is your canvas with a control bar at the bottom that allows you to zoom in and out, edit and view your object or scene in 3D space.

Drawing

If you tap the paint brush icon, you'll see a selection of pens, pencils, crayons and markers down the right hand side of the window. Underneath you can change the thickness of the pen and select a colour.

Select a pen from the icons on the right hand side. Choose from felt marker, calligraphy writing pen, oil brush, watercolour brush, pencil, eraser, wax crayon, pixel pen, air spray and paint fill.

Adjust the thickness using the slider.

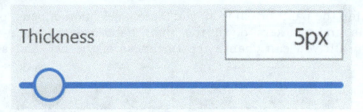

Select a finish from the drop down menu (matte, gloss, dull metal or polished metal). I'm using matte.

Select a colour from the palette. If you want a colour that isn't on your palette, tap 'add colour' and select one from the colour spectrum.

Draw directly onto the white canvas with your stylus pen or finger.

3D Objects

Tap the 3D cube logo, you'll see a selection of 3D models and objects down the right hand side of the window.

To add an object, select some from the objects section on the right hand side. In this example, I'm going to add a donut shape.

Select a finish from the drop down menu (matte, gloss, dull metal or polished metal). I'm using matte.

Select a colour from the palette.

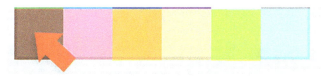

Now, draw a diagonal line across the area on your canvas you want the object to appear.

321

3D Models

Tap the 3D cube logo, you'll see a selection of 3D models and objects down the right hand side of the window.

To add a model, select some from the models section on the right hand side. In this example, I'm going to add a fish model.

Select a finish from the drop down menu (matte, gloss, dull metal or polished metal). I'm using matte.

Select a colour from the palette.

Now, draw a diagonal line across the area on your canvas you want the model to appear.

Manipulating Objects

You can rotate objects around the centre point of the object, around the vertical axis and the horizontal axis. To do this, tap on the image, you'll see a resize box appear around the object. The small white squares are the resize handles, you can tap and drag these to resize your image. Also on the edges of the resize box, you'll see four controls. These controls allow you to rotate the object. Just tap and drag these left to right or up and down.

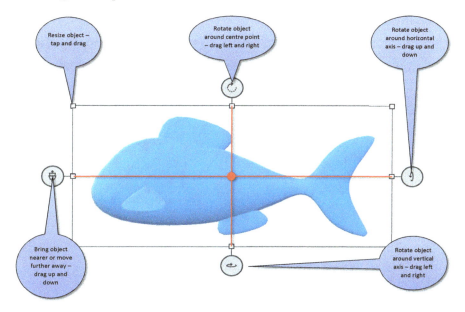

You can also move the object nearer or further away from your point of view.

2D Shapes

You can create 2D shapes such as triangles, circles, squares, stars and lines. You can create the shapes and add them to your scene, or you can stamp the 2D shape onto a 3D model.

Choose a shape from the pallet on the right hand side, tap on the canvas to create your shape. You can also add lines and curves. Tap the curve icon, then tap on the canvas to add your curve. Tap and drag the centre circle on the curve to adjust the arc. Tap the stamp icon to paste the shape in.

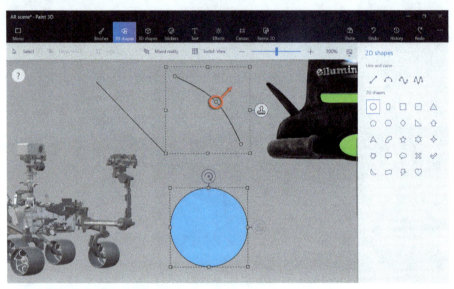

You can also pin your 2D shapes onto a 3D model. To do this, drag the shape over the 3D model, you'll notice the 2D shape will mould itself around the contours of the 3D model. Tap the stamp icon to paste the shape in position.

Stickers

Tap the sticker logo. Down the left hand side you'll see some sub categories.

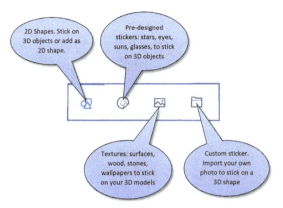

If you select pre-designed stickers from the sub category icons, underneath you'll see some stickers. For this example, I am going to add some eyes and a mouth to my fish model.

When you tap on the sticker, it will appear on your model. All you need to do is resize it using the resize handles, drag it into position, then tap the stamp icon to paste the sticker onto your model.

Custom Stickers & Textures

Tap the sticker logo. Then from the sub category icons on the right hand size, select the custom sticker icon. Tap the + to create a new sticker. From the popup window, navigate to your pictures folder and select an image.

Resize your image until it covers your model using the resize handles.

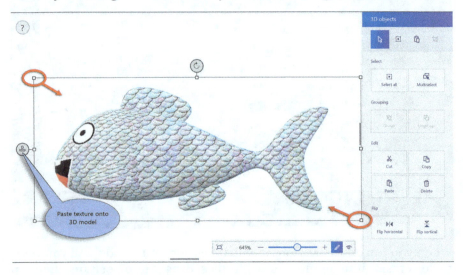

Tap the stamp icon to paste the texture to your model.

3D Doodles

Tap the 3D cube logo. You'll see, on the right hand side, a list of 3D models and objects. If you scroll down you'll see another section called 3D Doodle. The first icon converts your doodle into a 3D object with sharp edges, the second icon converts your doodle into a 3D object with soft edges.

To draw, select one of the doodle options and draw directly onto the canvas. You can only draw sections at a time, as when you start to draw on the canvas, you'll notice a light blue circle appear where you started to draw. For Paint 3D to create your 3D doodle, both your start point and end point will need to be in this light blue circle.

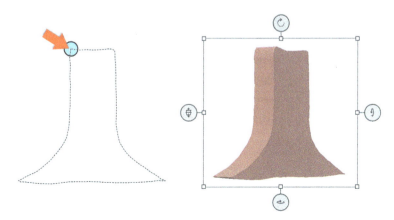

Chapter 7: Fun with 3D

If you want to create a doodle with soft edges, choose the second icon from the 3D doodle section.

Again to draw your doodle, your start and end points need to be in the light blue circle.

Here is an example of what you can build using simple doodles and arranging them in your 3D space.

These are very simple examples to demonstrate the procedures. I can't draw and yet I can create something reasonably good, imagine what you can do!

3D Text

To insert some 3D text, select the text icon on the top of the screen. Then from the 3D text options on the right hand side, click the 3D text icon. Draw yourself a text box.

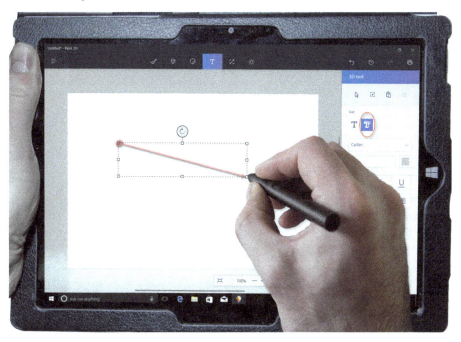

Type your text into the text box. You can change your font, size, colour and alignment, using the controls on the right hand side, as labelled below.

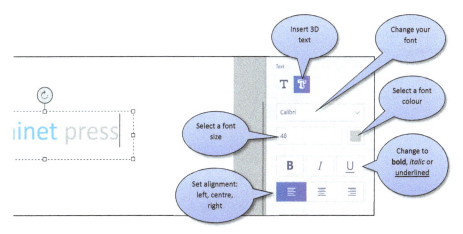

Click outside the text box to create the text.

You can manipulate the text as you can any other 3D object or model.

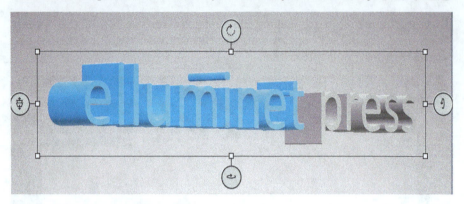

Share your Creations

You can share your creations on social media or email. To do this, click the menu icon on the far left hand side of your screen. From the drop down select 'share'. From the popup window, select where you want to share your creation.

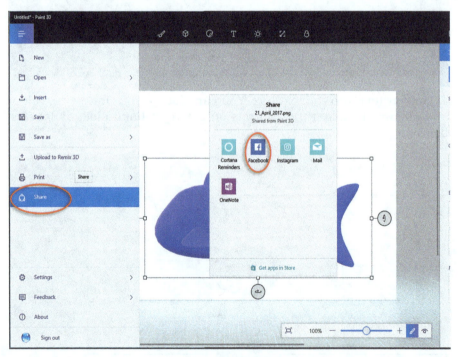

In this example, I am posting on facebook. You may need to enter your facebook login details before you can post on your timeline.

330

Magic Select

Magic Select is a feature that allows you to use your own photographs in a 3D scene. You can import a photograph and remove the subject from the background then paste into your scene.

For example, take our underwater scene. To insert a photo, tap the file icon on the top left of the screen, then from the backstage select 'insert'.

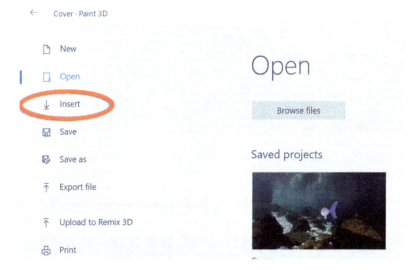

Browse for your file, select it, then tap 'open'.

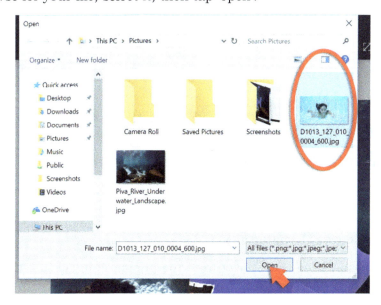

Paint 3D will paste your photograph into your scene. Now you can resize the image if you want by dragging the small white squares surrounding the image.

To remove the background and blend the subject in the photograph into your scene, tap 'magic select' on the right hand side of your screen.

If you look closely, you'll notice a box surrounding your photograph with 8 large white circles.

Drag these circles inwards around the subject in the photograph, as shown above. This is a mask that tells Paint 3D the part of the image you want to keep, and the part you want to discard. Tap 'next', on the right hand side. Then tap 'done'.

You can now drag the subject from the photograph you just removed anywhere in your scene.

Remix 3D site

Remix 3D is an online community where you can post your models you have created using Paint 3D.

Open your browser and navigate to the following website

`www.remix3d.com`

On the homepage, click 'sign in to remix 3D'.

Once you've signed in, you'll see two tabs at the top, 'discover' and 'my stuff'. If you click 'discover', you'll be able to browse a library of pre designed 3D models and those created by other people.

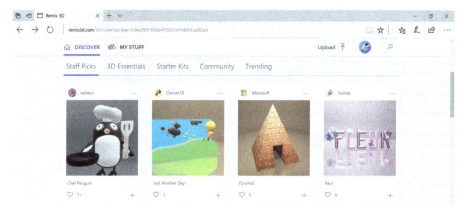

Click on the groups: 'Staff Picks', '3D Essentials', 'Starter Kits', 'Community' and 'Trending'. Have a browse through these groups to see what 3D models are available. If you see one you like, click on the thumbnail.

Then from the model information page, click 'remix in paint 3D' to open up the model.

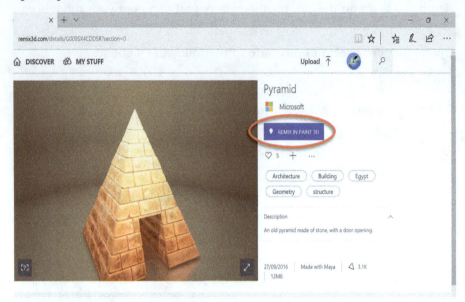

The model will open in Paint 3D, where you'll be able to edit it, resize it and add it to your scene.

Using these objects you can build up a 3D scene.

334

Mixed Reality Mode

Once you have created your 3D model or built a 3D scene, you can view it in mixed reality mode, meaning you can place your work in a real world environment captured with the on-board camera on your device or headset.

To do this, tap 'mixed reality' on the top of the screen.

In the mixed reality app, you'll see your model or scene appear with a live shot from your rear camera on your device. Tap on the screen to drop the model or scene onto the live camera shot.

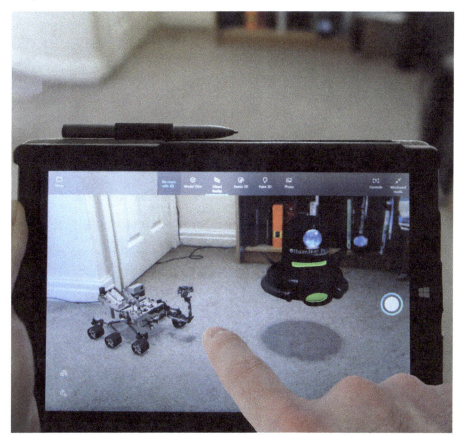

Tap 'Paint 3D' to go back to the Paint 3D app.

Holographic Interface

An interesting component of Windows 10 is Windows Holographic, using the HoloLens headset.

HoloLens

The HoloLens is a visor you wear over your eyes that covers your entire field of vision, and overlays digital images, 3D objects, apps and windows interface components such as your start menu, on your real world view. This is known as augmented or mixed reality.

HoloLens is a completely standalone device with its own CPU and GPU.

If this is the first time turning on your HoloLens, hold the power button down for 3 seconds.

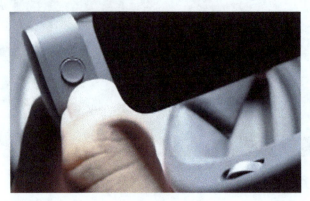

Attach the overhead strap if the headset doesn't stay secure on your head.

Put the device on your head, use the adjustment wheel on the back to tighten the headset so it fits securely around your head.

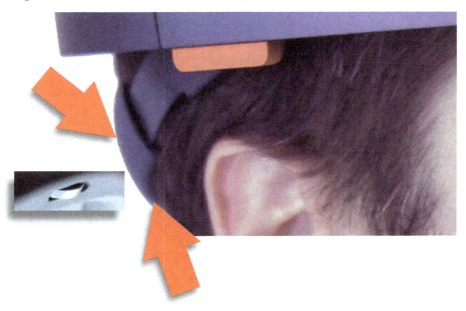

Next adjust the angle of the visor so the holographic display is centred in your view and comfortable.

Run through the setup and calibration steps displayed on your HoloLens. Once you're happy, we can start exploring your holographic space.

Getting Around the Interface

Lets have a look at some of the basic components of the holographic interface. These are similar to Windows 10's touch-screen interface.

The Start Menu

The start menu appears when you make the bloom gesture.

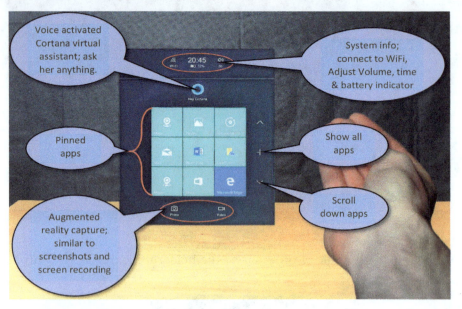

The App Bar

Also known as the 'holobar' and appears on the top of each app you launch in your holographic space.

Hololens Gestures

Much like tablets have hand gestures to manipulate objects on your screen, HoloLens has hand gestures to interact with objects in your holographic space. Lets take a look at some of the common ones.

Gesture Frame

This is the space in front of you where the sensors from the headset will detect your hand gestures in order to manipulate the holograms in your holographic space.

Gaze

The HoloLens tracks the objects you're looking at within your holographic space. This is similar to moving your mouse pointer in Windows 10. To move your cursor, you gaze or look at an object, tile or icon and 'air tap' to select it. You'll need to move your whole head rather than just your eyes.

Air Tap

This is equivalent to your left mouse button and you use it to select and manipulate objects in your holographic space. First, set your gaze on an object, then raise your forefinger and thumb and tap these two fingers together.

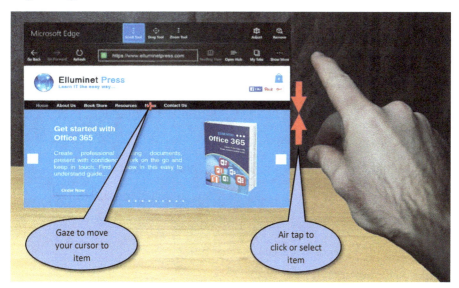

Gaze to move your cursor to item

Air tap to click or select item

Air Tap & Hold

This is equivalent to click and drag. First, set your gaze on an object, then raise your forefinger and thumb and tap these two fingers together. While holding your thumb and forefinger together, move your hand and arm over to the position you want to drag the object.

Bloom

Returns to the start menu. It is similar to the windows key on your keyboard or clicking the start button in Windows 10. Close your hand with your finger tips together, then open your hand spreading your fingers apart.

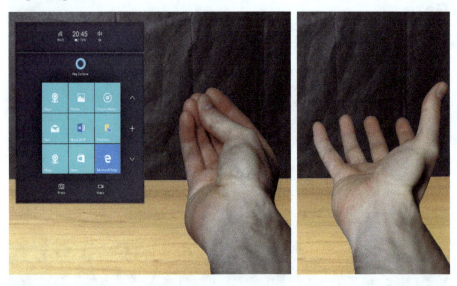

Voice Commands

The HoloLens will respond to voice commands such as

"select" instead of an air tap

"place" to place a hologram in your holographic space

"hey Cortana!" to get Cortana's attention to ask her something

"face me" to turn a hologram around so you can see it

"bigger/smaller" to change the size of holograms

So for example, gaze at an object and say "select".

Mixed Reality Headsets

There are a lot of mixed reality headsets available. Some ranging between £300-£400, such as one from Dell and Lenovo.

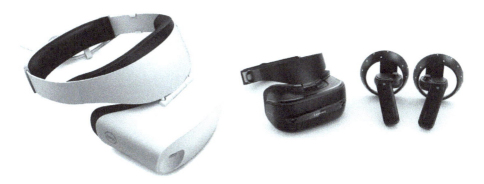

There are also other offerings from Acer which are roughly the same price.

You'll need an HDMI port on your graphics card and a USB 3 port to use most of these headsets

Windows Ink

Windows Ink will run on Windows 10 devices that are touch screen enabled. You might not find this feature on some desktop or laptop computers.

Windows Ink is integrated into apps like Maps, Microsoft Edge, Office and OneNote.

These apps allow you to draw and write directly onto the screen using a pen or stylus, meaning you can annotate maps, documents, web pages, photographs, math apps and in some cases even hand writing recognition.

Take a look at the demos in the multimedia section of the video resources. Open your web browser and navigate to the following website:

```
videos.tips/win-10-mm
```

Microsoft Whiteboard

Microsoft Whiteboard is useful when giving presentations, teaching, online collaboration, or drawing. You can also save and share your illustrations created while using Whiteboard. You'll find the whiteboard app on your start menu.

On the start screen, you'll see a thumbnail list of all the whiteboards you have created. Click on one to revisit. To create a new whiteboard, click 'create new whiteboard'.

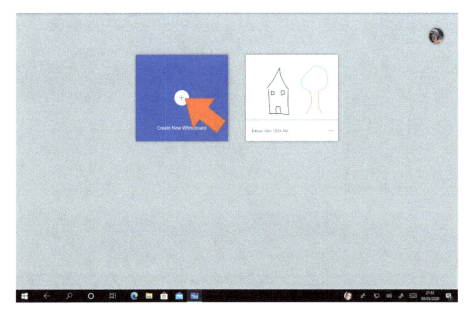

Chapter 8: Windows Ink

Getting Started

Select a template from the panel on the left hand side, or tap on the blank screen to start from scratch.

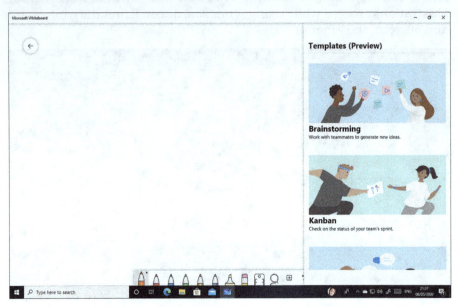

In the screen that opens, you'll see a tool bar appear along the bottom of your screen. Here, you'll find your pencils, pens, and highlighters you can use to draw onto the screen. Let's take a look:

If you want to choose the pen, tap on its icon, on the tool bar.

To change the colour and size, tap on the pen icon until the popup menu appears. Use the four circles on the left to select the thickness of the pen, then tap on a colour.

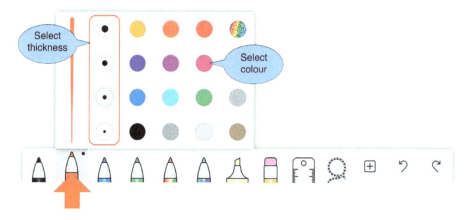

Now you can draw directly onto the screen with your pen.

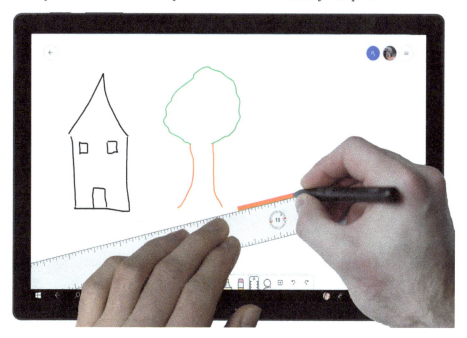

Inserting Objects

You can insert objects such as photographs, diagrams, tables, notes, as well as insert office documents and PDFs. To do this, tap the insert icon on the toolbar along the bottom of your screen. Select the object type you want to insert (eg an image)

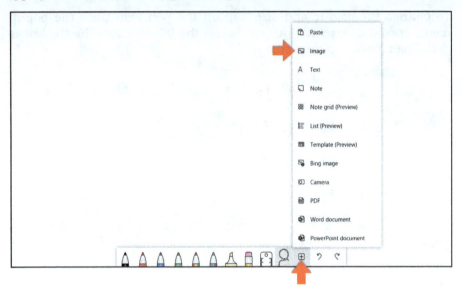

From the dialog box, select the image you want to insert.

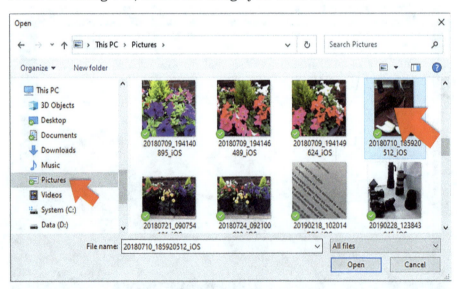

Click 'open'

Place the image on your whiteboard. Click and drag the image into position. You'll see a toolbar appear above the image.

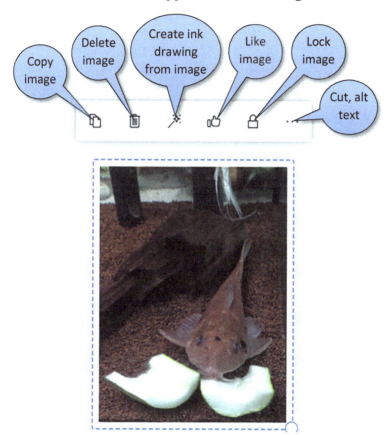

Inviting Collaborators

To invite other people to your whiteboard, click the sharing link on the top right of the screen.

Turn on 'web sharing link'. Whiteboard will generate a link you can send to other people.

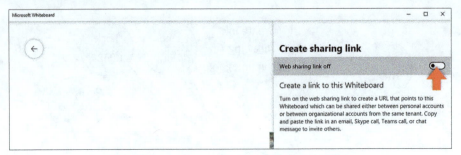

Now, once the link has been generated, click 'copy link' and paste it into an email or message to send to other people.

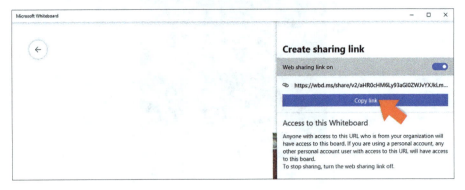

Once other people join, you'll see their contributions marked with their badge.

Ink to Shape

This feature creates clean geometric shapes from your drawings, such as squares, circles, etc. To enable ink to shape, click the hamburger icon on the top right.

Select 'ink to shape'.

Draw your shape on the canvas.

Ink to Table

This feature allows you to create clean tables by drawing them on your screen. To enable ink to table, click the hamburger icon on the top right.

Select 'ink to table'.

To draw your table, first draw a square. Then divide the square in half.

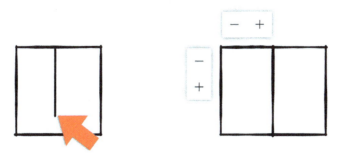

Sticky Notes

Sticky Notes allow you to hand write or type notes that you can pin to your desktop. You'll find sticky notes on your start menu.

If this is the first time running notes, you'll be prompted to enable insights. If you enable this, Cortana will be able to interpret your notes and create reminders and read the information you write in your notes.

You can write notes, delete notes, and add new notes using the icons indicated below.

Take a look at the demos in the multimedia section of the video resources. Open your web browser and navigate to the following website:

`videos.tips/win-10-mm`

If I write 'pick up kids at 9pm', Cortana will interpret this and prompt me to add a reminder. Tap 'add reminder'.

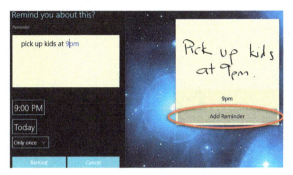

Cortana will remind you at the time you entered, and will display your reminders on your action centre in the usual way.

Sticky notes can also interpret to-do lists as well as looking up information. For example, if I am going to pick a friend up at the airport, I could write their flight number on a sticky note and use insights.

You can see below, I have written the flight number on a note and Cortana has interpreted and found a matching flight telling me the arrival time, gate and terminal number.

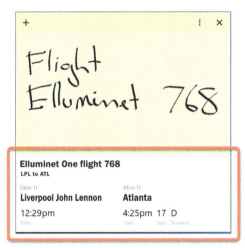

Quite a useful feature, and can also be used to look up definitions of words, stocks, exchange rates and so on. Give it a try.

Also included in Windows 10, is a sticky notes app. You can find this on your start menu. If you click on the app, your sticky notes you created in Windows Ink will appear.

Snip & Sketch

With Snip & Sketch, you can take a screenshot of whatever app you have open and handwrite annotations onto it with your pen. You can 'snip' the whole screen or just a section of it. You'll find the 'snip & sketch' app on your start menu.

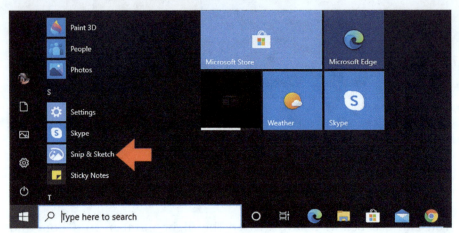

When you start the app, you'll see a toolbar at the top of your screen. This is where you'll find pens and highlighters for you to annotate the screenshot.

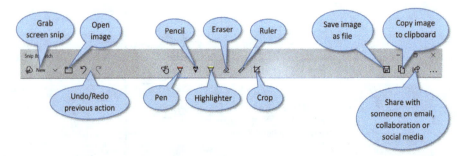

If you want to choose the pen, tap on its icon, on the tool bar. To change the colour and size, tap and hold your pen on the pen icon until a drop down menu appears. Tap on the colour and sizes you want.

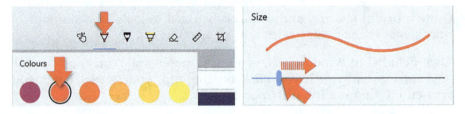

Draw directly onto the screen with your pen. If you want to change colour or size, select the pen icon again then choose a colour. You can also use a highlighter, to do this click the highlighter icon on the toolbar, select a colour and size from the drop down.

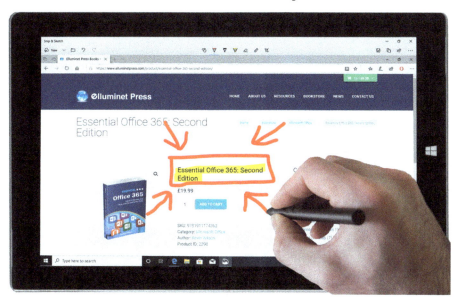

You can **save** your annotation as an image. To save, tap the 'save' icon on the top right of the screen. Enter a filename, then tap 'save'.

To **share**, tap the 'share' icon on the top right of the screen. Tap the app you want to use to share, eg mail.

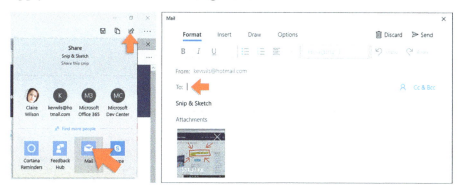

Fill in the email address and write a message, then tap the send icon.

OneNote Support

Using OneNote 2016, you can use the handwriting recognition feature on the draw ribbon to convert handwritten notes into text.

Just write your notes directly onto the page using your pen.

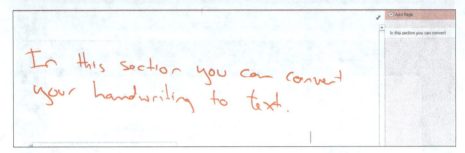

Then on the draw ribbon, tap 'ink to text'.

The conversions aren't always 100% and you'll get a few minor errors from time to time, but the software did pretty well on my handwriting.

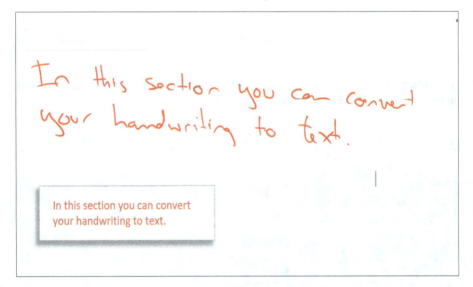

You can always go back and edit minor errors with your keyboard.

Microsoft Word Pen Support

In Microsoft Word, you'll see an additional ribbon menu called 'draw'. This has all your drawing tools such as pens, highlighters and an eraser for you to annotate your Word documents.

Select the 'draw' ribbon.

Select a pen from the selections in the centre of the ribbon. Then select the colour and thickness of your pen from the drop down menu.

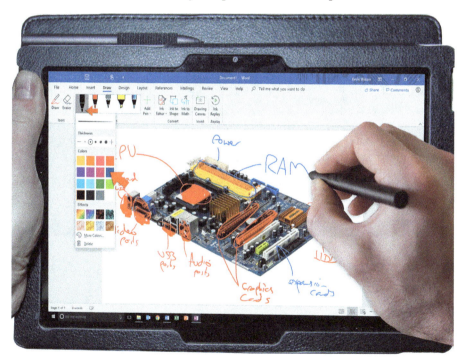

With these tools, you can draw directly onto your Word document, as shown above.

This means you can label diagrams, handwrite notes, make drawings and so on, all using your stylus or finger on your tablet.

You will then be able to save the document including all the annotations or drawings you have made.

Chapter 8: Windows Ink

Here you can highlight and annotate a typed Word document directly on your tablet using your stylus pen.

You can then save the document with all the annotations and highlights as well as share these with colleagues or friends.

Either use the share icon on the top right of your screen, or you can email the document over.

Microsoft PowerPoint Pen Support

In Microsoft PowerPoint, you'll see an additional ribbon menu called 'draw'. This has all your drawing tools such as pens, highlighters and an eraser for you to annotate your presentations.

Select the 'draw' ribbon and select a pen colour from the selections in the centre of the ribbon. From here you can select the colour and thickness of your pen.

You can annotate and draw on your slides in preparation for your presentation and when you save your presentation, PowerPoint will save your drawings and annotations as well.

You can also use your pen tools while you are presenting.

All your annotations and illustrations will appear on your presentation for your audience to see.

PowerPoint will also give you an option to save your annotations added during your presentation.

Windows 10 Apps

There are thousands of Apps available for download from the App Store.

You can get an app for virtually anything, from games, entertainment to productivity apps for graphics, writing, drawing, typing and word processing.

You can download utilities such as calculators, unit converters for length, volume, currency etc.

It is definitely worth browsing through the app store.

As well as apps available in the app store, Windows comes with a few pre-installed. Such as maps, weather, news, photos, movies and music.

Microsoft Store

You can purchase and download a wide variety of Apps for productivity, games, as well as film and television programs directly from the App Store. You can also buy Microsoft devices, such as surface tablets, laptops and other accessories right from the app.

You can find the app store by tapping on the icon on your start menu

Browsing the Store & Downloading Apps

Once the store opens you'll come to the main screen. Here you can search for apps by typing in the name in the search field. Or you can browse through the different categories.

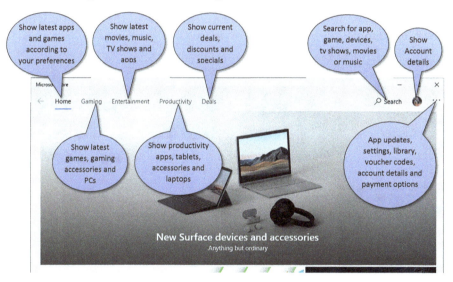

Some apps and games you will need to pay for so you'll need to add payment details - see page 364. Some apps are free.

Click 'gaming' to browse through the latest games, consoles, gaming PCs and accessories. Click 'entertainment' to browse through the latest films, TV programmes and music albums. Click 'productivity' to browse through various different apps from productivity, social media, to photography, as well as tablets and laptops for sale. Click 'deals' to view the latest tablets, laptops, PCs and accessories.

Select a category from the options along the top of the screen, eg 'entertainment'. Scroll down the page, click on an app/game to view details and buy/download the app.

Scroll down the page and you'll see an overview of the app and what it does, system requirements and reviews.

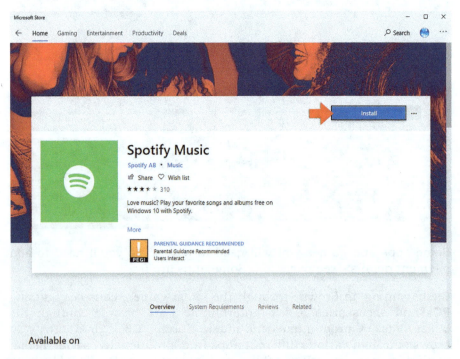

To install the app on your device, click 'install'.

Searching the Store & Downloading Apps

You can also search for specific types of apps by using the search field on the top right of the screen. Type what you're looking for into the search field, eg 'theory test'.

Click on the app's icon to show a summary of what the app is and what it does.

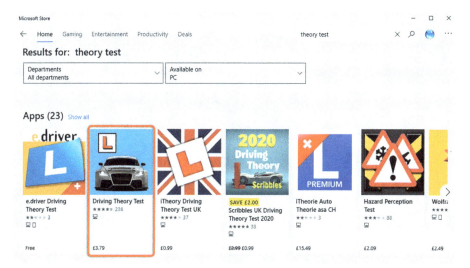

Select the app/game you want. Click the price tag to purchase and download the app. You'll need to enter your Microsoft Account email address and password.

Once the app has downloaded and installed, you will be able to start your app using the start menu.

Browsing Deals

The deals section of the store shows Microsoft's current deals and specials. Here you'll find discounted games and apps, as well as current deals on surface tablets and laptops. Select 'deals' from the menu across the top of the screen.

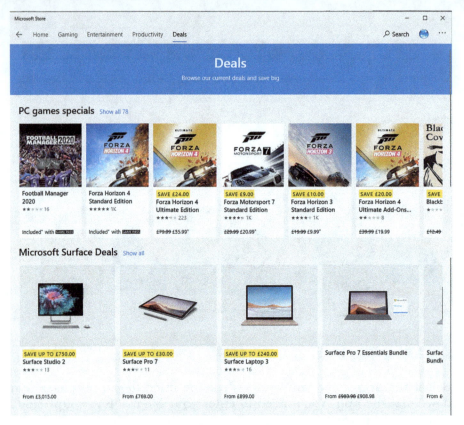

You can select any of the devices and buy them from the store.

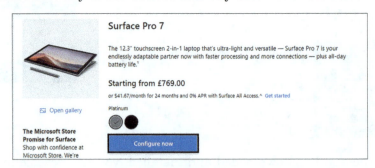

Click 'configure now' or 'build bundle'.

Here you can see reviews, technical specs and descriptions of the products. You'll also be able to configure your machine

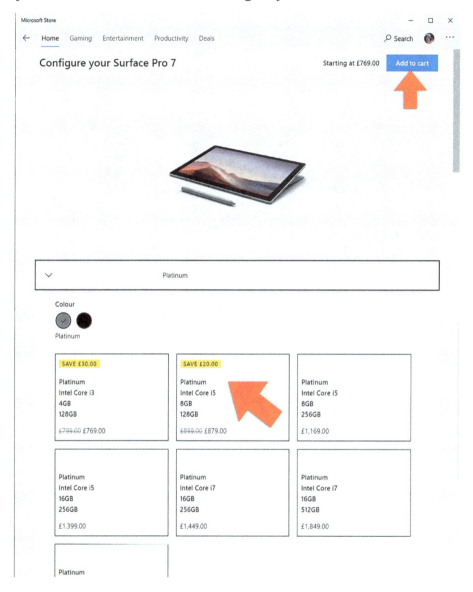

Select a configuration or build your bundle by clicking on the options you want.

Click the 'add to cart' button to buy the product. You'll need your Microsoft Account email and password, as well as a valid payment method set up in your Microsoft Account. Follow the on screen instructions to do this when prompted.

Payment Options

To enter or check your payment method, click the three dots icon on the top right of the screen and select 'payment options'.

When your web browser opens, sign in with your Microsoft Account username and password.

Select 'add a payment method', then select the type of payment, eg credit card.

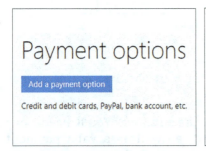
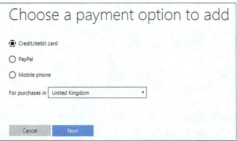

Follow the instructions on the screen to enter your payment details.

364

Maps App

You can find the maps icon on your start menu.

The maps app is useful for exploring parts of the world, landmarks and famous places. It is also useful for finding driving directions to different locations.

You can search for pretty much any address, country, place or landmark. Just type it into the search field on the top left.

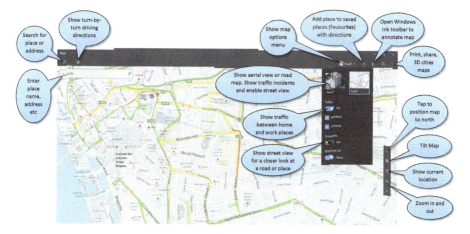

Maps App has an aerial map, and a road map. You can enable traffic flow, incident reporting, speed camera locations and street level view. To do this, select the 'map options' icon on the toolbar to reveal the popup menu.

Get Directions

You can get driving directions to any location or address you can think of. You can get directions from your current location or you can enter a start location and a destination.

As well as driving directions you can get local bus routes and in some places even walking directions.

To get your driving directions, click or tap the turn-by-turn driving directions icon on the top left of your screen, labelled below.

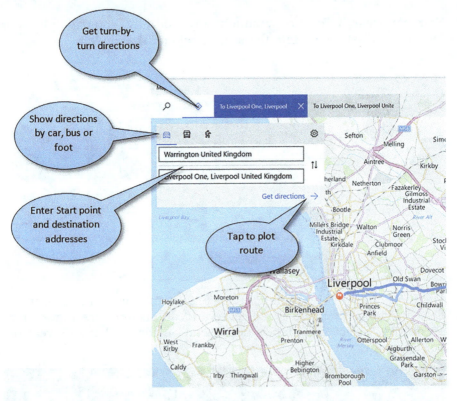

The first field will show your current location (Warrington in this example). You can also type in a location if you need to.

The second field is where you can enter your destination. Liverpool One Shopping Complex in this example. This can be a post code/zip code, residential address, town/city or place name.

Once you hit 'get directions' or tap the right arrow (next to your destination field), the maps app will calculate a route and display it on a map.

You'll see a map on the right hand side with a list of driving directions listed down the left hand side. You might see a choice of different routes, the quickest one is usually at the top.

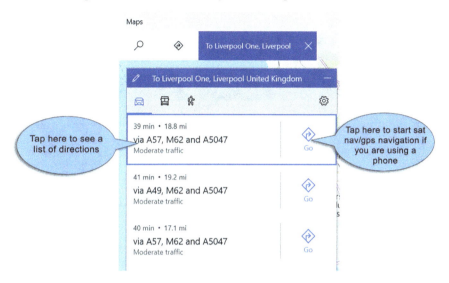

You can click on any of these directions and the map will zoom in and show you the road on the map.

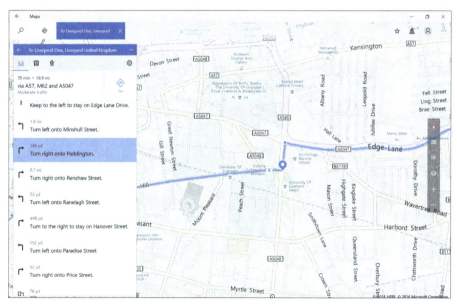

There is also an option to print the directions if needed but if you are using the maps app on your phone or tablet you can use it as a GPS or SatNav and the maps app will direct you as you drive.

Street View

Tap the map options icon on the tool bar on the top right hand side. From the popup menu turn on 'streetside'. You'll notice some of the roads will be highlighted. Main roads and highways are in blue, minor roads are in light green. To go into street view, tap on the part of the road you want to see.

You'll see a street view of that section. To move forward, tap on a part of the road. To "look" left and right tap and drag your view to the left or right.

You can tap the part of the road you want to view on the map in the bottom pane.

Ink Directions

If I wanted to find some quick directions from my location or a specific location, to somewhere close by, I can draw directly onto the map and the Maps App will calculate a route. So in this example, I want to get from Westfield Primary School to Birch Road. Tap the Windows Ink icon, then select the directions icon from the drop down. Draw a line between your start and end points.

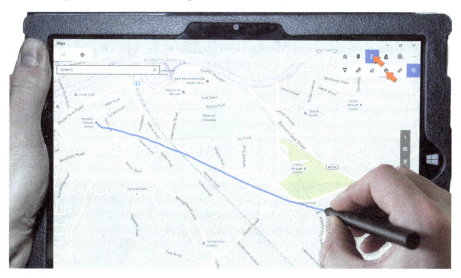

The Maps App will calculate the quickest route between your start and end points.

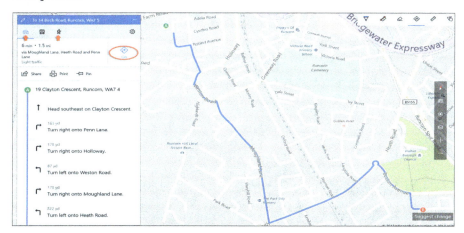

Down the left hand side, you'll see your turn-by-turn directions. Tap, the car icon for driving directions or tap, the little man icon for walking directions. Tap 'go' to start the navigation.

Measure Distances

Using the Windows Ink features, you can also measure distances between two points on the map.

Tap the Windows Ink icon, top right. Then from the drop down, select the measure tool.

Now with your pen, draw a line between the two points on the map, you want to measure.

Remember this tool doesn't take into account roads or paths on your map, just the relative length of the line you have drawn in relation to the scale of the map.

Annotations

Using the Windows Ink features, you can draw directly onto the map with your finger or pen.

Tap the Windows Ink icon, top right. Then from the drop down, select the ball-point pen tool.

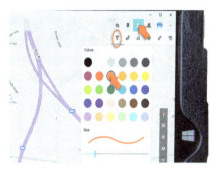

From the drop down menu, select a colour from the palette and adjust the size using the slider underneath. Drag the bar to the right to increase the thickness

Now with your pen, draw directly onto the map.

You can share these annotations with friends/colleagues or print them out.

Explore in 3D

This feature can come in handy if you want to explore landmarks or areas of interest. To start exploring 3D cities, click the 3 dots icon on the top right of the screen, then select '3D Cities'.

Down the left hand side you will see a number of famous landmarks cities, and areas you can explore in 3D. Not all cities will be in 3D yet but the ones that are will appear in this list.

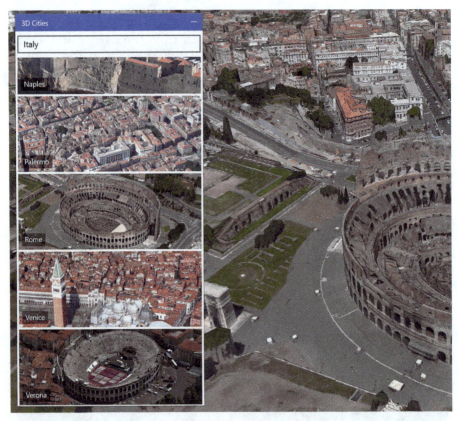

Perhaps you are going on holiday/vacation and you want to explore certain parts of the world you haven't been to - just remember the images you see aren't live and can be out of date.

Here you can see a fly-over view of a landmark. You can zoom in and out, rotate the map and move around as you explore.

Tap or click and drag the map around to explore, use the '+' and '-' icons on the right hand side to zoom in and out. Or use a pinch & spread gesture if you're using a touchscreen.

Try also searching for your favourite place by typing it into the search field.

Weather App

The weather app can give you a forecast for your current location or any location you choose to view.

You can find the Weather app on your start menu. It is usually disguised as a live tile showing you weather summary for your current location.

When you first start weather app it will ask for your location, unless you have location services enabled, then it will automatically find your location. If not, type it into the field in the middle of the screen.

Once you have entered your location the weather app will show you a summary of the local weather conditions.

You can tap on each day to see more details, you may need to scroll down the page to see them.

Down the left hand side you have your navigation icons where you can see local weather, animated radar weather maps, historical weather and view your favourite locations list.

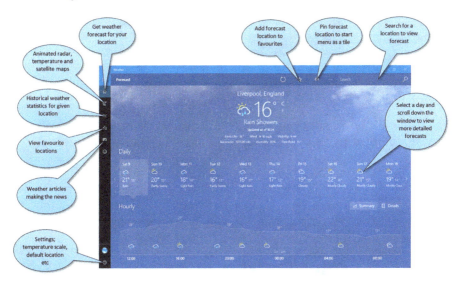

You can also find weather forecasts for other places. If for example you are going on holiday/vacation, you can enter the location's name into the search field and get a weather forecast.

You can also add forecasts for locations to your favourites list so you don't have to keep searching for them. To do this, just tap the 'add forecast location to favourites' icon along the top of your screen.

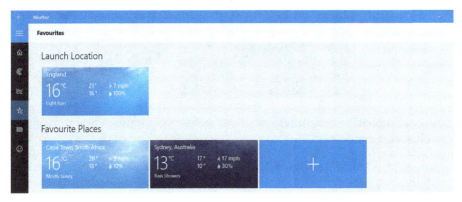

News App

You can find the news app icon on your start menu. It is usually a live tile and has up to date news headlines and images on the tile instead of an icon

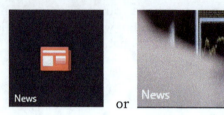 or

The news app brings you local news headlines and stories from around the world.

Down the left hand side you have your navigation icons where you can browse different news sources such as news or sports channels.

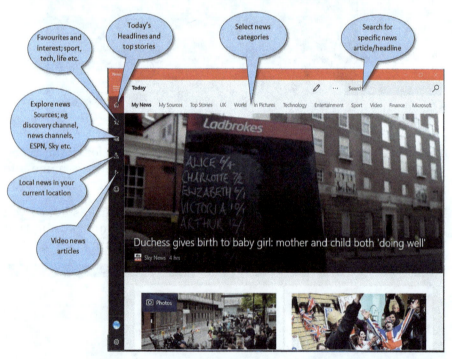

You can read the headlines, or local news, you can also watch video articles and reports.

You can find trending topics and news stories. Tap on the headlines to read the articles.

Alarms & Clock App

You can set alarms on your device, pc or phone to alert you. For example, setting a time to get up in the morning.

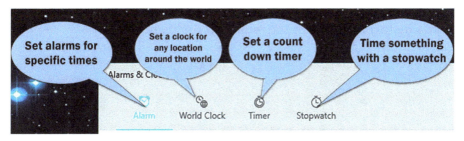

To do this tap the alarm tab, then tap the plus sign at the bottom of the window

Enter the time you want the alarm to sound. Then click in the 'alarm name' field and enter a name.

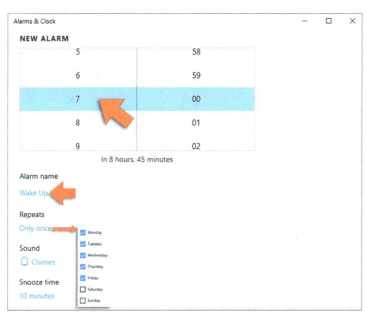

Click in the 'repeats' field, select the days you want the alarm to sound, eg week days (monday - friday).

Click the disk icon on the bottom of the window to save the alarm.

377

Similarly if you wanted to add a clock for another city in the world, tap 'world clock', then tap the plus sign and enter the city/country name in the search field.

This can be useful if you have colleagues or family in other countries, or just want to know what time it is there so when you skype them you aren't disturbing them in the middle of the night.

You can also create countdown timers, for example, to boil an egg for 3 minutes, time an exam for 50 minutes and so on.

Just tap timer, then tap the plus sign and enter the length of time.

Hit the play button to start the countdown.

Tap stopwatch to time something, for example, a race, lap times and so on.

Hit the play button to start the clock. Hit the flag icon to mark a lap.

Voice Recorder

Voice recorder is your on-board dictation machine. You can make voice notes, record lectures, interviews and so on. To start recording just hit the microphone icon on the screen.

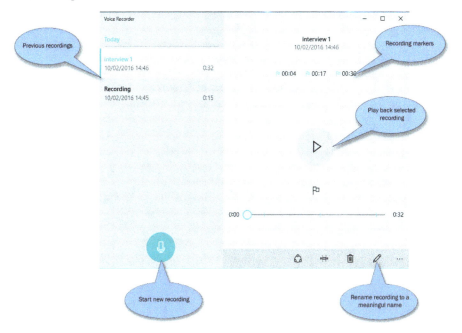

You can even add markers at important points during a recording.

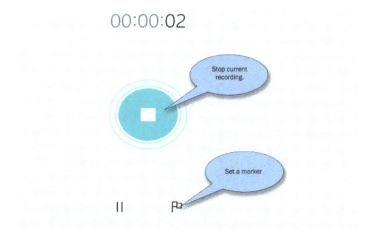

This way when you play back the recordings, you can go directly to the important points by clicking on these recording markers, illustrated in the top diagram.

379

Calculator App

The calculator app works like any calculator. You'll find it on your start menu

You can choose the type of calculator you want; just a standard calculator for adding a few numbers together or a full scientific calculator for working out more complex equations.

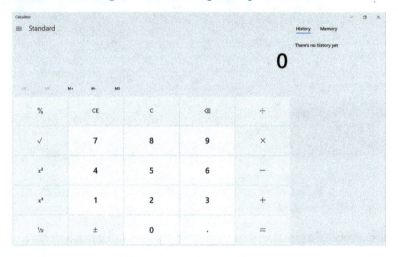

To change the calculator click the icon on the top left of your screen, and select 'scientific'.

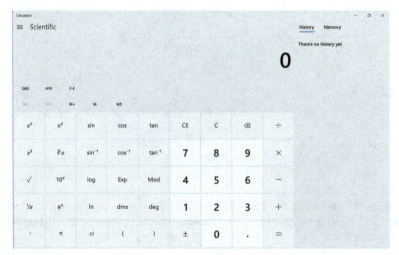

Unit Converter

You can also convert different units. You can convert between different currencies, weight, length, temperature, energy and so on. To open the converter, click the icon on the top left of your screen, shown below. Scroll down the list to the converters and select one, eg 'length'.

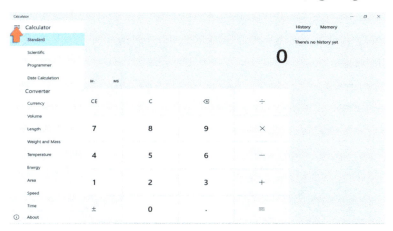

Useful if you want to convert metric measurements to ones you're familiar with. Eg: To convert from millimeters to inches, change the first one to millimeters and the second one to inches - indicated by the red arrows below.

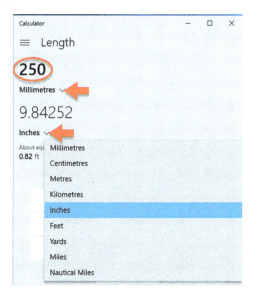

Click on the top number, circled above, usually 0 if you haven't entered anything. Now type in a value.

Chapter 9: Windows 10 Apps

Currency Converter

Click the icon on the top left of your screen and select 'currency' from the drop down menu.

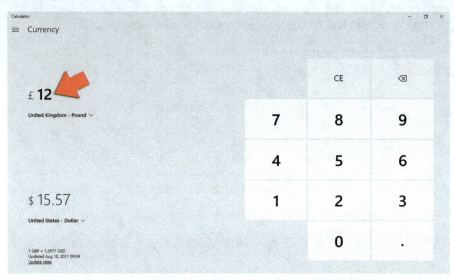

Tap on the currency numbers and enter a value using the on screen keypad, as shown above.

To change the currencies, click the currency name under the value, shown below. From the popup menu, select the currency you want.

In the example below, I'm converting from British Pounds to US Dollars.

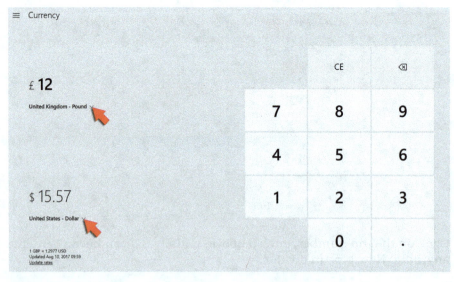

Graphing

With the graphing feature, you can plot various equations on the graph. To use the feature, click the icon on the top left of the screen and select 'graphing' from the menu.

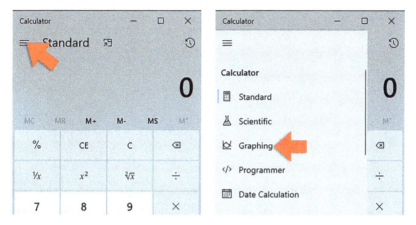

Make the window bigger, or go into full screen. As you do this, you'll see the graphing functions appear on the right.

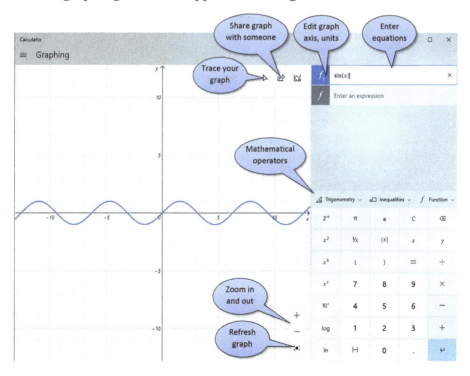

On the top right, enter your equations. Press enter to plot on the graph.

Maintaining your Computer

Computer maintenance keeps your computer in a good working order.

Using anti-virus software, backing up files, keeping your computer up to date.

Also more technical issues such as file de-fragmentation, disk clean-ups and start-up programs.

System backup and recovery procedures and advice when your PC has problems.

Here we will take a look at some common areas and procedures to keep your machine running smoothly

Take a look at the video demos in the maintenance section of the accompanying video resources. Open your web browser and navigate to the following website:

videos.tips/win-10-sys

Anti-Virus Software

A lot of this software is sold pre-installed on the machine you buy and is offered on a subscription basis. So you have to pay to update the software. Don't buy it! There are plenty of safe free options to choose from, including Microsoft's Windows Security.

Windows Security

Windows 10 comes pre-installed with Windows Security, formerly known as Windows Defender, is Microsoft's free anti-virus software. It does a pretty good job at protecting your machine as is frequently updated by Microsoft.

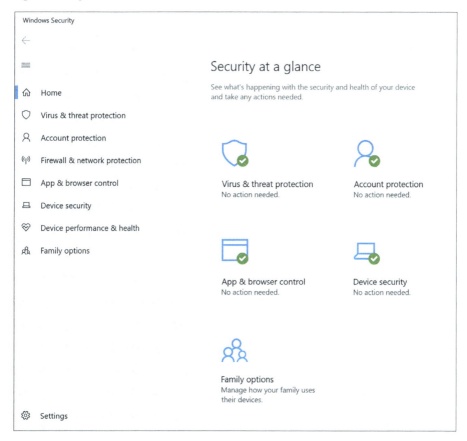

Two free ones that are a good place to start are Avast and AVG. Both of these packages are very good. The free one is basic, but you can upgrade if you need something more.

Avast

Avast scans and detects vulnerabilities in your home network, checks for program updates, scans files as you open them, emails as they come in and fixes PC performance issues.

You can download it from their website.

www.avast.com

Scroll down the page until you find 'free download'.

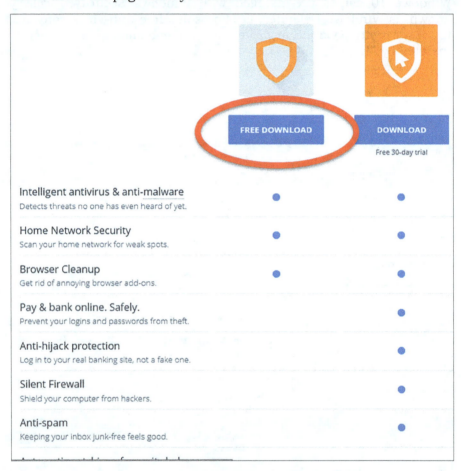

The other two versions here are 30 day trials and will expire after 30 days. You will need to pay a subscription to continue.

When prompted hit 'install'. If the installation doesn't run automatically, go to your downloads folder and run 'avast_free_antivirus_setup.exe', follow the on screen wizard.

AVG

AVG blocks viruses, spyware, & other malware, scans web, twitter, & facebook links and warns you of malicious attachments.

You can download it from their website.

www.avg.com

Scroll down and click 'free download'.

The other versions here are 30 day trials and will expire after 30 days. You will need to pay a subscription to continue.

The free version is good enough for home users.

Windows Security

Windows Security is the hub for all security features including virus protection, device health, networking, firewalls, internet security, app control and family safety options. Open your start menu, scroll down the list of apps on the left hand side, then click 'windows security'.

Down the left hand panel and on the 'home' page, you have some options:

Virus & Threat Protection. From here you can scan for threats with a full system scan which scans system files, apps, as well as your files. You can also perform an 'offline scan', where your system will restart into a 'secure mode' to scan for threats. This scan is useful for removing malware that isn't removed with a full or quick scan. Most detected threats are automatically quarantined.

Account Protection. Security settings for your Microsoft Account, manage sync settings between devices, adjust windows hello sign in options, enable/disable dynamic lock.

Firewall & Network Protection. Here you can troubleshoot network issues with WiFi or internet connectivity and adjust your firewall settings. You can also access firewall settings.

App & Browser Control. Here you can adjust your browser and application security settings such as SmartScreen filter that helps protect you against malicious websites, apps and downloads.

Device Security. Enable/disable core isolation and memory integrity preventing and attack injecting malicious code into processes.

Device Performance & Health. Here you can see any issues arising with drivers, updates, battery life and disk storage space. You also have the option to refresh Windows 10, meaning you can re-install Windows if it is not running smoothly while keeping your personal files safe.

Family Options. This section links you to your family options using your web browser and allows you to monitor your kids' online activity.

Running a Virus Scan

You can run a quick scan that checks your folders, or a full scan that scans every file on your PC. To start, select 'virus & threat protection' from the panel on the left hand side

From the 'scan screen' click 'scan options'.

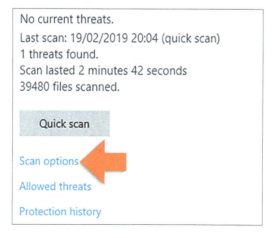

Select either 'quick scan' to scan system files as well as your personal files. Click 'full scan' to scan every file on your PC.

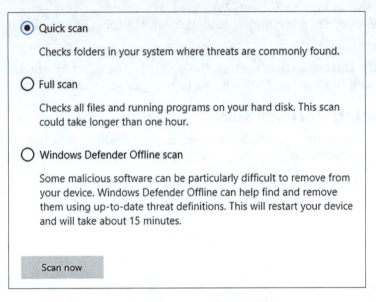

If you are trying to remove malware or a virus and the quick or full scan doesn't remove it, use 'windows defender offline scan' to restart your PC in a secure environment.

Click 'scan now'.

If you selected the 'windows defender offline scan', windows will reboot into a secure environment and scan your system

Any malware or viruses that are found will be removed or quarantined. You'll find the results in 'virus & threat protection' under 'protection history'.

Scan a Specified File or Folder

To scan a particular file or folder, open up File Explorer and navigate to the file or folder you want to scan.

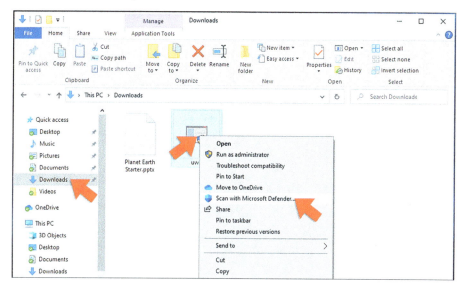

Dealing with Threats

If any of the virus scans detect a threat, they'll appear on the 'scan options' screen. Click on the threat to view details. Select an action, eg 'remove'.

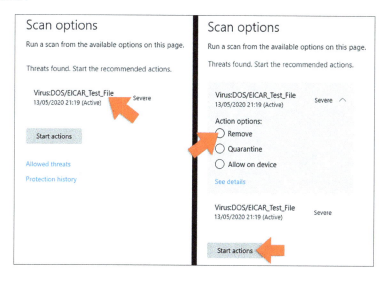

Click 'start actions' to clean.

Threat Protection Settings

Open windows security app, then select 'Virus & Threat Protection'. Scroll down to 'virus & threat protection settings', then click 'manage settings'.

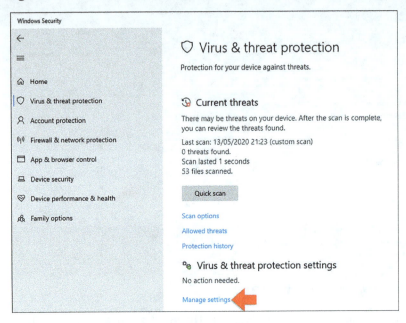

Here, you can enable/disable 'real time protection', 'cloud delivered protection', 'automatic sample submission', 'tamper protection', 'file exclusions', and 'notifications'.

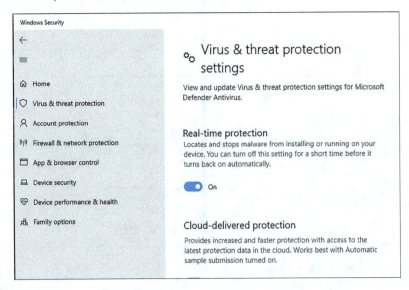

Controlling Folder Access

This feature allows you to protect files & folders from modification by unapproved applications and malware. If any of these applications try to modify files, you'll get a notification allowing you to block the action.

To enable this feature, open Windows Security, Click 'virus & threat protection', scroll down the page, then select 'Manage Ransomware Protection'. Set the 'controlled folder access' switch to 'On'.

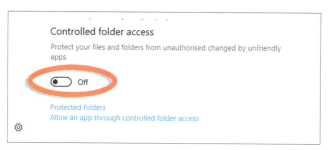

Windows Security will normally allow most known applications to access and change data in the folders on your machine. If Windows Security detects an app it doesn't recognise, you'll receive a notification that it has been blocked. Some of the time this will be a legitimate application, so you might need to add the application to the safe list.

To add other applications to the 'safe list', click 'allow an app trough controlled folder access'. Then click 'add an allowed app'.

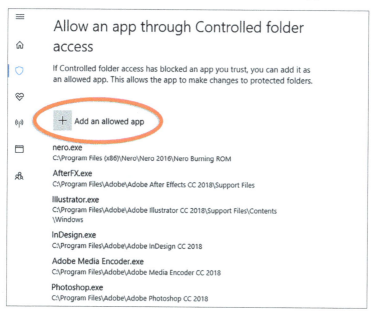

Now in the dialog box that appears, navigate to the folder where the application is installed. This will usually be "C:\Program Files". In this example, I'm going to add 'Adobe After Effects'. So navigate to the folder in 'program files'. Make sure you select the file with the EXE extension, as shown below.

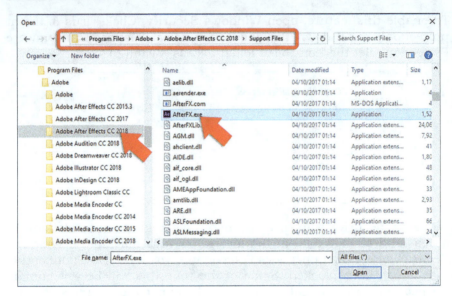

Windows Security will automatically add your system folders and most of your personal folders. You can add any others if you need to. To do this, click 'protected folders' on the 'virus & threat protection' screen.

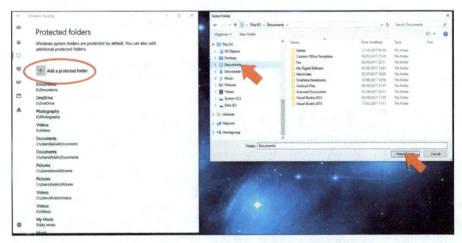

Click 'add a protected folder', then from the dialog box that appears, navigate to the folder you want to protect, click on it, then click 'select folder'.

Exploit Protection

This feature is designed to protect your PC from various types of exploits out of the box and shouldn't need any configuration.

To find this feature, open Windows Security, click 'App & browser control' then select 'Exploit protection' at the bottom of the page.

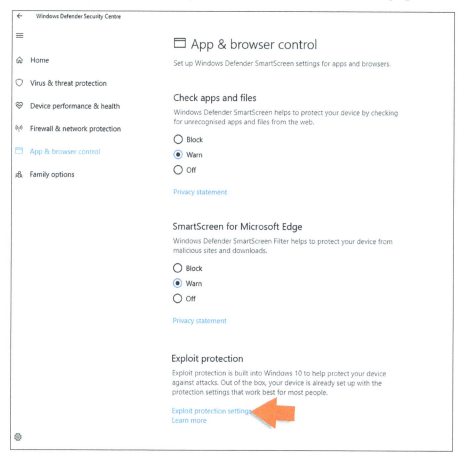

The exploit protection settings are divided into two categories: system settings and program settings.

System settings allows you to set the exploit protection globally - for all the programs.

The program settings allows you to override the global system settings for an individual program.

Most of these settings can be left on the default.

Windows Firewall

Windows Firewall is a security feature built into Windows 10. It is designed to filter network traffic to and from your computer and block any malicious attempts to connect to your machine or potentially harmful programs attempting to transmit data.

To open the firewall settings, start windows security - you'll find the icon on your start menu. Select 'firewall & network protection'

Enable or Disable

Select the network profile. The one your PC is using with have 'active' written next to it. Home networks use the 'private' profile.

Private. Networks where computers at home or office connected to a private, internal network usually a small workgroup.

Domain. Networks where computers are part of an Active Directory domain usually found on large networks in schools, colleges and businesses.

Guest or Public. Networks that are not secure such as wifi hotspots you'd find in a coffee shop, library or any public place.

It's best practice to enable the firewall on all three profiles.

To enable/disable, click on the network profile. Eg 'private network'.

Set the slider to 'on' to enable, 'off' to disable.

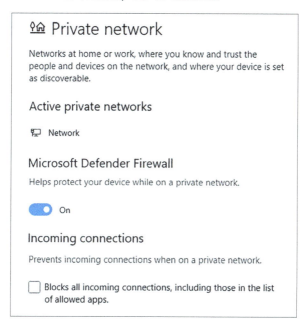

If you're on a public wifi network, enable 'block all incoming connections' on the active network profile.

Allow or Block an App

Select 'firewall & network protection' in Windows Security, then click 'allow an app through firewall'.

Click 'change settings', enter your administrator password if prompted.

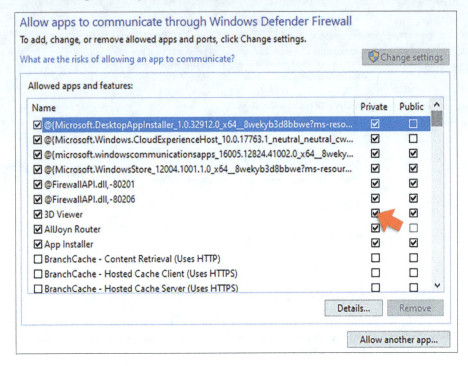

Scroll down the list, click the box next to the app name. Add the tick to allow the app on private and public networks. Remove the tick to block the app.

If you app isn't in the list, click 'allow another app'.

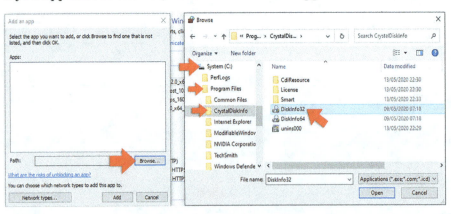

Navigate to the app. This is usually in the 'program files' on the C drive.

Click 'open', then back on the 'add an app' screen click 'add'.

Windows Sandbox

Windows Sandbox is a desktop app for safely running applications in isolation, without the risk of virus or malware infection. This is particularly useful for testing apps and software downloaded from the internet or email attachments that you are unsure of. You can also open a file using Windows Sandbox to test whether it is safe to open or not. Windows Sandbox tends to run a little bit slower than usual, but this is normal.

To start, open your start menu, scroll down the apps on the left hand side, then select 'windows sandbox'.

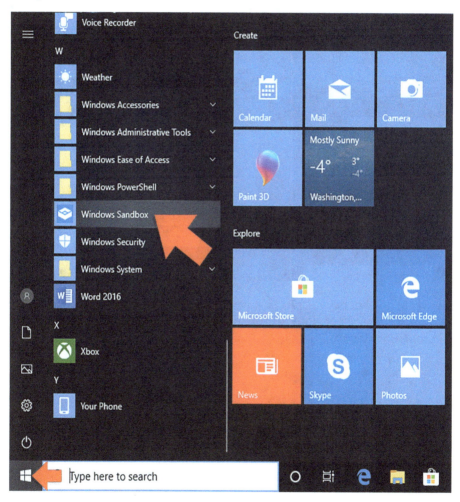

Click 'yes' on the confirmation dialog box, and enter your admin password if prompted.

Once sandbox opens, you'll see a window pop up with its own desktop and start menu. Here you can run apps, or open files in complete isolation.

Opening Files

To use sandbox, you can copy and paste files from your PC directly onto the sandbox desktop. To do this, first open your file explorer on your PC. Click the file explorer icon on your taskbar.

Navigate to where the file is saved. If you've downloaded something from a web browser, look in the 'downloads' folder. Right click on the file and select 'copy'.

Open windows sandbox, right click on the desktop within the sandbox app, then click 'paste'.

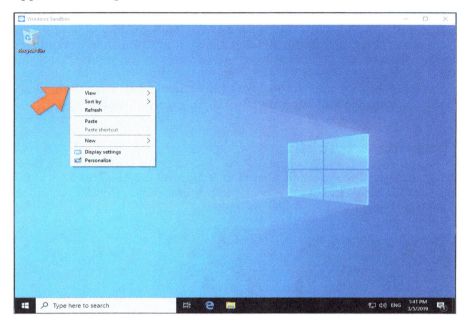

To test the file, double click on the icon you just pasted onto the desktop.

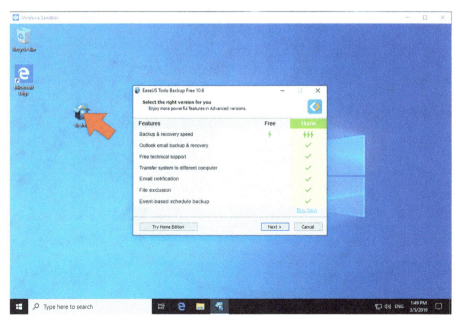

You can run through the program without affecting your system.

Backing Up your Files

If you have ever lost data because of a computer glitch or crash you know how frustrating it can be. So we all need a good backup strategy. I'm going to go through the strategy I have found that has worked well over the years.

Windows 10 has a built in backup utility called FileHistory that allows you to select files and back them up to an external hard drive.

Creating a Backup

First of all go buy yourself a good external hard disk. This is a small device that plugs into a USB port on your computer. Below is a typical specification for an external hard disk

Plug in your external drive into a free USB port.

In the search field on the task bar type 'file history'.

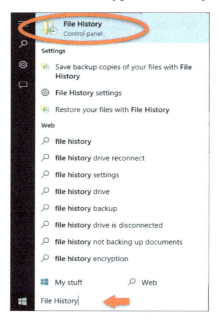

Click 'File History' in the search results, circled above.

On the screen that appears, click 'Turn On' to enable File History.

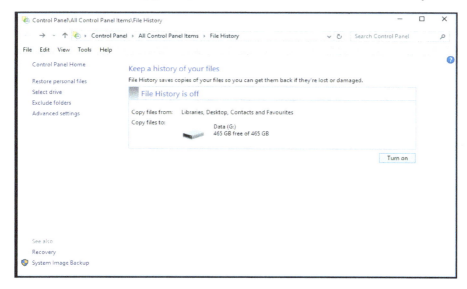

Once you have turned on File History, Windows 10 will start to copy files from your libraries (documents, pictures, music etc) onto your external hard drive.

Adding Folders

If you want to add folders to your backup, just add them to your libraries. Remember your desktop, documents, photos, music & videos folders and their contents are already included.

For example, if I wanted to include my photography folder which is on another hard drive, open file explorer, right click on the folder and go down to 'include in library'. Then from the slide-out menu, click 'create new library'.

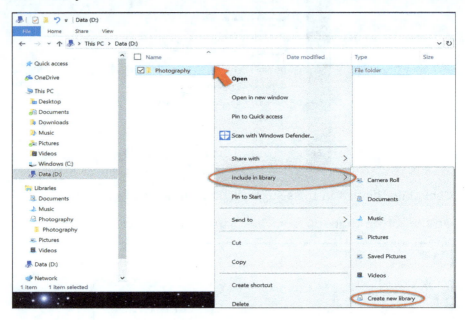

You'll see your libraries listed in the left hand pane.

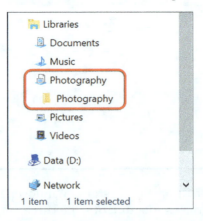

This folder will now be backed up with the rest of your libraries.

404

Setting Backup Schedules

By default, File History saves files every hour, but you can change this by clicking on "Advanced Settings" listed down the left hand side of the screen.

A good guide is to set how often File History saves files to "Daily". This will tell File History to save copies of your files once a day. For most users this is sufficient.

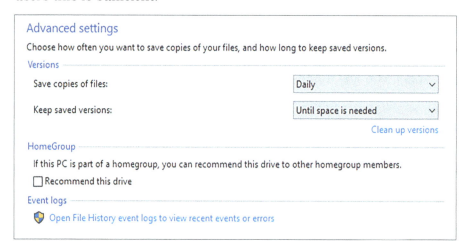

Set 'keep saved versions' to 'until space is needed'. This means that File History will keep creating backups while there is sufficient space on the hard drive, then once the drive fills up, File History will start to delete the oldest backups to make space for new backups.

Good practice would be to plug in your external drive at the end of each day to back up what you have done throughout the day.

Backups can take a while depending on how much you have done.

Restoring Files

Plug in your external Hard drive. Open up File History and click 'Restore Personal Files'

Use the left and right arrows at the bottom to navigate to the date backed up when you know your file still existed or was working.

Then in the library section double click in the folder the file was in eg pictures if you lost a photo.

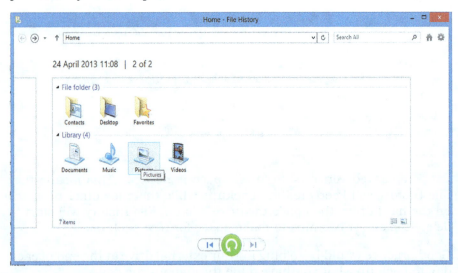

Select the photo and to restore it click the green button at the bottom of the window.

Password Recovery

You can recover a forgotten Microsoft Account password from the login screen. Click 'I forgot my password' underneath the password field. If you don't see this field, it usually appears after you've entered an incorrect password.

Here you'll be asked to verify your identity. You'll need your alternative email address. This is the email address you entered when you signed up for a Microsoft Account. Select the email address from the drop down box, then type the full address in the field underneath. Click 'send code'.

Now, go and check that email address - the account for the email address you just entered above. You'll see an email from 'microsoft account team' with a code. Enter the code in the field below and click 'next'.

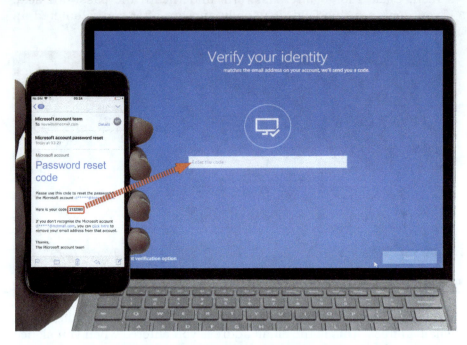

Enter your new password in the field, then click 'next'.

You will now be able to log on using your new password. Click 'sign in' to go back to the lock screen.

Now, sign in with the password you just entered.

If you're still struggling, you can reset your password for a Microsoft Account from a web browser on another device or phone.

Open a web browser and navigate to the following website.

```
account.live.com/password/reset
```

or

```
account.live.com/acsr
```

Follow the instructions on the screen.

PIN Recovery

You can recover a forgotten Microsoft Account password from the login screen. Click 'I forgot my PIN' underneath the password field. If you don't see this field, it usually appears after you've entered an incorrect PIN.

Enter your Microsoft Account Password.

Click 'sign in'.

Select your recovery email address. This is the email address you entered when you signed up for a Microsoft Account. Select the email address, then type in your email address to confirm. Click 'send code'.

Now, go and check that email address - the account for the email address you just entered above. You'll see an email from 'microsoft account team' with a code. Enter the code in the field below and click 'verify'.

Click 'verify'. Click 'continue' on the 'are you sure' confirmation screen.

Now enter your new PIN, then click 'ok'.

Windows Update

Windows update usually automatically downloads and installs all updates available for windows.

The Unified Update Platform or UUP allows targeted updates meaning Windows Update will only download the changes and updates included since the last update that are relevant to your version of Windows 10. This will mean smaller downloads and quicker updates.

Settings

You can find Windows Update in the Settings App on the start menu. Select 'update & security'.

Select 'windows update' from the panel on the left hand side.

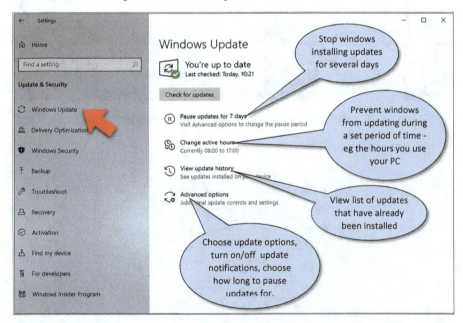

Pause Updates

You can pause updates for a set period of time up to 7 days. This means that Windows won't download or install an update for this period of time.

To pause updates click 'pause updates for 7 days' on the Windows Update screen.

To change the number of days you want Windows to pause the updates for, click on 'advanced options' on the Windows update screen.

Scroll down to 'pause updates' and select a date from the drop down box.

Active Hours

Once Windows Update has downloaded the updates, it will schedule a system restart if one is required to install the updates. This is usually scheduled according to your specified 'active hours', which means Windows Update will not restart during these hours.

To change the active hours, click 'change active hours' at the bottom of the windows update screen.

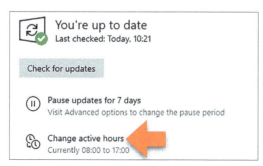

Click 'change', next to your 'current active hours'.

Click in the 'start time' box.

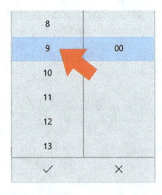

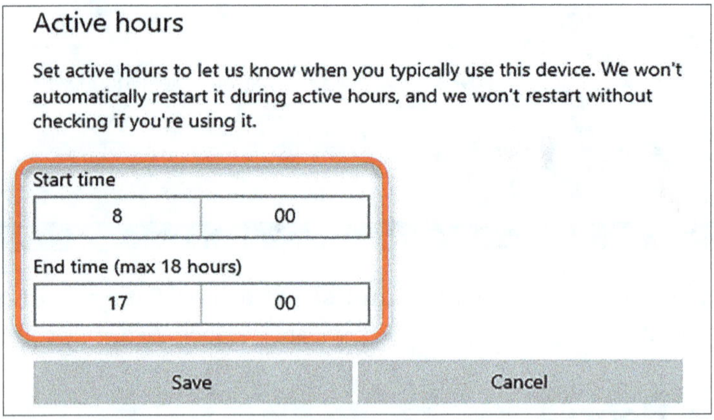

Select a start time from the dialog box that appears. Click the 'tick' to confirm.

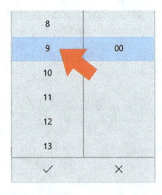

Do the same for the end time.

Click 'save' when you're done.

Update History

To see what updates have been installed, click 'view update history' on Windows Update's main screen.

Here you'll see a list of all the updates that have been installed

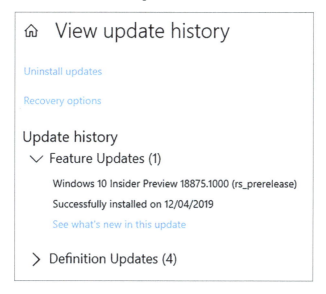

You can also uninstall updates from here. To do this click 'uninstall updates. Select an update from the list and click 'uninstall'

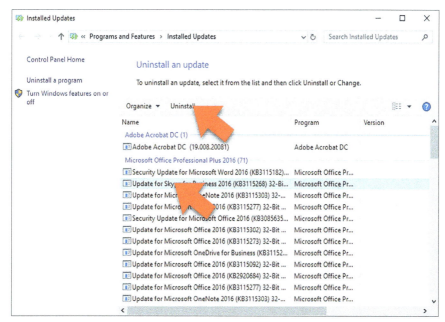

Bandwidth Limiting

Constant updates can eat up your internet bandwidth leaving very little for you to browse the web, skype and do your work.

With this in mind, Microsoft have introduced a bandwidth limit to windows update, which means you can allocate a percentage of your bandwidth to windows update so it doesn't use your entire bandwidth to download updates

The settings for this are buried inside windows update and you can find them here..

Settings app > update & security > windows update > advanced options > delivery optimization > advanced options.

Here you can change the settings by dragging the sliders and selecting the check boxes to enable/disable limiting.

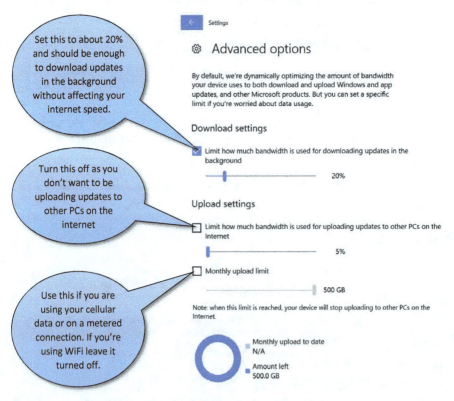

Update Delivery Optimisation

If you have multiple windows 10 devices on your home or office network you can use Delivery Optimization to reduce internet bandwidth consumption by sharing the downloaded updates among the multiple devices on your network. This means that the update packages are downloaded from the internet to a device on the network, the update packages are then shared from this device and made available to other devices on the network, so they can update without having to download the package again from the internet.

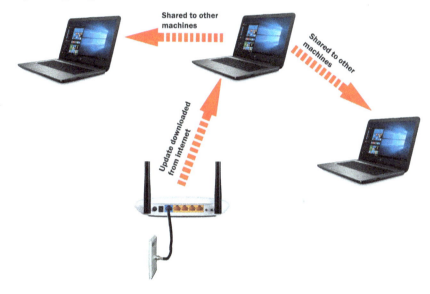

To enable delivery optimisation, open your settings app and select 'update & security'. Select 'advanced options' from the list, then 'delivery optimisation' at the bottom

Click the slider switch to turn it on and select 'PCs on my local network'.

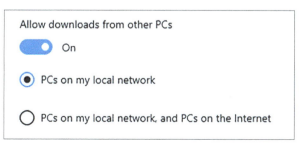

417

Fonts

You can download and install new fonts. This is useful if you are a designer or want a different font for a document you are working on.

You can download endless types of fonts from various websites on the internet. Many of these are free, but there are one or two you'd have to pay for. Here are a few useful sites offering fonts to download.

```
fonts.google.com
www.dafont.com
www.fontsquirrel.com
```

To install fonts you have downloaded, open File Explorer and select your 'downloads' folder from the left hand side

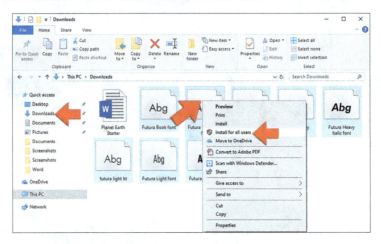

Select all the font files you have downloaded, right click on the selection, them select 'install for all users'.

You can see all your installed fonts using the settings app. Click the settings app icon on your start menu and select 'personalisation'. Select 'fonts' from the list on the left hand side.

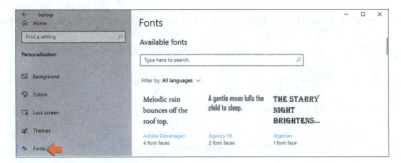

Disk De-fragmentation

Data is saved in blocks on the surface of the disk called clusters. When a computer saves your file, it writes the data to the next empty cluster on the disk, even if the clusters are not adjacent.

This allows faster performance, and usually, the disk is spinning fast enough that this has little effect on the time it takes to open the file.

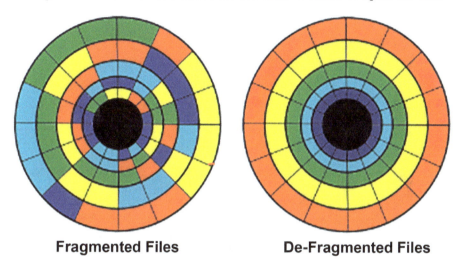

Fragmented Files   **De-Fragmented Files**

However, as more and more files are created, saved, deleted or changed, the data becomes fragmented across the surface of a disk, and it takes longer to access. This can cause problems when launching software (because it will often load many different files as it launches).

So bad fragmentation just makes every operation on the computer take longer but eventually fragmentation can cause applications to crash, hang, or even corrupt the data.

It's a good rule of thumb to do this roughly once a month, to keep things running smoothly.

Disk defragmentation only applies to hard drives with mechanical spinning disks (HDD). If you have a solid state drive or SSD, then you don't need to worry about defragmentation. Defragging has no effect on performance with a SSD.

Windows 10 will usually detect a SSD and optimise the drive itself using the TRIM command rather than defrag.

To de-fragment the disk in Windows 10, type 'defragment' into the search field on the taskbar. Click 'Defragment and optimise your drives'.

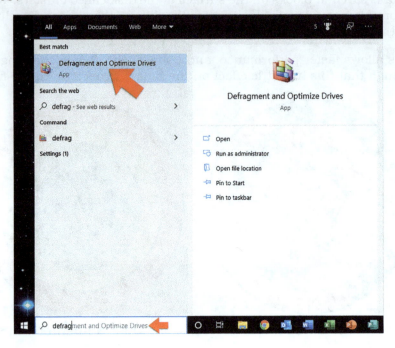

Select the drive you want to defrag. Click the 'optimize' button.

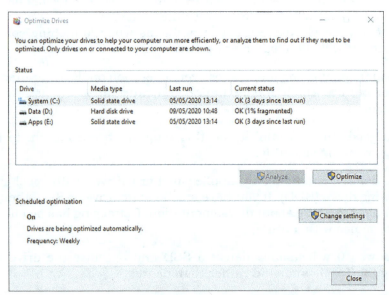

This will start de-fragmenting your disk. This process can take a while.

Disk Clean-Up

Over time, windows gets clogged up with temporary files from browsing the internet, installing and un-installing software and general every day usage. Doing this once a month will help keep things running smoothly.

Type 'disk cleanup' into the search field on bottom left the taskbar.

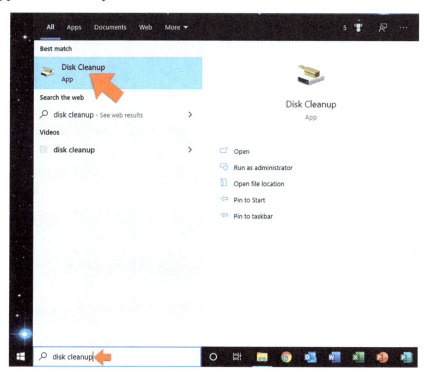

Click 'clear disk space by deleting unnecessary files'

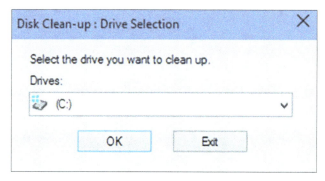

Select drive C, click ok.

In the window that appears you can see a list of all the different files and caches. It is safe to select all these for clearing.

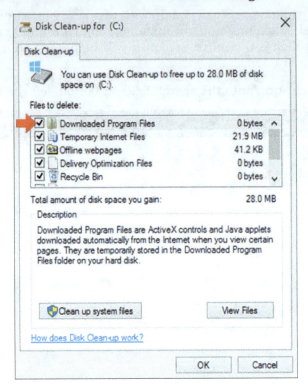

Once you are done click ok and windows will clear out all those old files.

Click 'delete files' on the confirmation dialog box to clear out all the old files

Do the same with the system files. In the window above, click 'clean up system files'.

This helps to keep your system running smoothly. A good rule of thumb is to do this about once a month.

Start-Up Programs

Start up programs automatically start when you start up Windows - this can cause Windows to become very sluggish during start up. These are usually 'helper' apps that are installed with certain pieces of software and most can be disabled without any problem.

Hit **control-alt-delete** on your keyboard and select task manager from the menu. Click more details if you don't have the screen below.

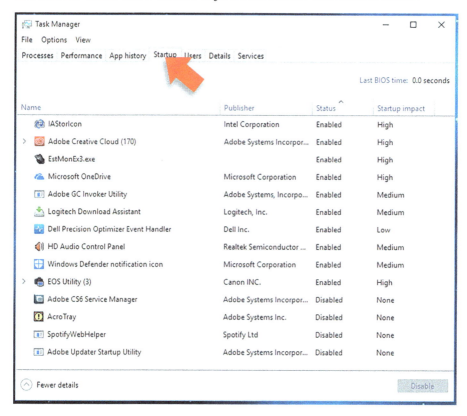

Click on the startup tab. Most of these programs can be disabled with the exception of your sound, video and network devices.

You will also see the startup impact this shows how much the program slows the machine down.

These are the programs that show up in your system tray on the bottom right hand side of your screen.

As you can see above, this system is quite clean – only essential icons appear in the tray.

Chapter 10: Maintaining your Computer

Introduced in the Spring Creator's Update, you can now access start up programs from the settings app

Go to your settings app, select 'apps'. From the list on the left hand side, select 'start-up'.

On this screen you'll see a list of apps that are configured to start when Windows starts. Click the sliders next to each app to either enable or disable them - you can turn then on or off.

Remove Programs and Apps

There are two ways you can remove programs, through the control panel or directly from the start menu.

For desktop apps such as anti-virus software, Microsoft Office, Adobe Creative Suite and similar apps, you should remove these from the 'programs and features' section of the Control Panel.

As an example, I am going to remove 'avast antivirus' from my computer.

First you need to open the 'programs and features' section of the control panel. The quickest way to do this, is to search for it using the search field on the bottom left of your task bar.

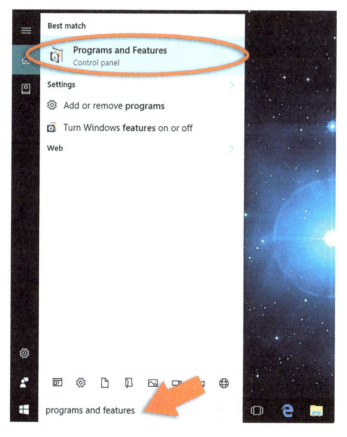

In the search field, indicated by the red arrow, type

```
programs and features
```

Click 'programs and features', circled above, from the search result.

Select the application you want to remove from the list, then click 'uninstall', circled below.

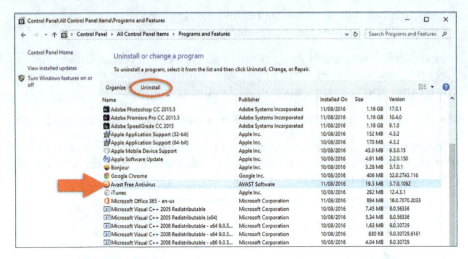

Now, depending on what program you are trying to remove, you might get a screen asking you what you want to do. In this case, avast is giving me options of what I can do.

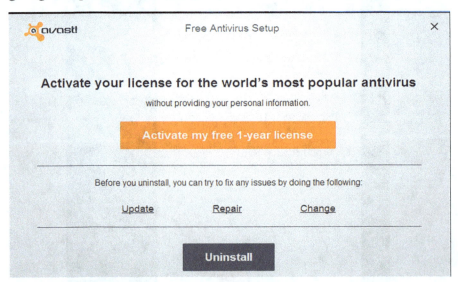

In most cases you just have to click the 'uninstall' button, also sometimes labelled 'remove'.

Once you have done that, the install wizard will run and start to remove the software you have chosen. Depending on what you have chosen to remove, you might need to restart your PC.

This is a similar process for removing old versions of Microsoft Office or Adobe Creative Suite and any other desktop applications.

It's good practice to go through the apps and programs installed on your device, and remove the ones you don't use anymore and any old apps. This helps to keep your device running smoothly.

For apps that you have downloaded from the App Store and ones that come with Windows 10, you can remove them directly from the start menu.

To do this, right click on the icon on the start menu and select 'uninstall'. Tap and hold your finger on the icon, if you are using a touch screen tablet.

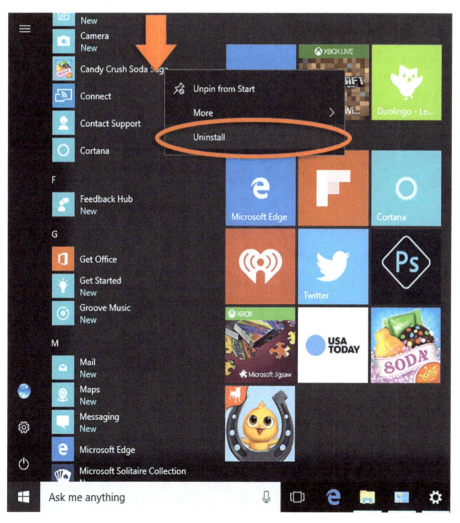

Resetting Apps

Sometimes apps can become slow and unresponsive, so in Windows 10, you have the option to reset the app. This will clear all the App's data, history lists, caches, settings and so on. This doesn't clear any of your personal files etc.

Settings App -> Apps -> Apps & Features.

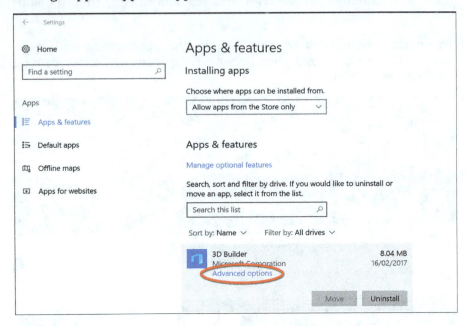

Tap on an App in the list, then tap 'advanced options'.

From the advanced options, tap 'reset'. Then tap 'reset' again to confirm.

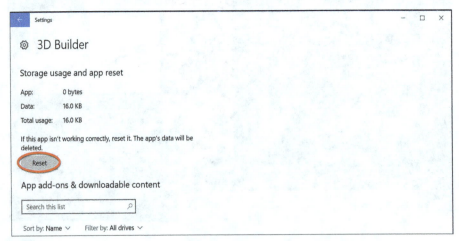

Task Manager

The task manager shows you all the processes, services and apps that are currently running on your machine, as well as some performance statistics of your processor, memory, hard drives and graphics cards. The task manager is also useful if a program stops responding and freezes up - you can terminate the program from the task manager.

To open task manager, press **control-alt-delete** on your keyboard and click 'task manager' from the options. If you see the reduced task manager as shown below, click 'more details'.

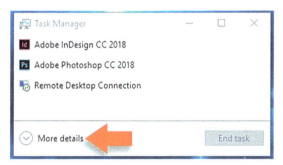

Here you will see some tabs along the top of the window. This will show you running processes, computer performance, a history of apps, apps that run at start up, apps used by a specific user, details of apps and services running.

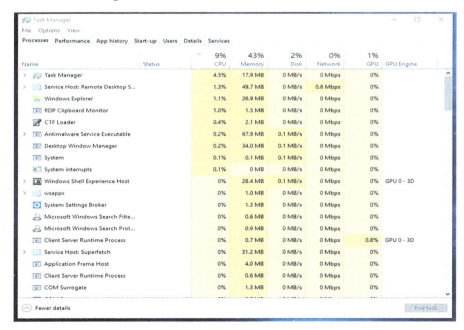

Chapter 10: Maintaining your Computer

You can also terminate some of these apps - to do this click the service/app then click 'end task'. You should only do this if the particular app/service is causing a problem. Don't start terminating services as it can cause your machine to become unstable.

Task manager is useful to terminate apps that have crashed or 'not responding'.

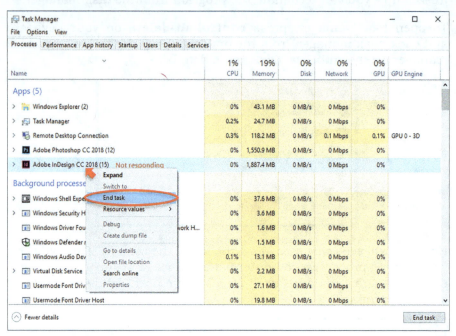

To do this, find the app in the 'processes' tab. The app that has crashed is usually marked with 'not responding'. Right click on the app and from the popup menu, select 'end task'.

You can also sort the processes according to the resources they are using. For example, if you want to see what processes are hogging all the CPU resources, click the CPU column. As you can see, the photos app is using a lot of the CPU.

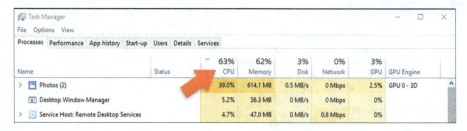

You can do the same for memory, disk, network and GPU.

You can also check the performance of your machine. To do this select the 'performance' tab.

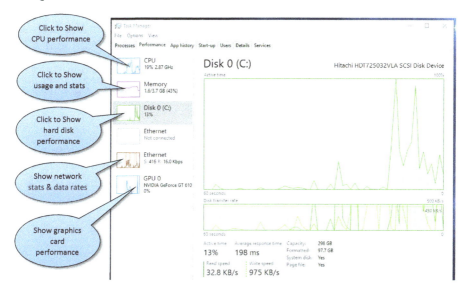

Here we can see the CPU time. On the right hand side you'll see the cores of the CPU and the graph indicates the activity - how much each core is being used to execute various tasks.

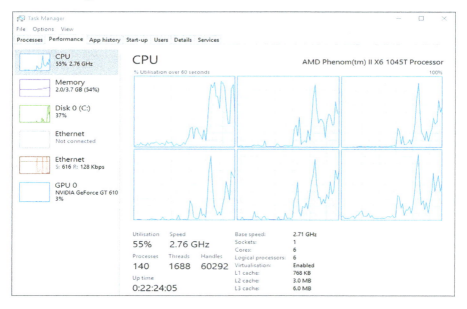

Underneath you'll see some stats for clock speed in GHz, cache sizes, cores and sockets, the up time, as well as the number of processes currently running.

System Recovery

If you are having problems, Windows 10 has a section to recover your computer. You can boot to the recovery environment from the settings app. Windows 10 will also startup into the recovery environment after two failed attempts to restart.

To open the recovery options in Windows, type 'recovery options' into the search field on the bottom left of your taskbar. Select 'recovery options' from the search results.

In the first section you can reset your PC - this re-installs windows 10 leaving all your personal files intact. To do this click 'get started'.

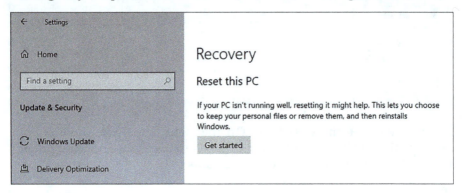

Scroll down to the next section. Here, you can go back to a previous version of Windows 10 - useful if you've installed an update but are having problems. To do this click 'get started'.

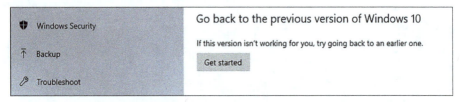

In the section at the bottom, you can boot to the recovery environment under the 'advanced startup' section. To do this click 'restart now'.

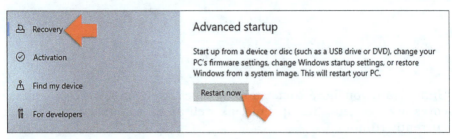

Force Windows into the Recovery Environment

If you're having trouble starting Windows, you can force windows 10 to boot into the recovery environment.

To do this, start your machine, then when you see the start up logo screen, hold down the power button until your screen goes blank. *If you don't see the logo you'll need to boot from the installation media - see 'boot from external drive' on page 436 for details.*

Wait a few seconds, then press the power button again to start your machine.

When you see the start up logo screen, hold down the power button again until your screen goes blank.

Wait a few seconds, then press the power button again to start your machine.

This time, allow your device to fully restart. You should see this screen.

Once the WinRE environment starts, you'll see the 'automatic repair screen'.

Click 'advanced options' to begin.

Reset your PC

Boot into the recovery environment as shown in the previous section.

To reinstall Windows 10 for your PC, click 'troubleshoot'.

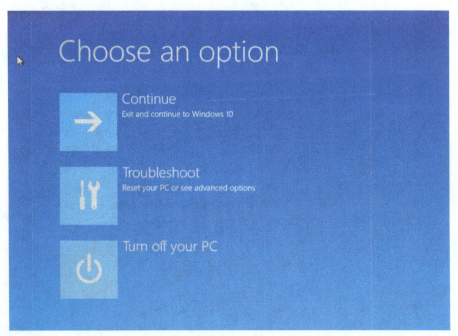

From the 'troubleshoot' screen, click 'reset this PC'.

From here you can do a complete re-install by clicking on 'remove everything'. This will remove all your files and applications and reset Windows 10 back to its factory default.

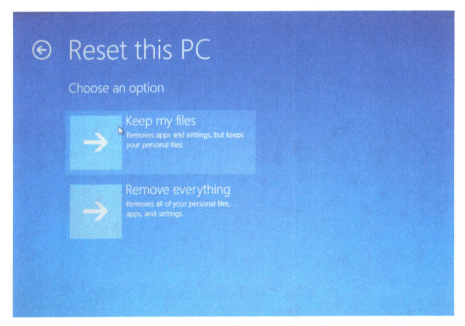

Click 'keep my files' to refresh Windows 10. This will delete all your installed applications and settings. Your personal files and data will remain intact.

Select where you want to download the installer from. You can download from the cloud meaning the installer will download the installer files from Microsoft's servers to re-install windows. Select this one if you are connected to the internet and have a fast internet connection.

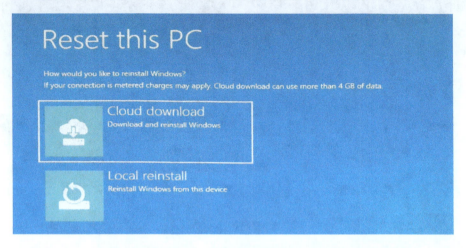

If not, click 'local reinstall' to reinstall Windows 10 from the recovery partition on your hard drive.

Boot from External Drive (USB)

First insert the USB drive into a USB port on your PC.

Start up your machine. As the machine boots, have a look at the start up screen for the hot key that displays the boot menu. This key is usually Esc, F8, F10, F11 or F12.

On this particular machine it's F11. *If you're using a surface tablet, press and hold the volume-down button, then press and release the power button.*

Once you find the boot menu select the USB drive, press 'enter' on your keyboard.

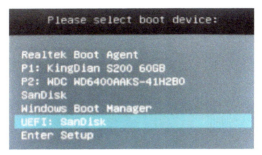

Re-install Windows from USB Installation Media

Boot your PC from the USB drive as described in the previous section.

Select language, time format and your keyboard layout. Click 'next'.

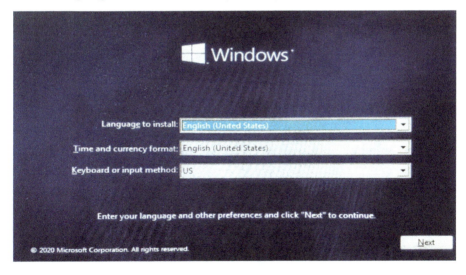

Click 'install now' to re-install windows 10.

Chapter 10: Maintaining your Computer

Click 'I don't have a product key'. No need to enter a product key, you can activate later.

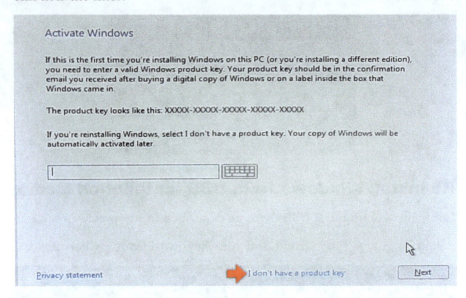

Select the version of Windows 10 you want to install. Eg 'Windows 10 Home', or 'windows 10 pro'. Click 'next'.

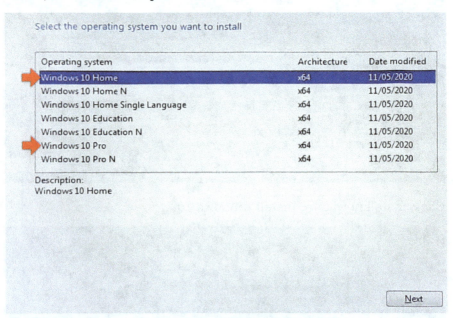

Accept the license agreement on the following screen.

Click 'next'.

Click 'custom: install windows only'.

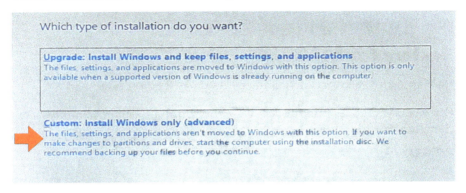

If you see 'partition 1', 'partition 2', and so on, click on each of these then select 'delete'. *Note that this will delete all the information on these partitions - so use with caution. Make sure all this data is backed up if you want to keep it.* This ensures you have a clean drive.

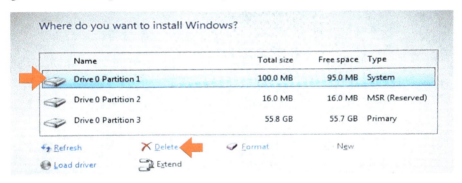

Once all partitions have been deleted, select the drive you want to install windows onto. You should see 'unallocated space' next to the drive.

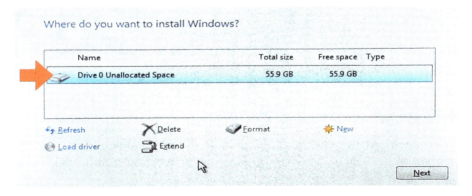

Click 'next' to begin.

The setup will begin the installation. When the restore finishes, you'll need to go through the initial setup again. See "Running Windows the First Time" on page 43.

Restore from Recovery Drive

Boot into the recovery environment as described on page 433.

Once your PC boots into the recovery environment, select 'troubleshoot', then 'advanced options'.

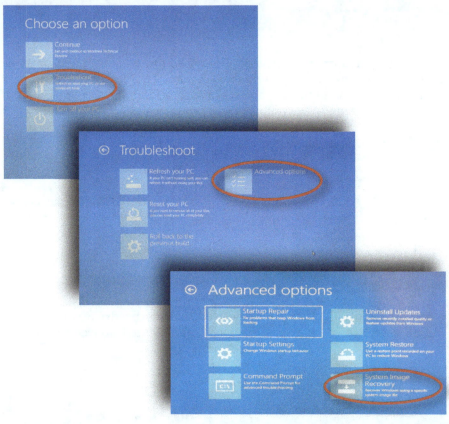

Insert your recovery disk and click 'system image recovery' to restore from a disk.

For information on creating recovery images, see the next section.

Take a look at the maintenance demos in the 'windows maintenance' section of the video resources. Open your web browser and navigate to the following website:

```
videos.tips/win-10-sys
```

Create a Recovery Drive

A recovery drive or recovery disk is an exact copy of your entire system often referred to as a 'system image'. This image contains your operating system (windows 10), settings/preferences as well as any applications. This is useful if your computer crashes and you can't start it up again.

In the search field on the bottom left, type 'backup'. Select 'backup settings' from the search results. In the backup options select 'go to backup and restore (windows 7)'.

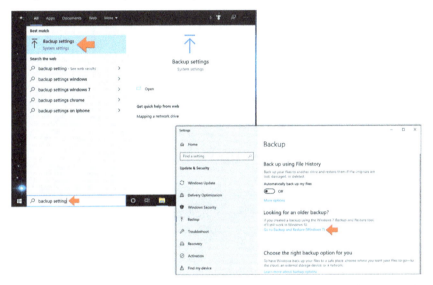

Plug in a portable hard drive (a 500GB capacity is usually more than enough).

Chapter 10: Maintaining your Computer

Click 'Create a system image', then select "on a hard disk".

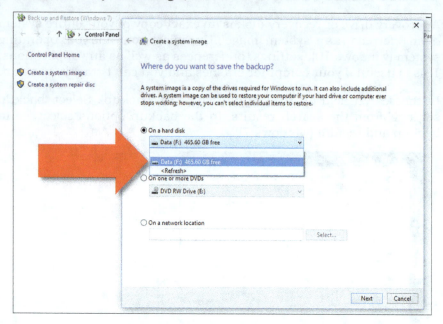

Click next. Make sure only 'system reserved', 'system' & 'windows recovery environment' is selected. Click next.

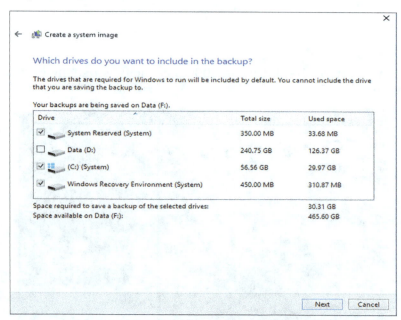

You will be able to start windows with this drive if your computer fails. See "Restore from Recovery Drive" on page 440.

Activate Windows

To activate windows, you'll need a license with a product key or a digital license. If your machine came pre-installed with windows 10 or you purchased windows 10 from the Microsoft Store, you most likely have a digital licence meaning Windows 10 will automatically activate.

To activate Windows, type 'activation' into the field on the bottom left of your screen. Select 'activation settings' from the search results.

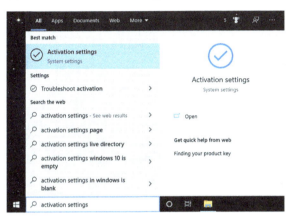

Click 'change product key'.

Enter your product key into pop-up box. Click 'next'.

Video Resources

To help you understand the procedures and concepts explored in this book, we have developed some video resources and app demos for you to use, as you work through the book.

To find the resources, open your web browser and navigate to the following website

`videos.tips/win-10`

At certain points in the book you'll find a website link that will allow you to navigate to the relevant video demo.

Type the website url into the address bar at the top of your browser.

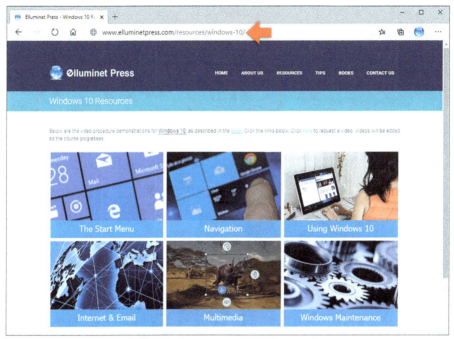

You'll see different categories. Click on these to access the videos.

When you open the link to the video resources, you'll see a thumbnail list at the bottom.

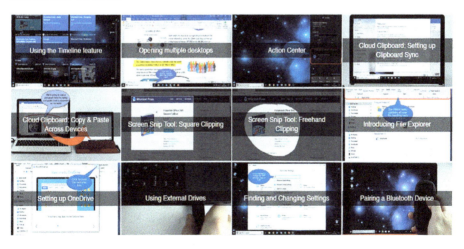

Click on the thumbnail for the particular video you want to watch. Most videos are between 40 and 90 seconds outlining the procedure, others are a bit longer.

Appendix A: Video Resources

When the video is playing, hover your mouse over the video and you'll see some controls...

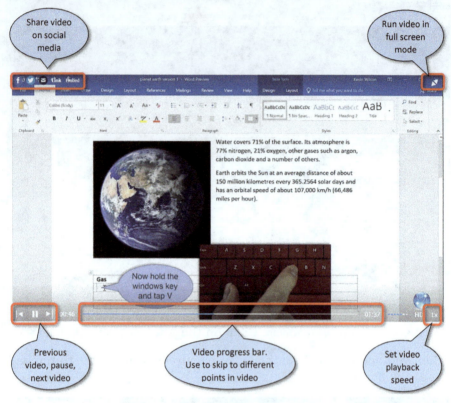

Here, you can share the video on social media, make it full screen. You can also play/pause the video, jump to a particular part of the video using the progress bar and set the playback speed.

You'll also find cheat sheets

Here, you'll find short-cuts, updates and tips.

You'll also find a tips section. Here, we'll keep you up to date with the latest tips and tricks to help you get the most out of windows 10.

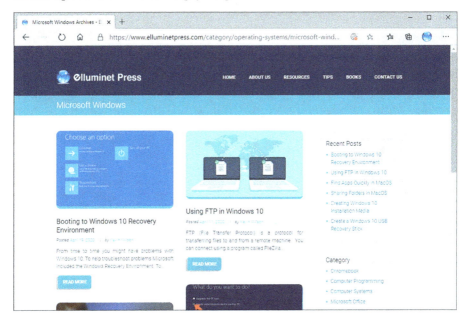

Finally, you'll find a glossary of computing terms.

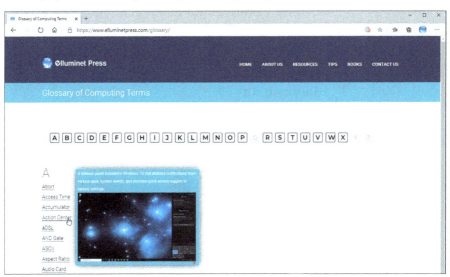

You can find the index here:

www.elluminetpress.com/glossary

This is integrated into the resources section.

Index

Index

Index

N

Index

Y

www.ingramcontent.com/pod-product-compliance
Lightning Source LLC
LaVergne TN
LVHW052124070326
832902LV00038B/1741